No. 160488

Certificate *under s. 87 (2) of the Companies (Consolidation) Act, 1908 (8 Edw. 7, c. 69), that a Company is entitled to commence business.*

I hereby Certify, That the

Northern Counties Motor & Engineering Company Limited

which was incorporated under the Companies Acts, 1908 to 1917, on the Eleventh day of November 1919, and which has this day filed a statutory declaration in the prescribed form that the conditions of s. 87—1 (a) and (b) of the Companies (Consolidation) Act, 1908, have been complied with, is entitled to commence business.

Given under my hand at London this Twenty-third day of January One Thousand Nine Hundred and Twenty

Registrar of Joint Stock Companies.

(28290) Wt. 2438—3177. 1000. 4/19. Sir J. C. & S. Gp. 117. C330.

A Reading VRLL admirably demonstrates its extra length in this view of No. 27 turning at the Three Tuns terminus in Wokingham Road in 1971. *(RGR)*

ISBN 1905304021
ISBN 9781905304028

This handsome Daimler had been delivered to Youngs' Bus Company in 1949, but by now is operating with Western SMT who bought out Youngs' in 1951. The design clearly follows on from that developed from the relaxed utilities as seen on page 59. ***(IGS)***

The British Bus and Truck Heritage

NORTHERN COUNTIES

of Wigan

A history of the Company

and its products from 1919 to 2005

by

Bob Rowe

Venture *publications*

Foreword

by David Cherry

When Bob Rowe and John Senior told me they were embarking on the production of a definitive history of Northern Counties from its inception, I was delighted to know that the Company would have its place in the history of the bus building industry alongside other well-known and respected names, many of whom have also ceased trading and are now just a part of that history. I was also pleased that they wanted me to contribute a Foreword to the book. Having now read it I am happy to do so.

I was lucky to have been part of the bus industry for over 40 years, both in manufacturing and on the operating side. Those years we can surely consider to be some of the most interesting of the 20th Century, years which saw major changes in both arms of the industry, but unfortunately not all to the good.

Perhaps the change I found most disconcerting was the closure of the Northern Counties Company and its successors in 2005 after such a long and distinguished history supplying bodies to all parts of the UK and beyond, and in so doing providing significant employment in the Wigan area.

I consider myself fortunate to have been associated with 'Counties' for over 30 years until 1992 and to have been involved with its splendid staff and the many loyal customers without whom the Company could not have flourished for so many years.

Congratulations to both Bob and John on their efforts during the past year or so in examining records, talking to employees and customers of the Company, and involving other enthuiasts resulting in such a comprehensive account in both narrative and photographic form which I commend to all those interested in our industry.

It is good to know that whilst passenger transport is operated, and enthusiasts continue to maintain their interest, the name Northern Counties will not be forgotten.

David Cherry, seen below, and with a group of employees following the completion of one of the Kuwait contracts. ***(JAS/STA)***

Introduction & Acknowledgements

When, in 2004, the *Venture* Board learnt of the impending closure of the Northern Counties factory located at Enfield Street, Wigan, it seemed inconceivable to them that a final book on the company should not be produced. John Senior recalled that the first manufacturer's history, which he had produced with Eric Ogden thirty years previously, was about Northern Counties. Since both were prepared to assist in providing information that had come to light since the publication of the earlier volume, it seemed unworthy to decline the suggestion that I should attempt to assemble the story.

John Senior kindly contacted David Cherry, who had been Director and General Manager of Northern Counties when the original volume was published, and David's support during the period the book has been under preparation has been invaluable. I suspect that at times he, like me, never thought the publication day would arrive. John Senior has continued to be either across the desk or at the end of a telephone throughout the many long months the book's gestation has taken and, has, even to his surprise I suspect, mastered every quirk which Word, Excel, Page Maker, Paint Shop Pro and Photoshop threw at him, in addition to changing to digital photography part way through the project. Mark Senior has also been at hand to assist, in particular with the construction of the appendices.

Geoff Lumb rose manfully to the challenge of adding to the archival data we held by providing a steady stream of cuttings from contemporary trade magazines – to ensure we understood the circumstances pertaining at the time – and Chris Taylor was also especially helpful in this connection.

Harry Postlethwaite also provided material and help at an early date, while without the copious lists provided by Bob Smith, it simply would not have been possible to come to terms with the output of the two factories involved in this story. An appeal in the local paper, the *Wigan Observer*, brought forward a number of

Amongst the many preserved NCME vehicles, this former Wigan Corporation Leyland PD2, which resides at the Boyle Street Manchester Museum of Transport, is a particularly fine example. ***(JAS)***

former employees who were only too willing to answer my questions. Arising from this I thank Norman Green, Bev Proctor, Brian Rignall, Dennis Smith, Alan Spencer and Ossie Wright.

David and Mary Shaw, our indefatigable proof readers, burned much midnight oil to ensure that the finished work was ship-shape, and, hopefully, watertight.

Finally, John Senior and I acknowledge the long-suffering forebearance of our respective wives and assure them that rumours about a follow-on book on Massey from Harry and Eric and myself can be totally discounted – well for 2006 anyway! Readers with Massey material which we might like to see should, however, send it to me at Venture's Glossop office, just in case we allow ourselves to be pursuaded.

Of the other organisations that have been contacted, the help of the following is most gratefully acknowledged:–

Central Reference Library, Manchester
Cardiff Reference Library
Wigan History Shop
Companies House, Cardiff
Manchester Museum of Transport

Other thanks are due to the following for their help during the book's production:–

Elaine Altman, John Banks, Richard Bean, Stewart Brown, Gavin Booth, David Cole, Philip Groves, Mike Haddon, Robin Hannay, David Kent, Terry Lawrenson, Neil MacDonald, Ron Maybray, Elizabeth Mobey-Gilbert, Neil Scales, Ian Stewart, George Wedlake, Tony Wilson.

Photographic acknowledgements

ABC	Alan Cross	JAS	John Senior
AWD	Alan Drabble	JMB	John Banks
DBC	David Beilby collection	JMBC	John Banks collection
DC	David Cole	KT	Ken Taylor
EO	Eric Ogden	NGC	Norman Green collection
GC	Geoff Coxon	RGR	Bob Rowe
GHFA	Geoffrey Atkins/© John Banks collection	RNH	Robin Hannay
GLC	Geoff Lumb collection	STA	Senior Transport Archive
IGS	Ian Stewart	TW	Tony Wilson

If I have inadvertently overlooked anyone in these lists I trust they will accept my apologies for their omission

Cardiff Corporation was unique in being the only operator to receive trolleybuses bodied by Northern Counties. Number 203 has, fortunately, been preserved and is seen here at the Trolleybus Museum at Sandtoft. *(JAS)*

Contents

Southdown 864 was one of the third batch of Leyland PD3s delivered to the company in 1961 and which were to total 285 units. It is seen here on the A27 at Fareham Railway Station in September 1966, en route from Warsash to Southsea on the busy service 45. *(RGR)*

The pre-war AEC Renown was one of the more successful three-axle double-deckers built in the 1930s, which were never very numerous. Leicester 329, which entered service in 1939, carries a Northern Counties body of the distinctive style introduced in 1938. The restoration work on this bus, which has been with the Leicestershire Museum of Technology for over thirty years, is a credit to that organisation. ***(STA)***

Prologue

January 2005 saw the final sad closure of the last bus building premises in Wigan, Greater Manchester (although for most of this story during the 20th Century Wigan was in Lancashire) after almost one hundred years of continuous trading. And for the vast majority of its life the Northern Counties Company was under the control of successive generations of the Lewis family. Our narrative therefore commences in 1872, when Queen Victoria had completed only 35 of her 64 years as Monarch, and William Gladstone was in the middle of the first of his periods as Prime Minister. The founder of Northern Counties, Henry Gethin Lewis, (usually known as H G Lewis Senior) was born on 5th April that year in Pontlotyn, Glamorgan, the son of James and Margaret Lewis. He attended Lewis School Pengam and subsequently began his business career at Cardiff Docks, entering the office of an uncle (a Mr Gethin Lewis) who was at the time head of the influential Bute Works Supply Company of Cardiff.

He served here for 21 years, eventually becoming a partner and, when the business was formed into a limited liability company, a director and its secretary. In 1897 he married Annie Llewellyn, daughter of Jenkin Llewellyn of Penarth. They went on to raise eight children, four boys and four girls the eldest of whom, born in 1899, was also called Henry Gethin (usually known as Junior during the lifetime of his father). During his time with this company, H G Lewis Senior compiled a series of tables which were published in 1899 under the title of Redemption hire, deferred purchase and easy payment tables; these were adopted as a standard by the Wagon Building and Financing Corporation, a trade association of the day.

This was not his only connection with the coal wagon industry; an early photograph exists (c1903) of a coal wagon carrying the name of Hall Lewis. We shall come across this organisation again later, but this Lewis was part of the same family. It is hardly surprising, therefore, that in 1911 he founded the firm of Henry G Lewis and Co Ltd, Cardiff, rolling-stock proprietors. He was also associated with the Taff Wagon Company and from 1914 with the Glamorgan Wagon Co and the North Glamorgan Wagon Company. During World War 1 his own company specialised in supplying the Admiralty with rolling stock for the conveyance and stocking of coal for the naval fleet on the East Coast. At the close of hostilities, he was reputed to be one of the largest wagon hirers in Great Britain.

Once peacetime conditions returned following the signing of the Treaty of Versailles in 1918 by the then Prime Minister, David Lloyd George, a fellow countryman of H G Lewis of course, the opportunity arose to experience a more relaxed lifestyle again in company with colleagues from the railway wagon industry. During the latter part of 1919 he was to be found enjoying the hospitality of Sir Archibald Bell, who was a director of the Ince Waggon & Ironworks Co Ltd of Wigan, on the occasion of a shooting party, quite probably on 'The Glorious 12th'. Also amongst the party, apparently, was a Mr T G Bell, a garage proprietor who had premises in Wigan. Whether it was over the port and cigars we shall never know for sure, but the upshot of this liaison was that on 11th November 1919, a company named the Northern Counties Motor & Engineering Company Limited was formed, initially with the registered office at 27 King Street, Wigan.

The implication has to be that H G Lewis Senior was providing the capital for the expansion of the business.

An early view inside the Wigan Lane body building area taken about 1924 clearly shows motor-car body construction taking place alongside that of motor buses, although construction of the former was being phased out around this time.

The full size bus in the background had been new in 1921. Registered DJ 1240, it was operated by St Helens & District Motor Services; it was presumably back for repair. *(STA)*

Chapter One

1919 - 1934

The original directors of the new Northern Counties company, who were required to own a minimum of £3,000 in shares to qualify, were, besides H G Lewis, who became Chairman, T G Bell, (Managing Director), D G Hall and S H Lewis. These latter two gentlemen lent their names to the Hall, Lewis company we have already met and of which more in due course. The company secretary was F T Hanson. The authorised capital of the new company was £100,000, although at most, only £30,000 was ever issued. The business was formed to 'acquire certain freehold land and hereditaments in Wigan Lane, Wigan' and was authorised to carry on the business of motor-body building, repairs, painting of motor cars, lorries, etc, and the buying and selling of such vehicles as an agent.

Since the previous industrial experience of three of the directors had been allied to the railway wagon and coal industry, it seems clear that Bell's contribution to the venture was a garage business and premises, and explains why the fledgling operation was established in Wigan. Bell's garage had been operating from Wigan Lane since before the First World War. Hall, Lewis, of which Messrs Hall and (S H) Lewis were directors, had been established in the Cardiff area at the turn of the century and was the owner of a large fleet of railway wagons, with workshops to repair and maintain them. After the end of the First World War, the Hall, Lewis Company also developed road transport interests and by 1924 had gone on to develop premises at Park Royal in North London to further the wagon repair business. It was on this site that Hall, Lewis Limited, a separate company from the parent, commenced the activity of coachbuilding, having been registered in that year. Hall, Lewis Limited was to be succeeded by Park Royal Coachworks Limited and the story of this company has been documented by Alan Townsin in the book

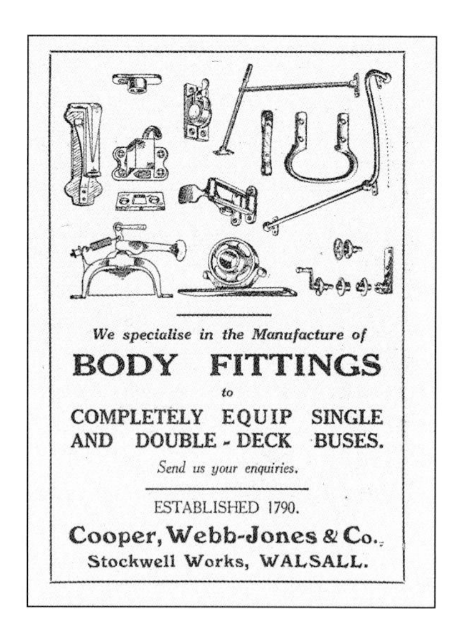

Another early view of the Wigan Lane works, with a variety of timber framing being produced ready to be passed through for vehicles under construction in the assembly area. The traditional belt-drive system for the woodworking machinery may also be seen on the wall. *(STA)*

of the same name, published by TPC in 1979. It had generally been felt that Northern Counties was an offshoot of Hall, Lewis, but from the above chronology, whilst closely connected, it is now clear that it was legally independent and in business long before Hall, Lewis the coach builder was registered in 1924.

The site in Wigan Lane, which was described in the 1920's local street index as 146 Wigan Lane, comprised two adjoining houses, standing back from what would become the A49 Wigan to Ormskirk Road, with extensive gardens and a substantial orchard behind. It was here that a new works was constructed, with the original intention of building bodies on all types of vehicle chassis and initially quality coachwork for private cars was the main intended production. A certificate issued by the registrar of Joint Stock Companies dated 23rd January 1920 confirmed that the various regulations concerned with the establishment of a company had been complied with and that it was, therefore, now entitled to commence business. The first advertisement that has been traced in the local press relating to the new company advised the readers of the *Wigan Observer* on Saturday 14th February 1920 that the largest provincial garage for pleasure cars and commercial vehicles would be 'open shortly'. By May 1920, both the local and national trade press were carrying advertisements for bodywork from Northern Counties. Such rapid growth in availability of products was a feature of this immediate post-war period. Members of the armed forces were returning from active service, sometimes complete with a gratuity. Before the war, expensive motor vehicles had generally been beyond their reach, but now the man-in-the-street was returning with more skills and money than had previously been the case.

It would seem, therefore, that the very earliest Leyland passenger vehicles supplied by Northern Counties in 1919 to Mid-Cheshire of Northwich and described as having bodywork built by them, were in fact sub-contracted, it even having been suggested that Massey Brothers were the builders. As was the case with many car builders of the period, Northern Counties were also agents for other manufacturers, so it is not always easy to establish whether vehicles supplied by one firm were actually their products, or supplied as agents. In any event, the two Leylands concerned were both taken into North Western stock when that company acquired Mid-Cheshire in 1924. Early photographs of the company's activities found by the author so far show Italian Fiat and American Ford motor car chassis with, or awaiting, new Northern Counties bodies. Even an example of the rare American

The forge was at the heart of the manufacturing process at the works to make the iron brackets and other fittings which were very much a feature of the charabancs of this period, and this assortment has been carefully selected for the photographer's visit to include, amongst other bespoke items, some of the components for supporting the canvas roofs of the day. *(STA)*

A high proportion of imported chassis is evident in this view. In the foreground, from left to right, are a Ford, an Austin and a Manchester registered Moon chassis of American origin. The registration mark dates from 1920. Note the curious tread on the tyres of the Austin and the octagonal frames of the Moon's circular headlamps. The Moon carries a temporary wooden seat and the three visible tyres each have a different tread! In the background are two Vauxhalls. At the right, the vehicle with the alarming front suspension is a Ford with what appears to be funeral hearse body under construction. *(STA)*

Although bodywork on motor-cars appears to have finished c1924, bespoke coachwork continued to be built to customers' requirements, and one such vehicle was another funeral hearse, this time for G Ward & Sons of Ashton-under-Lyne, apparently carrying an early form of trade plate issued by the County Borough of Oldham. *(STA)*

By 1923 Fiat motor-cars were a popular choice of chassis for Northern Counties customers. In some cases the left hand drive was even retained; electric lighting and pneumatic tyres were nevertheless fitted. In the this picture the Fiat landaulette is posed outside the impressive archway to Haigh Hall Park, still to be found on Wigan Lane and where many of the official company photographs were taken being a little way along Wigan Lane not far from the company premises. *(STA)*

British manufacturers did not have things all their own way in the 'twenties, and imports of lightweight chassis took a sizeable proportion of the market away from them. The French manufacturer Berliet was just one of many, and this example was supplied to Brookside Garage of Chorlton-cum-Hardy, Manchester. The NCME body, supplied in September 1923, seated 16 and the chassis was fitted with pneumatic tyres. It was quite customary to charge a premium fare if a vehicle was so equipped. The close relationship between a large motor car and a motor coach of this type can clearly be seen. *(GLC)*

Moon chassis was fitted with a car body. When production switched to commercial passenger vehicles a similarly wide variety of chassis were involved and whilst the old established companies such as AEC, Leyland and Daimler were producing, in the main, robust and solid chassis, there was a wider market for the lightweight chassis used for small buses and charabancs. In the early 'twenties and indeed until the effects of the 1930 Road Traffic Act took place, there was a growing number of imported chassis for such work, with Lancia and Fiat being amongst the front runners, and Northern Counties were quick to advertise their bodywork on such chassis.

Other, home-produced, chassis which passed through the Wigan Lane works included Albion, Bristol, Commer, Karrier, Pagefield, Thornycroft and Vulcan, but of these, the Albion marque was to become the most important to Wigan Lane's output and it appears that possibly some hundreds were bodied before Albion gradually dropped down the popularity stakes in the 'thirties. Many of these Albions were for Scottish customers, but the reasons for this solid and valuable relationship are clearly deeper rooted than just the fact that Albion was supplying clients on their own patch, as it were. There appear to be no obvious family or financial ties between the two organisations, and the precise date when the Albion Motor Company's first chassis was bodied remains, regrettably, unclear. It may have been a saloon car, it might have been a charabanc, it might even have been a lorry. Whatever it was, it paved the way for Northern Counties to become a major bodybuilder for the Scotstoun-based company when Albion offered complete vehicles for its customers.

Northern Counties geographical situation was convenient; close to the A6 and on the main London to Glasgow railway line. It offered, by the standards of the day, good access to and from Scotland, through bringing open chassis down from Scotstoun and over Shap, especially in the winter, is perhaps better left to the imagination. Maybe the railway had a part to play. Significantly at this time, there were very few other bodybuilders in England north of Wigan who were involved in the production of bus bodies for sale on the open market. Maybe the astute Henry Gethin Lewis had recognised this when he established the Northern Counties Motor & Engineering Company.

The earliest body, on what would later be described as a 'public service vehicle' chassis, appears, not surprisingly perhaps, to have been a charabanc. The overseas connection was still present however; imported lightweight examples such as Berliet and Lancia being fitted with single-decker bus bodies. The very first motor buses for Aberdeen Corporation on Thornycroft J chassis, supplied in 1920, received dual-door bus bodies from Northern Counties and the following year a Daimler CK was delivered to St Helens & District Motor Services. This Daimler, along with a Leyland C7 supplied in 1925, passed to St Helens Corporation on acquisition of the company in June 1927, but no orders were ever supplied to that Council other than wartime allocations – surprisingly perhaps, in view of the town's proximity to Wigan.

Thornycroft was another make of chassis which came to Wigan Lane for passenger bodywork in the 1920s and this 40hp model was supplied to the Lake District Road Traffic Co in spring 1922, being purchased for operation between Grasmere and Windermere. *(STA/GLC)*

NORTHERN COUNTIES
SUPERIOR MOTOR
COACHWORK.

Notice this Advertisement Weekly!

The illustration shows light 20-Seater Saloon Bus, suitable for pneumatic-tyred chassis. We have designs for every requirement. The best selected materials used in construction. Accurate work and prompt delivery.

Coachwork for PASSENGER CARRYING, COMMERCIAL and PRIVATE.

The Northern Counties Motor & Engineering Co., Ltd.,
Phone 310 WIGAN. Phone 310

From the *Commercial Motor* of October 1922. These small Vulcan saloon buses represented one of Northern Counties' earliest psv-bodying projects, the six forming one of the first batches of buses to be purchased by Ribble Motor Services of nearby Preston. At this time Ribble's fleet consisted of less than 30 vehicles. It would be a long time before any more orders came from Ribble, however, as the book eventually reveals . . . *(GLC)*

By 1922 a batch of Vulcan VSD chassis (built in Southport) was being supplied to Ribble Motor Services of nearby Preston. Apart from an allocation of Second World War Guys, it would be 1967, however, before a repeat peacetime order arrived! Almost as long a period was to lapse before the recipient of two more normal-control Vulcan chassis delivered in August 1923 was to receive further bodies from Northern Counties. The two buses in question were supplied to Manchester Corporation by Lancashire Motor Traders, further evidence of the state of the fledgling industry at the time in that manufacturers and agents were all involved in the growing business. Within a year the last car body was to be produced, following which the manufacture of public service vehicle bodywork became the main, but not exclusive, activity. It is interesting to note that by 1924, T G Bell had ceased to be a director, thus underlining, perhaps, the move away from the car trade which had brought him into business with Lewis. By this time the registered office was at the Wigan Lane premises. Interestingly, living at 146 Wigan Lane by 1922 was one Alfred Alcock. Harry Postlethwaite, in his history of East Lancashire Coachbuilders, published by *Venture Publications* in 2000, indicated that prior to joining that company in 1938, Alcock had worked for Massey Bros (who will appear again later in this story) and prior to that with Northern Counties. Quite what Alfred Alcock's position which led to his 'living over the shop' was, is not absolutely certain, but we know he had distinguished himself in the 1919 City and Guilds of London Institute examination in Road Carriage Building and it could well be that this success

Two Vulcans were also supplied to Manchester Corporation by the dealer Lancashire Motor Traders and were registered ND 2777/8 as seen. The bodies included features for which Vulcan held Patents, such as the oval window on the offside. *(GLC)*

had led to his appointment at Wigan Lane, with accommodation to go with it. When discussing this matter many years later, his grandson confirmed that prior to moving to Massey Brothers, he understood that his grandfather had been employed by Northern Counties as either works foreman or manager.

The parent Hall, Lewis company in South Wales, which, as has been indicated, had branched out into road transport operations after the war, ordered several bodies from Northern Counties during 1923, which included three 18-seat normal control Guy chassis, the remainder being 4/5 ton tipper lorries. It may have been that the absence of 'in house' body building facilities further encouraged the setting up of a coach building factory at Park Royal. Contemporary accounts reported that one of the Guys had been exhibited on the stand of the chassis builder on the occasion of the then recent Scottish Show in Glasgow. The report went on to describe how the 18 passengers were accommodated in armchair seats, these being covered front and back with antique leather and provided with pneumatic cushions. The inside lining boards of the body were covered in antique leather so far as the waist rail, and the pillars and roof with Bedford cord. The instrument board, garnish rails and legs of the seats were of polished walnut. Special attention was given to the ventilation of the interior, eight drop windows having been included in the design of the body, as well as two large roof ventilators. The body was panelled throughout in aluminium, which enabled the total weight to be kept down to 1ton 19cwt 2qtr, thus permitting the vehicle to travel at a speed of 20 mph, as its total weight fell below the two ton limit prescribed by the then law. By this time Northern Counties had commenced giving names to their various styles of body; this vehicle was known as the 'Northern'.

Whilst contemporary advertisements are an important reference for researchers of history, at a distance of 80 years some have to be viewed with a degree of scepticism. This Albion announcement from a 1925 issue of *Commercial Motor* falls into such a category. The reader can draw his or her own conclusions about the possibility of any vehicle achieving an average speed of over 33 mph on the roads of the time for a continuous period of 24 hours, including stops for refuelling and changes of driver. And as for admitting non-compliance with the then maximum speed limit for such vehicles of 20 mph, one wonders what today's legal eagles would make of this – after the Trades Descriptions people had finished, of course! *(STA)*

It was reported that one of the models upon which the company was concentrating during 1924 was a special one-man controlled saloon bus and it was noted that the general appearance of the vehicle followed that associated with a high-class private car, (which was hardly surprising given the origins of the company!), although it obviously incorporated several features that were only found on the one-man bus used on regular service. It was described as being built on most distinctive and graceful lines, the streamlining of the bonnet, scuttle and body assisting to create this effect, which was aided by the bulbous construction of the rear and the fully domed roof. The body, which was built with a low loading line and a single running board gave access to the door providing entry to the interior. The door was of the usual half-folding and half-sliding type under the control of the driver. A special feature of the door were the nickel plated piano hinges which ran throughout its full length, these being used in place of ordinary butts, so that passengers did not run the risk of damaging their fingers in the division of the door. An emergency door was incorporated in the rear panel, and its design was a departure from standard practice in that the door was hinged from the rear offside pillar and opened from the centre.

This construction permitted two large lights to be fitted at the rear instead of three small windows, and not only improved the general appearance of the body, but also provided passengers with a better view to the rear. It also resulted in the saving of a certain amount of weight in the body by dispensing with the special pillar on which the emergency door was usually hung. The windows on each side of the body were arranged to be lowered, with special balancing devices fitted. The windscreen was V-shaped, and both upper portions, which were fitted with envelope shaped glass, (ie of rectangular overlapping configuration) deflected outwards. The interior finish of the body was somewhat unusual in that the underside of the roof was fitted with a large oval panel in walnut veneer, which was surrounded by a lighter grained veneer, extending to the cantrails. These rails carried walnut mouldings, which linked up with the centre panel. A large sunken light was fitted in the centre panel and two ornamental lights were embodied in the quarter panels, giving the whole a very handsome effect. The 18 seats were upholstered in antique leather, the back rests being of sprung steel and the cushions being described as deep and well sprung. A large locker was provided on the undercarriage which accommodated a spare wheel and tyre. Finally, a running board extended from front to rear wing, and leather valances were fitted to the length of the body. Whilst such elaborate fittings might seem somewhat excessive today, it has to be remembered that such finishes were common place on contemporary tramcar bodies. The particular bus described

Buses entering service in this country today are required to have low floors to ease boarding and help less able passengers. Eighty years ago Northern Counties was extolling the virtue of its innovative patented design which met with the contemporary low loading requirements of 1926.

Amongst Northern Counties' patent applications at this time No. 19184 was lodged jointly by the Company and Messrs BH Davies and RF Fone, this being the earliest reference so far found to Mr Fone at NCME. *(STA)*

48 Advts. (Supplement.) THE COMMERCIAL MOTOR February 9, 1926.

LOW LOADING

The simplest solution yet evolved.

DESPITE all the arguments which can be brought forward both for and against low frame chassis, one fact stands out clear and unchallenged, viz., that Northern Counties Low Loading Saloon is the simplest solution yet evolved for providing an omnibus with a low loading line. Moreover, it possesses one distinct advantage over all others, in that it is adaptable to any high frame chassis.

Your present vehicles, therefore, can be converted to real low loaders without any mechanical rearrangement whatsoever, and at a minimum cost to yourself.

We shall be pleased to send fullest possible particulars of this unique coachwork upon request.

NORTHERN COUNTIES
MOTOR & ENGINEERING COMPANY, LTD.

London Sales Office: 14, COCKSPUR ST., LONDON, S.W.1. 'Phone: Gerrard 8933. Works: WIGAN LANE, WIGAN. 'Phone: Wigan 310

was, in fact, fitted on a 30cwt Fiat chassis for the Harrogate Road Car Company and was registered in the batch WY 6249-54.

Throughout the 1920's the Scottish Albion Motor Company's products were seen regularly at Wigan Lane, with bodies being fitted to chassis for Ayrshire Pullman, Kilmarnock Corporation, Midland Bus Services, Scottish General Transport and Young's of Paisley, (all of whom eventually became part of Western SMT), Aberdeen Corporation, Mullen & Thomson of Elgin, Northern General of Arbroath, Port Glasgow Motor Company, Scottish General Omnibus, Scottish Motor Traction (which later became the holding company for Alexanders, Central SMT, SMT and Western SMT), Stewart & McDonald of Carluke (later part of Central SMT) and W Alexander. Many, if not all, of these vehicles would have been ordered by Albion Motors, who were based at Scotstoun, to enable them to supply complete vehicles to its customers. Indeed, from time to time, Albion Motors themselves were customers of Northern Counties, ordering buses which then acted as demonstrators. This arrangement, whereby Albion Motors obtained orders for complete vehicles and then sub-contracted the body work to Northern Counties, was to continue up to the late 1930's.

By the time of the 1925 Olympia Motor Show in London the trade press were commenting favourably on what was described as 'clever construction' by Northern Counties on a Daimler single-decker, which by employing a special channel steel under-framing dropped over the sides and between the chassis members, allowed the floor level to be kept two or three inches lower than was the case with conventional bearers. In addition, the back of the chassis frame was dropped behind the back axle to permit easy steps up into the body, resulting in practically low-loading level on a normal chassis. It was, in fact, some years later before the idea of using a dropped frame extension to create a large luggage area in the boot of coaches was patented by Orange Brothers, thus tending to suggest that there is nothing new in this world to the automobile engineer! Northern Counties also exhibited a one-man-operated service bus body on an Albion chassis and a 20-seater pay-as-you-enter service bus body on a Thornycroft chassis.

Another contemporary review reported favourably on the practice of extending the body sides right down to the step boards thus improving the appearance, citing the Northern Counties 'Windermere' body fitted to a Lancia chassis as a good example. It further indicated that this combination was being standardised on by the Curtis Automobile Company. This firm was the agent for Lancia, who also ordered 'Windermere' bodies from Hall, Lewis, indicating another close link between the two organisations. Curtis Automobile was situated less than a stone's throw away from Hall, Lewis in Abbey Road, London NW10. This Abbey Road should not be confused with the other Abbey Road in NW8 which is in St John's Wood, where the house at No. 3 was purchased by EMI in 1929. Used by many famous recording artists, it is still the Beatles album of 1969 which probably has given the road its greatest fame.

Towards the end of this year, 1925, the delivery of four Thornycroft BX chassis to an operator in the North West of England was to commence a relationship that continued right up to the demise of that undertaking. The buses concerned were normal-control two-door 26-seat saloons for the Stalybridge, Hyde, Mossley & Dukinfield Tramways and Electricity Joint Board (subsequently referred to as SHMD), an interesting example of municipal co-operation on the borders of Cheshire and Lancashire. The buses themselves soon had the rear door sealed and the steps removed, whilst the connection between the two organisations was to become far more durable. Apart from purchases of second hand buses (both former demonstrators), wartime and early post-war deliveries, when other factors tended to influence purchasing decisions, the bodies for all buses delivered to SHMD from 1925 until 1968 were built by Northern Counties. Anyone familiar with the history of the Trade Union movement during the 20th century will know that 1926 was, of course, the year of the General Strike. Whether this had any significant effect on the trading situation of the Northern Counties Motor & Engineering Company has not been recorded for posterity. It is quite possible that by the very nature of the business, the impact was likely to be minimal. The same, however, was unlikely to be the case with the associated companies owned by the Lewis family, indescribably linked as they were with coal mining production and the South Wales industry on which it relied so much.

Part of the Stalybridge, Hyde, Mossley and Dukinfield Tramways & Electricity Joint Board's fleet of buses referred to in the advertisement opposite, proudly placed by Northern Counties in the *Commercial Motor* early in 1930, included this Thornycroft A1 which was delivered in 1927. Its body seated only twenty and No. 88 (TU 2094) was to remain in service with the Board until 1932. *(STA both)*

NORTHERN COUNTIES COACHWORK.

Among Municipal and similar important Transport Undertakings Northern Counties Coachwork enjoys an enviable reputation for consistent good quality.

Good quality means satisfaction, and satisfaction means repeat orders.

Stalybridge, Hyde, Mossley & Dukinfield Tramways & Electricity Joint Board operate a fleet of 59 Passenger Vehicles —all Thornycrofts.

The first 5 Bus Bodies purchased were built by two well advertised Coachbuilders in the South.

The remaining 54 bear the nameplate "BUILT BY NORTHERN COUNTIES."

Specify Bodywork by Northern Counties.

Built to the highest standard for those who require the best.

Northern COUNTIES COACHWORK

NORTHERN COUNTIES MOTOR & ENGINEERING CO., LTD., COACHBUILDERS, WIGAN.

TELEPHONE: 1265 & 1266. TELEGRAMS: "COACHWORK."

The link between the various 'Lewis' companies would never seem to have been very far below the surface; at the time of the Olympia Motor Show mentioned above, the two bus manufacturing businesses linked to the Lewis family were sharing the same address at 14 Cockspur Street, Westminster as a Sales Office for both Northern Counties and Hall, Lewis Limited products. In April 1926, the month before the General Strike started, SHMD took delivery of its second order from Northern Counties, this time for eight of the smaller A1 model Thornycrofts, which were suitable for one-man operation and having only 20 seats. A study of the picture of one of these vehicles, No. 88, suggests that it was perhaps more functional and less ornate than the saloon which had appeared at the 1924 show in Scotland and which has been described in detail previously. By 1927, SHMD was taking delivery of its third batch of Northern Counties bodies and was joined that year in the list of customers supplied by them by two more English municipal operators. The first was Bradford Corporation, who took seven AEC 413 models, and much nearer to home, the first bodies for Wigan Corporation. They numbered two in total and were fitted to Thornycroft LB chassis. Records indicate that Wigan also received Thornycrofts bodied by Massey and Santus that year, but a trade press reference indicates that at the 1927 show a **Hall, Lewis**-bodied Thornycroft was present! It would seem that some work was being sub-contracted by Northern Counties to Hall, Lewis at this time; another example of the closeness of the two companies that has not previously been fully appreciated. Later that year six further chassis were bodied for the Corporation, this time on the Bristol B model, followed by three Karrier WL6/1 chassis, which, as their chassis type indicated, were based on three axles. One of the Bristol chassis had been exhibited at the 1927 Motor Show, described as being 32-seat front-entrance saloon omnibus on a Bristol light passenger chassis. Also at the 1927 show was a 30-seat saloon omnibus for Huddersfield Corporation mounted on a three-axle Karrier chassis (another WL6/1) and a 38-seat rear-entrance saloon bus to the order of Walker Bros (Wigan) Limited, this being mounted on a Pagefield six-cylinder low level passenger chassis, which was, in fact, a product of Walker Brothers. The following year two of these rather rare Pagefield chassis were also supplied to Wigan Corporation (see page 22). They also took into stock the previous year's demonstration model which they had operated for three months before assuming ownership. Because the initial Pagefield was ordered by Walker Brothers for their own demonstration purposes, the body has been attributed by some sources to Walkers themselves; but it is clear from a reference taken from the *Tramway and Railway World* of November 1927 that the body was contracted to Northern Counties.

(Upper) Visitors to the 1925 Show would have been able to examine a variety of small coaches, including this example on the Northern Counties stand. *(STA)*

(Lower) By the mid-1920s pneumatic tyres were becoming more popular, being able to withstand the rigours of the poor roads of the time, though punctures would unfortunately be commonplace. *(STA)*

20 Advts. THE COMMERCIAL MOTOR October 27, 1925.

Thirty-five!

Make a note of the number, if you are at all interested in bodies! Make certain of examining the wonderful examples of modern Commercial Coachwork on the Hall, Lewis Stand No. **35.** Here are some brief details :

32-Seater Rear Entrance Single Deck Bus, mounted on a Thornycroft "J.B." Type Chassis. The low platform step and wide door at the rear afford great ease of entrance and exit to the Saloon, which is very tastefully finished inside. Ventilation is provided by frameless drop windows and swivel type ventilators. Seats with spring steel backs are fitted, comfortably upholstered with best quality leather; adequate interior lighting is also provided. Fully domed wings and life guards, driver's mirror, and illuminated destination route indicator box comprise part of the equipment.

26-Seater Standard One-man Operated Single Deck Bus, mounted on a Lancia "Pentaiota" Chassis. The door at front is of the half-folding pattern, totally enclosing the steps mechanically controlled by a patent door operating gear, which automatically locks the door in either an open or closed position. Eight windows drop into sides in felt-lined channel and can be secured in any desired position; besides these windows extra ventilation is afforded by a row of ventilators operating on spring swivel joints. Adequate interior lighting is provided by means of seven lights. Seats with spring steel supported backs, fully upholstered in a comfortable manner with real leather, are provided. The emergency exit at the rear is controlled by means of a specially designed 3-point lock, allowing for easy operation from either inside or outside of the bus. A complete set of fully domed wings, life guards and driver's mirror comprise part of the equipment.

20-Seater One-Man Operated Lightweight Bus, mounted on Albion 24 h.p. Chassis. A wide entrance, provided with a driver controlled panelled type door fitted at the front nearside. The emergency door is controlled by a special 3-point lock. Seats with spring steel backs are provided, upholstered with best quality leather. Adequate ventilation is afforded by a row of ventilators situated above the side windows.

22-Seater Specially Constructed Coach, mounted on the low Loading Maudslay Chassis, affording the most complete comfort possible with beautifully upholstered squabs and deep spring cushions. A boot at the rear, affording accommodation for passengers' luggage and the storage of the rigid, special steel framed side curtains. This vehicle is finished in the most luxuriant manner and is of the latest design yet produced.

If you cannot pay a visit to the Show, write to us for a copy of our Special Show Brochure.

HALL, LEWIS
AND COMPANY, LIMITED,
14, Cockspur Street, LONDON, S.W.1.
Works: Park Royal, Middlesex.

A20 ADVERTISERS APPRECIATE YOUR MENTIONING "THE COMMERCIAL MOTOR."

91 Advts. (Supplement.) THE COMMERCIAL MOTOR October 27, 1925.

Be Sure

to examine these three bodies on the Northern Counties STAND (No. 24). They will repay your visit to the Show.

28-Seater Single Deck Rear Entrance Bus
mounted on Daimler 'C.M.' Type Chassis.

The entrance is designed so as to facilitate safe and easy entrance and exit. Chassis provided with a specially dropped extension behind the rear wheels, which permits of a single entrance step, 15 in. from the ground. Fully domed wings are provided with running boards extending from wing to wing. An all-metal staggered windscreen with quarter lights and sun vizor is incorporated. Adequate ventilation of a special nature is provided, and the interior is tastefully finished. Seats are of the semi-bucket type, with spring stee. backs, comfortably upholstered with leather. In addition to the usual equipment a "First Aid" outfit is provided.

24-Seater One-man Operated Front Entrance Single Deck Lightweight Bus
mounted on a 24 h.p. Albion Chassis.

The weight of this body is 20 cwts., including all fittings. The door is mechanically operated and automatically locked by exhibitor's patent one-man door gear. The emergency door is fitted with a special three-point fastener, capable of easy inside and outside operation. Ventilation is provided for by frameless drop windows and special roof ventilators.

20-Seater "PAY-AS-YOU-ENTER" Single Deck Bus **mounted on 'A.1' Type Thornycroft Chassis.**

NORTHERN COUNTIES STAND 24

If you cannot visit Olympia, ask us to send you a copy of the handsome Portfolio we are distributing there.

Northern Counties Motor & Engineering Co. Ltd., 14, Cockspur St., London, S.W.1.
Works: WIGAN LANE, WIGAN.

C24 ADVERTISERS APPRECIATE YOUR MENTIONING "THE COMMERCIAL MOTOR."

The strong links between the two Lewis companies are demonstrated here, although, despite sharing a common sales office in London, both Hall, Lewis and Northern Counties were keen to attract prospective customers to their respective stands at the 1925 Commercial Motor Show.

Originally built in 1926 as a demonstrator for Thornycroft, in which condition it is seen here, and promoting the 'Low Loading' feature then the latest development in single-deck bus design, this normal control A1 was, perhaps not surprisingly, to later find its way into the SHMD fleet as No. 91. It retained the registration mark allocated by Hampshire County Council, HO 6347. *(STA all)*

Karrier Motors Ltd.

cordially invite your attendance at

Stand
No. 83

(Tel.: Riverside 4307)

during the forthcoming Olympia Commercial Motor Vehicle Show, where KARRIER models for 1926 will be exhibited.

□ □ □

KARRIER MOTORS Ltd., HUDDERSFIELD.

London Office: Windsor House, Victoria Street, Westminster, S.W.1.

Wigan Corporation did not take delivery of its first order from Northern Counties until 1927, when nine buses were delivered. Six were based on Bristol B chassis, but there were also three magnificent Karrier WL6/1s, of which No. 29, pictured above, was the last. The two door body was divided into two compartments. An interesting feature of the chassis was that it lacked any brakes on the front wheels, although since it was limited to 12 mph (as indicated on the guard rail) this might well have not been too much of an operational problem.

Karrier Motors of Huddersfield were working hard to extend their customer base in the mid-twenties, and were successful in obtaining orders from several major municipal customers. Sadly, the product lacked the reliability of competitor's products from Leyland and AEC, for example, and Karrier faded from the scene. By 1935 they had ceased bus manufacture.

Somewhat rarer than the Bristol and Karrier chassis taken into stock by Wigan Corporation were two Pagefield chassis, being assembled locally in Wigan by Walker Bros. *(STA all)*

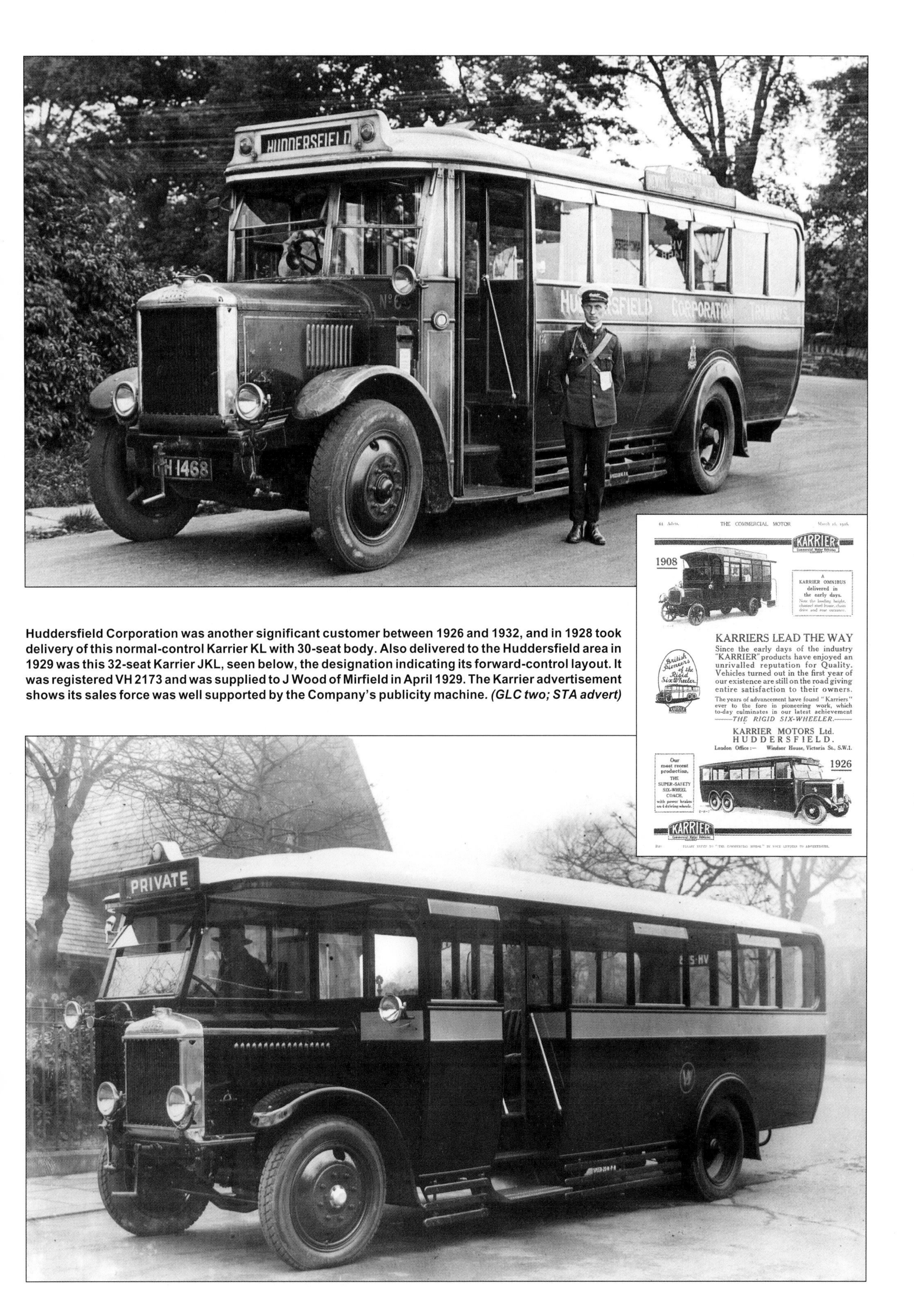

Huddersfield Corporation was another significant customer between 1926 and 1932, and in 1928 took delivery of this normal-control Karrier KL with 30-seat body. Also delivered to the Huddersfield area in 1929 was this 32-seat Karrier JKL, seen below, the designation indicating its forward-control layout. It was registered VH 2173 and was supplied to J Wood of Mirfield in April 1929. The Karrier advertisement shows its sales force was well supported by the Company's publicity machine. ***(GLC two; STA advert)***

STEWART & McDONALD LTD.
49

No 62 CORPORATION MOTORS

ENTERPRISE
C. & D.

(Opposite) Albion Motors of Scotstoun had developed a significant association with Northern Counties by the time this 1928 PM28 entered service with Stewart and McDonald of Carluke. The chassis was of the low-frame type, having been introduced in 1926. The cutaway rear nearside corner of the body around the entrance was typical of Scottish practice, although more unusual in England. Stewart and McDonald were purchased by the London Midland and Scottish Railway Company in 1930, and from 1932 the Scottish Motor Traction Company managed the Scottish railway interests. In 1932 Central SMT was formed and the company was later to become a significant customer of Northern Counties products. This Albion, therefore, passed to them, being withdrawn in 1937. Lest it should be imagined that Northern Counties only supplied to company operators in Scotland, this Aberdeen Corporation example, also on an Albion PM28, should disprove such a thought. The lower view show a Thornycroft A6, one of four, supplied to Griffiths & Davies of Abercarn. It was delivered with a 24-seat body in December 1929 and registered WO 3449.

(Above) Normal-control Albions were also supplied to the Carlisle, Dalston & District Motor Services Limited. Not quite another Scottish order, but not so very far off.

When Eric Ogden included the picture below of the Glossop Carriage Company's Karrier K4 in the original history of Northern Counties, it was not appreciated that it never actually entered service with them, the necessary licence to operate in the Glossop area being refused by the local authority. *(STA all)*

(This page) Among the variety of chassis from various manufacturers upon which Northern Counties bodies were mounted were Bristol and Morris Commercial. The upper picture depicts a Bristol B for the Bristol Tramways & Carriage Company whose specification called for 31 seats in a dual-door body. The picture below shows a Morris Commercial Dictator, originally built as a demonstration vehicle. Morris Commercial Cars Limited had entered the PSV market in 1929, utilising the old Wolseley works at Adderley Park, Birmingham. Few passenger chassis were built after 1934.

(Opposite) This Thornycroft was built for the Kendal Motor Bus Company. Huddersfield Corporation built up a sizable fleet of Northern Counties bodied buses from 1926 to 1932. This Karrier KL with 30-seat body was delivered in March 1928. *(STA all)*

KENDAL
KENDAL MOTOR 'BUS COMPANY, LIMITED.

HUDDERSFIELD
HUDDERSFIELD CORPORATION TRAMWAYS.
No 58

Northern Counties reached a landmark in 1928 when the first double-deck body was constructed at the Wigan Lane factory. It was built on a Maudslay chassis with the intention of being used by the Coventry based manufacturer as a demonstrator and first appeared at the 1928 Olympia Motor Show.

It is known that it at least operated in Morecambe for a short while, but its subsequent history has not been confirmed. From its appearance the lowbridge body could be said to have some similarities with the bodies being built at the time by Leyland Motors, and which Northern Counties would later build under licence from that company for Wigan Corporation. Maudslay was never a large builder of PSV chassis and double-deck versions were even rarer. *(STA)*

When consideration was given to tramway replacement by the Corporation in Wigan, it was inevitable that Northern Counties would figure again. However, before this took place, Northern Counties reached another landmark when the first double-deck body was constructed at Wigan Lane and was exhibited at the Olympia Motor Show in 1928. It was constructed on a Maudslay chassis and was built as a demonstrator for the Coventry manufacturer. Because of its height, a special painting and varnishing room had to be erected around it. In view of the unique nature of this bus, it is strange that until recently little was known of it subsequent history. However, it appears that a demonstration Maudslay double-decker passed to York Brothers of Northampton in 1930 and with whom it stayed until it was sold (for scrap?) in 1939.

Having successfully placed a fleet of Leyland Titan double-deckers in service in 1929, when consideration was being given by Wigan's Tramways Committee in the following year to the replacement of the tram system, it was not surprising that Leyland Titans were again the committee's choice. The Leyland Society, in its history *The Leyland Buses of Wigan Corporation*, records that after agreeing a repeat order for Leyland bodied Leyland Titans, it was provisionally agreed that Leyland would supply 20 further Titan chassis for bodying by local coachbuilders, who would mount bodies to a design that would not infringe the patent rights held by Leyland. These buses were required for delivery by March 1931. Subsequently, it was agreed, in a meeting attended by Mr Fone of Northern Counties and representatives from Massey Brothers and Santus, (the other two local Wigan coachbuilders) that bodies would be built to the Leyland design (at a cost of £700 per body). Leyland Motors agreed to make a special concession in the case of these vehicles to be built for the Corporation by allowing the local bodybuilders to copy the 'Titan' design on payment of £1 instead of the usual charge of £50. This concession was a special one, it was stated, made on this occasion for the benefit of the Corporation, as a result of the relations existing between themselves and the Corporation as regards the employment of Wigan labour. From thence onward, Wigan Corporation only ever ordered Leyland chassis (apart from wartime allocations) and bodywork was always built in the County of Lancashire, and more often than not, supplied by either Northern Counties or Massey Brothers from Wigan.

This situation whereby other bodybuilders could reproduce other designer's work, usually for an agreed fee, was not unusual at this time. Indeed Leyland, unable to cope with demand for bodywork on its new Leyland Titan, in fact sub-contracted some work to Shorts of Rochester, Strachans of North West London, Weymanns of Addlestone and United at Lowestoft at least. Leyland's difficulties were caused

It was, perhaps, inevitable that Wigan Corporation would eventually take into stock double-deck bodies from the NCME Wigan Lane factory. However, these first examples delivered in 1930 were, by agreement with Leyland, to its design. *(STA)*

by a shortage of skilled body-builders, but they were anxious to avoid placing these contracts too close to home, for fear of losing workers to the other firms. This makes the Wigan deal all the more unusual. In a development that virtually mirrored this situation, Northern Counties were involved in a similar exercise later that year with Exeter Corporation, to whom they had been supplying single-deck bodies since 1929. Yet again, the reason for the order was in connection with tramway replacement. Exeter had taken a batch of AEC Regents to the London General Omnibus Company's Chiswick design in 1930, which had been built by Ransomes of Ipswich. Ransomes had already supplied the LGOC direct with AEC Regents with bodies to Chiswick designs, besides also supplying similar bodies to Lowestoft and West Bridgford. Metropolitan-Cammell was also to supply 'Chiswick' bodies to the LGOC, which were all metal. This time, in 1931, Northern Counties supplied the bodies based on the Chiswick design and were the first highbridge design vehicles constructed by the company. Such was the appearance of the buses in question, that for many years they were incorrectly attributed to Ransomes.

One event at this time which should not be overlooked, in the context of the effect on Northern Counties, was the passing into law of the 1930 Road Traffic Act. The provisions of this Act were many and various, (revising speed limits for example) and in summary introduced national regulations in place of local ones, (where they existed) and operationally introduced regulation into the bus industry. These changes were vast and extensive and are really too great to be included in this narrative. Where the impact on coach and bus builders came was in the area of the new Construction and Use Regulations, which also outlawed certain practices that had been permitted and rendered the operation of certain types of vehicle illegal. This, generally, was in connection with such matters as weight, braking and overhang. The enforced withdrawal of 18,000 mostly small vehicles rendered obsolete by the new regulations would have stimulated the market, but their replacements would have mainly been larger vehicles.

Although the General Strike had, perhaps, had minimal effect on the two bus building concerns, the effects following the Wall Street crash of 1929 must have had some impact and may have been at least partially responsible for the collapse of Hall, Lewis who were declared bankrupt that year. Out of the liquidation of this concern was born Park Royal Coachworks Limited, as mentioned previously, but HG Lewis was never to be involved with this company.

It was, in fact, in this year that the founder's son, also HG Lewis, commenced employment with Northern Counties, by which time the registered office had been changed to Imperial Buildings, Bute Docks, Cardiff.

The classic lines of the London General Omnibus Company's Chiswick designed body, but built by Northern Counties in this instance, and fitted here to an AEC Regent as one of a batch of nine for Exeter Corporation delivered in 1931, are shown well in these two views. Strachans, apparently, also built 50 bodies to this design. ***(STA both)***

For comparative purposes and in order to put the delivery of the Exeter vehicle shown opposite into perspective, three buses to identical design are shown here. At the top, West Bridgford Urban District Council also operated AEC Regents, this time the Chiswick design having been constructed by Ransomes of Ipswich, who also built the body for the Exeter AEC seen in the centre view. The lower photograph, taken outside Victoria Station in London, shows one of the London General's AECs with operator designed body a few years after entering service and following the formation of the London Passenger Transport Board. Note that Northern Counties fitted the side lights in the same position as on the London vehicle. *(GHFA)*

A second double-deck demonstration bus was built in 1930; this time for Daimler. Based on their CF6 chassis, 52 seats were accommodated in the body, despite the fact that in the upper saloon the seats were arranged centrally, with a gangway along each side. The style of the body closely resembled that constructed on the Maudslay built two years earlier. After use as a demonstrator, the bus passed to Lanarkshire Traction (predecessors of Central SMT), Motherwell, in 1932. As may be deduced from the above, double-deck construction was now assuming a greater proportion of the factory output, and besides orders from those operators already mentioned, others were received around this time from Young's of Paisley (naturally on Albion chassis), Barrow in Furness Corporation, on Crossley Condors and seven for Huddersfield Corporation on AEC Regent chassis. Nineteen-thirty-two also saw a repeat order from Wigan, as well as the first order for double-deckers from Cardiff.

A move towards a more standardised technical requirement could not have been a bad thing for the vehicle constructor and it may have been the stimulus which resulted in Northern Counties building its first steel framed double-deck body which appeared at the 1933 Commercial Motor Show at Olympia, being destined for Young's of Paisley. Whilst Northern Counties were by no means the first to construct such a vehicle, the innovation had been approached with a concern for simplicity and ease of maintenance. As a method of construction it was not universally accepted, however, and is said to be one of the reasons why Alfred Alcock, who by now was at Massey, later moved to East Lancs, the latter utilising the new methods whilst the former would not. A batch of vehicles to this new design was delivered to Birkenhead

Huddersfield Corporation's choice of Northern Counties bodies has already been mentioned. The final deliveries were made in 1932, when no less than 18 buses were supplied, carrying body Nos. 2697 to 2714. The lower picture shows four of the vehicles concerned, two AEC Regents and two AEC Regals. Nont Sarah's was a famous pub on the A640 used by travellers crossing the Pennines. The upper picture clearly shows the lettering and coats of arms carried by No. 151 as a result of the Corporation's joint operation with the LMS railway. ***(STA both)***

Northern Counties sales methods, certainly during the inter-war years, seemed to include building up close relationships with some of the more important families who were part of the developing bus industry. Perhaps not surprisingly, given the geography of the situation, the Watts family of Chepstow were among these, although one vehicle in particular, of which more shortly, appeared to strain this relationship. Here, two coaches based on Albion chassis and part of the Watts' Red & White empire are featured. Some of the bodies supplied to Red & White in 1931/2 were replacement ones on Albion PM28 chassis, the opportunity being taken to re-engine the chassis with Gardner units at the same time. It is understood that around 28 Albions were dealt with in this way.

A solitary Bristol double-deck GO6G, No, 254, was also supplied to Red & White in 1935, but unfortunately it seems its delivery was affected by the restructuring difficulties Northern Counties was going through at the time, being delayed in part, apparently, by a strike. One day, no doubt, a full Red & White history will cover all these matters. Once again, the pilastered arch leading into Haigh Hall Park, near the factory, features in these official views. *(STA Both)*

Although very few coach bodies had been produced by Northern Counties, the fact that the company could create designs of elegance and quality is clearly shown in these two 1934 examples. In the upper picture, Hebble Motor Services of Halifax took delivery of this solitary Albion Valiant PV70 with luxurious 28-seat coach body. The fittings included deep upholstered seats covered in moquette, window curtains, chrome window fittings and interior bevelled mirrors and clock.

In the lower picture is one of six Leyland TS6s with 32-seat coach bodies supplied to Belfast independent operator HMS Catherwood. They were for use on long distance services within Northern Ireland. Chrome plated steps to the front of the rear door permitted access to the roof mounted luggage locker, while the side window arrangement anticipated double-deck styles introduced after the Second World War. *(STA both)*

Corporation, another new customer, the following year on Leyland TD3 chassis. The end of 1933 had seen two rather unusual AEC Regents enter service with Bury Corporation, in that they were fitted with twin staircases and two doorways. The same year SHMD, who, as we have seen, had been a customer since 1925, also took their first double-deck bodies from the company in that year.

In spite of this relatively new market for double-deck buses, Northern Counties was not neglecting the market for saloons which had helped establish the company; indeed since 1930 it had been producing attractive coach bodies for long distance services which were being developed at the time. Amongst operators to take delivery of such vehicles was the Western Welsh Company of Cardiff, on both AEC and Leyland chassis, (almost certainly another example of the South Wales sales connections) and Greyhound Coaches of Bristol, in their case, perhaps predictably, on Bristol chassis. Red & White also took delivery of coaches and this was another example of a family controlled company, in this case the Watts, having links with the Lewis'. Arguably the most attractive coach body of all during the 1930s was supplied to HMS Catherwood of Belfast. A study of a picture of the body for this operator portrays elements of styling that was to be used in a different form 15 years later. Whilst not actually coach bodies, Northern Counties also bodied a handful of AEC Q chassis around this time as single-deckers, with centre entrance bodies. The existence of this combination has not previously been widely known.

Two products of vastly differing types from the AEC factory in Southall are shown here. The upper picture is of the classic Regent, one of two supplied to Douglas Corporation in 1933, the year in which Northern Counties all metal framed double-deck body, of which this is an example, had been introduced and which seated 52. The Corporation had been a Northern Counties customer since 1927. *(STA)*

The lower picture, on the other hand, depicts AEC's brave attempt at a side-engined chassis, the Q, which was introduced in 1932. Welsh Motorways No. 38 (ATX 338) has a 1935 body of a style that was perhaps not as elegant as either of the coaches shown on the opposite page. Northern Counties was not a name normally associated with bodies on AEC Q chassis. The AEC Regent, in various marques, was to continue in production up to 1968, but the Q was discontinued in 1937. *(GHFA)*

Chapter Two

1935 - 1939

The fall of the national Government, led by Britain's first labour Prime Minister, Ramsey McDonald, in 1935, led to a General Election late that year. It was held on Thursday 14th November and, as a matter of interest, all General Elections since have been held on Thursdays. The new Government was led by Stanley Baldwin and the change in leadership reflected the universal discontent in the country at the time, unemployment, which stood at two million, being amongst the many ills.

In a similar way, it appears that not all was completely well within the Northern Counties company. Since the end of the 1920's, the profit and loss account deficit had been increasing year on year, so much so that by the end of the 1932/3 financial year it stood at more than £34,000; not a large sum by today's standards, but a considerable figure considering the trading conditions of the time. Regrettably, surviving records, including those from Companies House, do not give a completely clear picture of contemporary events, but the upshot of all this was that a new company, still named Northern Counties Motor & Engineering Company Limited, was incorporated on 23rd December 1935, with the principal purpose of 'acquiring a company of the same name which had been formed in 1919'. The registered number of the new company was 308576 and the Capital authorised was £15,000, of which £13,000 was initially issued, compared to the £100,000 of the original company. Whereas the qualification for directorship of the original company had been £3,000 in shares, the requirement in the new one was one share and the

The introduction of all metal framed bodies was not to the liking of all customers, and Hebble Motor Services choose the traditional style, with six-bay bodywork, for this 51-seat lowbridge version, one of six supplied in 1935 on Leyland TD4 chassis. ***(STA)***

directors were HG Lewis (Chairman), HG Lewis Jnr and RF Fone. HG Lewis Jnr was Company Secretary. The latter two individuals had held similar positions in the original company since the late '1920s, but SH Lewis was no longer a director. Examination of company records indicate that the original company of 1919, number 160468, was eventually struck off in 1938.

What does seem to be clear is that the demise of Hall, Lewis in 1929, and the restructuring of Northern Counties in 1935, left lasting and unpleasant memories at Cardiff and were a direct cause of the understandable reluctance by older members of the Lewis family to permit access to, or disclose details of, the family's private and business affairs. Since Cardiff was the company's head office from where all invoicing and accountancy took place (presumably for both companies) and all financial records were kept, this made research and verification somewhat difficult.

The fact that a large number (80) of double-deck buses were built in 1935, including 35 for Nottingham, 15 for Birmingham and others for Birkenhead and Cardiff Corporations and (of course!) SHMD, does not really help clarify matters, as this figure was an impressive one by the company's standards, so it may have simply been a case of financial restructuring. Certain legal documents examined in connection with the production of this book appear to indicate that, concurrently with this change, HG Lewis was relinquishing some control of the company to his son, HG Lewis Jnr and this may have had something to do with the reorganization. In an interview with Jim Burns, who retired in 1979 after 50 year's service, he recalled that at the time of the restructuring, the factory was closed for a significant period and all the staff were finished for a while. This would appear to have been around the time that SHMD 150/5, their last Thornycroft Daring double-deck buses, were under construction, a photograph appearing in Eric Ogden's history of the undertaking showing uncompleted vehicles lined up in the apparently deserted factory.

The available production figures for 1936 certainly show a decline when compared with the previous year, being approximately 50% down when compared year on year. Yet the following year saw the introduction of a new style of double-deck bus body that has become, over the years, almost the most instantly recognisable pre-war Northern Counties body despite the passage of time. The first of these new bodies was, in fact, delivered to Cardiff Corporation during 1937. In

One of the largest deliveries made by NCME up to this time was in 1935 when no less than 35 AEC Regents with metal-framed highbridge bodies were supplied to Nottingham Corporation.

The somewhat unusual style of the body, with centre route number box at the front of the upper-deck, was also shared with buses suppied around that time to Cardiff Corporation. *(GHFA)*

Final single-deck deliveries for SHMD before the war comprised seven Daimler COG5s with streamlined style bodies in 1937. Seats were provided for no less than 38 passengers, which was no mean feat given the dimensions permissible at the time. The corresponding double-deck Daimler preference was for the COG6, almost identical examples being delivered each year from 1937 to 1940, although detail differences between the batches were made. The contrasting lighter green sweep against the dark green of the main colour scheme made these vehicles particularly eye-catching, helping them to stand out from the various other municipal operators in their territory. ***(STA both)***

view of the significant appearance of the design, it would be interesting to discover whether a new designer had recently joined the company's drawing office, or whether it was produced by existing staff. Claims have been made that the design and specification was that of W Forbes, the Cardiff Manager and Engineer, but most reports in those days tended to attribute a new vehicle's appearance to the recipient General Manager, whether or not he had actually influenced the design. Contemporary reports claimed that 'it embodied beauty of line as well as sturdiness of construction', but whether a view from the 21st Century would necessarily agree is open to debate. The bodies were described as being 'all-metal', which had virtually become Northern Counties' standard by this time, but since the trade reviews seem to dwell on this issue a little, it would seem that such methods of construction were still not universally embraced.

Indeed, Charles Roe, the body builder based in Leeds and who would have been direct competitors for some of the work going to Wigan Lane, eschewed such techniques, and held quite strong views on the issue. By way of highlighting the debate, *Transport World* reported that the all-metal bodywork was built of bright cold rolled steel of solid section, using no single section of less than 1/8 inch thickness and had no main structural members either shaped or bent. Accurate jigging was, therefore, simplified and 'the criticism so often levelled against the steel body that its greatest enemies are the rivet and the drill, did not apply'. Jigs were, in fact, used at all stages of the manufacture and every bolt hole was jig drilled and reamered and there were no punched holes in any unit of the body, the skeletons of which were built as a straight structure, whilst all of the longitudinal members were in one length from bulkhead to bulkhead with no notching or cutting away at pillar connections. This assembly was completed by means of nuts and bolts with hardened positive lock washers. Charles Roe, by contrast, continued to put his faith in the strength of teak.

This method of metal construction not only simplified the manufacture and erection of the bodies, but also offered exceptional advantages to the maintenance engineer when repairs due to accident damage became necessary. In order to provide the steel shells with the pleasing exterior contours, shaped and swaged steel plates were riveted to the main pillars before assembly and although the structural pillar was straight, the shaped plates could be to any desired contour, the hand-beaten upper saloon front canopy following the exact line of the windscreen and was duplicated at the back; this in turn was continued downward to an out-swept rear quarter panel. No structural details were welded and no self-tapping screws were used in any part of the body. Five half-drop windows were provided on each side of the body.

Besides taking delivery of no less than 35 double-deck bodies in 1937, Cardiff Corporation also took three AEC Regals with 35-seat bodies, generally conforming to the same specification as the double-deckers. A novel way of overcoming the problem of providing a full width intermediate step and a flush fitting folding and sliding door, was achieved by providing a slot in the steel-framed folding door, thus permitting the door to fold over the step. The single-deck buses were painted in a form of 'reversed' livery from the double-deckers, being cream with a crimson lake flare. SHMD also received eight similar single-deckers on Daimler chassis around the same time and again the livery received special treatment, being dark and pale green and cream. The 'streamline' flare on all these single-deckers was also repeated on three Daimler double-deckers delivered to SHMD that year (1937), which were also the first double-deckers of that make delivered to the undertaking and as a result they looked particularly smart. Meanwhile, dear old Wigan Corporation, when taking delivery of some Leyland TD5s the following year, preferred to keep to the 1929 Leyland based design – decidedly out-dated one feels by then, but in keeping with its faith in the composite body. However, it was when the Corporation determined to order metal framed bodies for the first time that 'modern' Northern Counties bodies first appeared in the fleet, so that in due course the final Leyland TD5 models it received sported the latest style, although perhaps in keeping with the rather conservative nature of the undertaking, they were of six bay construction, unlike the Cardiff design. They were also, in keeping with Wigan's normal requirements, of lowbridge construction, at the time Wigan being the only customer to require this type of body. Wigan also took three Leyland Lion LT9s in 1938, but as may have been expected, the style of body was rather more conservative than the contemporary single-deckers for Cardiff and SHMD.

8
DEPOT
WIGAN CORPORATION
98
JP 296

DEPOT
WIGAN CORPORATION
JP 2965

The last new customer for Northern Counties to receive a delivery before the outbreak of war was Eastbourne Corporation, which took five AEC Regents in January 1938. This particular batch of buses acquired a degree of fame than might otherwise have been the case when, in 1954, they were converted to open top form for use along the sea front, painted in a predominantly white livery and given names (by the then General Manager's daughter) inspired by Lewis Carol's *Alice in Wonderland*. One could, therefore, ride on *White Rabbit*, *White Queen* or *White King*, no doubt encouraged by young children, an inspired gesture long before such marketing ploys were common place. Perhaps the reader of the children's story was much taken by the Queen of Hearts cry "off with their heads" and determined to emulate it. These AEC buses were finally withdrawn in 1962, but were by no means the only Northern Counties bodies that were to receive such an 'after life' as will be seen later, in the next chapter.

(Opposite) One often hears the virtues of standardisation being extolled, and it must have been one of the reasons why Wigan Corporation retained the style of Leylass to this design were also supplied by three other builders may have influenced the decision. Wigan No. 96 (JP 2965) was one of four buses delivered from NCME during 1938. ***(JMBC)***

(This page) Introduced in 1937, Northern Counties' final pre-war double-deck model was perhaps one of the most distinctive of all designs to be introduced in this period. Two examples from the following year are seen here; appropriately both for local authority operators (indeed, this style of body was only supplied to such organisations in peace time). The upper view shows an AEC Regent for Eastbourne Corporation and the lower a Leyland TD5 for Birkenhead Corporation. ***(GHFA, STA)***

Chapter Three

1939 - 1946

Prime Minister Neville Chamberlain's radio broadcast of 3rd September 1939 that "consequently this country is at war with Germany" probably filled the directors and staff of Northern Counties with as much dread and fear of the unknown as it did most of the population of the United Kingdom. From purely a production point of view, Northern Counties prospects could have not looked too promising. Total output for 1938, the final full year of peace, had only been 43 units, the lowest annual figure since the company had been reformed in 1935. The total for 1939 was, in fact, only to be 29 buses shared amongst half-a-dozen local authorities. The final order delivered that year was for Newcastle Corporation, who received two Daimler COG5s in October; perhaps, unsurprisingly, the largest single order was for SHMD, who received 10 Daimler COG6s during the summer. But perhaps the most interesting vehicles bodied in that fateful year were nine AEC Renowns for Leicester Corporation, which were delivered in February and March, one of which survives in preservation today.

Generally, the bodies for Leicester followed the new design introduced in 1937, their all metal construction having been previously described in detail, with the exception that, being fitted to three-axle chassis and, therefore, that much longer, these had an additional bay. Not all the deliveries in 1939, in fact, utilised this style; the sole AEC Regent delivered to Douglas Corporation that year, was built to the earlier style of body without the thick corner pillars. The Regents delivered to Leicester in 1937 seated 56; these Renowns had seats for 64 passengers and were destined to be employed on the final pre-war bus-to-tram conversion in that City, the higher seating capacity doubtless matching more closely the capacity of the trams they were replacing.

Leicester's 1939 AEC Renowns are perhaps among the most well-known bodies constructed by Northern Counties on three-axle motor buses, no doubt due, in no small measure, to the fact that one of them, No. 329, has been in preservation for many years. Apart from the extra bay, they very closely resemble the design introduced in 1937. *(GHFA)*

Output in terms of buses from Wigan Lane in 1940 was down to a mere ten for SHMD (of course!) and five for Bury Corporation. Available records do not indicate precisely when Northern Counties war work commenced, but since the next bus body delivered following the completion of Bury EN 8523 in August was not until December 1941, it is inconceivable that work for the war effort was not taking place during this time. It is known that large quantities of general service wagons were built for the military on Albion chassis during the war, as well as the assembly of Dodge and Chevrolet military vehicles and Indian motor cycles supplied under the American lease-lend scheme. In addition to the assembly of vehicle chassis, a large number of army lorries were stripped down and packed in cases for transport to North Africa. Eric Ogden recorded an unusual wartime vehicle that was probably unique, being an ambulance built on a Scammell 'mechanical horse' three-wheeled tractive unit. In the event, it was not used as an ambulance, being stationed on Wigan Market Square at the time when the encased Dodge and Chevrolet vehicles, incoming from the United States, were stored there. A flat body was later fitted and the vehicle was employed on works duties.

An order that was certainly received before the outbreak of hostilities was one from Cardiff Corporation for ten trolleybuses, which were to remain unique right to the closure of the company, no other trolleybuses ever being built by Northern Counties. Whilst there is no obvious reason for this, it could have been due to Mr Lewis' unfortunate financial experience with this type of vehicle. Cardiff Corporation's Transport Committee had determined during 1938/9 on the eventual scrapping of all its trams and their replacement by trolleybuses and accordingly had placed an order with Leyland Motors Ltd for ten 70-seater three-axle vehicles to be fitted with General Electric Company equipment with bodies by Northern Counties. Owing to the circumstances appertaining at the time, Leyland were unable to build the chassis, but the Council were fortunate to find that AEC were in a position to complete the order, the company at the time still supplying large numbers of similar vehicles to London Transport. The first complete vehicle was delivered in September 1941, although body construction had initially commenced as early as November 1939, wartime delays and revised priorities obviously affecting progress. Indeed the first trolleybus chassis was not received at Wigan until 1st August 1941. The body

Leicester Corporation had presumably been sufficiently impressed with the Northern Counties bodies on its 1939 AEC Renowns that the style was replicated by Metro-Cammell when a further batch of Renowns was supplied the following year. *(GHFA)*

The entry into service of Cardiff's first trolleybuses coincided with the introduction of the Council's pay-on-entry flat fare scheme. Notices advising the public of the scheme may be seen in the two windows at the rear of the lower saloon. The allegation made even today that 'pay-on-entry' vehicles can delay services might well be substantiated by this photograph. *(GLC)*

had been designed very much in consultation with the Transport Department's then Chief Engineer WJ Evans, and was constructed to meet particular problems found in Cardiff, where a number of low bridges necessitated a low-loading chassis in order to achieve an overall height of the double-deck body of just under 15ft. Unladen weight was 9tons 8cwt. Interestingly perhaps, the body was not exactly similar to previous products and in time it would be seen to have anticipated the post-war style. Co-operation between manufacturers was apparent as the trolley bases were supported by means of Metropolitan-Cammell patent concealed gantries and further liaison had taken place with East Lancashire Coachbuilders of Blackburn. Not only had the Transport Committee wished to see the removal of trams, but it also decided to dispense with the issuing of tickets and Mr Evans had developed a pay-as-you-enter device as a means of fare collection jointly with East Lancs and this equipment was fitted to the trolleybuses. This enabled a flat fare of 1d to be charged on all journeys. Sufficient trolleybuses (five) had been delivered to enable Cardiff to implement the new arrangements with effect from, appropriately, St David's Day, 1st March 1942, and they entered service operating between Clarence Bridge (Docks) and Cathedral Road. The balance of the order was completed by December that year. One indication of the changed circumstances was that the vehicles were delivered in all-over grey paint, a feature that was to apply to a greater or lesser extent to nearly all wartime deliveries.

Two days after the first trolleybus was delivered, the first motorbus built under wartime conditions was dispatched to Sheffield Corporation. Throughout the country, bus production had virtually stopped by the end of 1940, as has been seen above. During 1941, the Ministry of Supply (MoS), who were responsible for the allocation of materials and the Ministry of War Transport (MoWT), who became responsible for the allocation of new buses, together with manufacturers in the bus industry, collectively began work on a specification for a wartime bus, which in line with the general austerity of the time and which also affected other diverse items such as furniture and clothing, became generally known as 'utility' buses. Before plans for these vehicles had been completed, it was possible to build a small number of vehicles from parts held by the various manufacturers and which previously had been 'frozen' by the government. The MoS indicated that this material could be

Despite the fact that the introduction of Cardiff's trolleybus system had been planned well before the outbreak of war, it was not until 1942 that the first entered service. By that time they were delivered in all-over grey paint, and it is difficult to appreciate, in black and white pictures, just how drab this was. However, reference to the colour photograph on page six indicates just how dreary it was.

The vehicles were noteworthy for a number of other reasons, too. They were built to a restricted height (by moving the motor and other components on the chassis to allow the body to sit lower) to cope with the many railway bridges in Cardiff, as shown by No. 200 (CKG 191), in Clare Road. The railway lines concerned were largely provided to allow access to the docks for the export of coal, and at one time no doubt many of Mr Lewis' wagons traversed the tracks concerned. Reference has already been made to their design to accommodate Cardiff's flat fare system.

On their withdrawal in 1963 one of the batch (203 – CKG 194) was presented to the-then Reading Transport Society (now the British Trolleybus Society) and is normally to be found at the Trolleybus Museum located at Sandtoft in north Lincolnshire. *(GLC both)*

The initial construction of bodywork by Northern Counties once the initial 'freeze' was lifted on war-time construction was fitted to a variety of chassis which had previously been assembled but not bodied. Among the first to receive such buses was Sheffield Corporation, who received three highbridge type AEC Regents in December 1941. Northern Counties had not supplied the Corporation previously, and, apart from four 'utility' Daimlers delivered in 1944, was not to do so again. *(GHFA)*

Lancashire United similarly had never taken products from Northern Counties before their No. 255 was delivered in April 1942, but in this case it was to be followed by many other deliveries over the next four decades. The lowbridge body on this Leyland TD7 has some features in common with the 'utility' design that was to appear from Northern Counties later that year, but the out-swept skirt was definitely a pre-war feature. *(JAS)*

The ‘unfrozen’ buses completed in 1941/2 went to a variety of operators. Stockton Corporation was the recipient of a solitary Leyland TD7 in February 1942. The body was of distinctly pre-war style, although the number of opening windows conforms to wartime regulations. EUP 598 was photographed not long after entering service, and has the customary white painted mudguards and hooded headlights found on vehicles of the time. The somewhat suspicious look from the man closest to the camera can be well understood; photography was certainly not encouraged during this time of conflict. *(STA)*

EAT
HUNTERS
BREAD
SOUTH SHIELDS
XG 7906

Crawford's Cream Crackers
LYONS
T
LYONS
T
BIRMINGHAM
GHA 793
SERVICE

(Opposite) Reference has been made in the text to the Leyland TD7 delivered to South Shields in 1942. After exchanging the chassis with a Middlesbrough Corporation Guy Arab, the result was as seen here – probably the only utility Guy to be fitted with a distinctly non-utility body during the war.

The allocation by the Ministry of War Transport of buses to operators was somewhat perverse, to say the least. (One can almost hear the man in Whitehall saying 'well, a bus is a bus, isn't it?'). To Midland Red fell the doubtful satisfaction of receiving three Northern Counties TD7s, also in 1942. Since the company was well known for nearly all its fleet at that time having been built 'in house', the allocation of such vehicles must have come as a bit of a surprise, although some Guy Arabs subsequently delivered to Midland Red also carried Northern Counties bodies. ***(RNH both)***

(Above) A subsequent delivery to Lancashire United was No. 294, which arrived in October 1943 by which time utility production was well under way. The bus formed part of a large MoS contract for 84 Guy Arabs with lowbridge bodywork, of which 15 went to Lancashire United, the balance going to no less than fourteen other operators. The wooden slatted seats fitted to many of these bodies are clearly visible in this view. ***(STA)***

unfrozen and thus a total of 30 chassis (nine AECs, six Bristols and fifteen Leylands) were delivered to Northern Counties between August 1941 and May 1942 for bodying and delivery to operators allocated by the MoWT. Utilising parts still available in the factory, 19 of these buses received highbridge bodies to almost pre-war style, but were destined for many operators who, under peacetime conditions, were most unlikely to have received such products, perhaps the most obvious examples being the Leyland TD7s delivered to Midland Red in February 1942, the chassis of which were originally intended for Oldham. Similarly, South Shields received the same combination in July that year. The body they liked; the chassis they didn't, so in February the following year they swapped the chassis for a Guy Arab with Middlesbrough, who ended up with a Leyland TD7 with a Northern Counties utility body. Another recipient of unfrozen TD7s was Western SMT, which was to be the first in a long line of deliveries from Northern Counties.

The remaining unfrozen chassis received low height bodies to a more austere style, but still with out-swept skirt panels which were strictly 'taboo' as far as the utility specification was concerned. By the time the last of these vehicles had been delivered, in November 1942, the first of the genuine utility buses were leaving the factory. The fact that Northern Counties had been selected to carry out this wartime work for the transport industry was perhaps a little surprising. The utility specification, as drawn up by a wartime technical committee set up under the collaboration mentioned above, was to produce serviceable buses at minimum cost in terms of materials. In terms of appearance, the most obvious feature was the elimination of the normal double curvature of front and rear domes, which would have involved work by panel beaters whose priority at this time, would generally have been needed on aircraft work. The specification required that the bodies were to be of composite construction and no window pans were to be used, so that the body framing itself would form the window pillars. Only one opening window per side per deck was permitted and this was to be of the half-drop type. To compensate for this, two

By the time this photograph of Coventry No. 353 (EKV 953) was taken after the war, the Corporation had replaced the rather less than adequate standard opening window arrangements with no less than eight sliding ventilators on each side of the body. *(STA)*

hinged ventilator windows were provided at the front of the upper deck. The seating was normally of slatted wood. Northern Counties ,however, who had been producing metal framed bodies since 1933, received dispensation to be allowed to continue using their standard metal-framed construction, which accounts for the surprise at their being included in the list of selected manufacturers, and they continued to include the pressed window pans with rounded corners which were generally forbidden to other builders.

This is not to suggest, however, that all the bodies built by them in the war were all-metal. Philip Groves recalls that not all of Coventry's Daimlers were totally metal-framed; the first two had wooden-framed top-decks, as did around seventy other Northern Counties bodies built in 1943 and 1944. They did not look immediately very different from those with 'metal top decks'. The form of construction was of metal pillars with wooden sleeves, although the wood did tend to rot after some years. The first utility chassis to arrive at the Wigan Lane factory on 21st May 1942 was a Guy Arab and it departed exactly two months later for St Helens Corporation. Guy had been selected, again rather surprisingly, (they had not built double-deck chassis since 1933) to produce motorbus chassis under wartime conditions and together with Daimler, provided all the utility chassis delivered to Northern Counties between 1942 and 1946. The two major bus manufacturers, AEC and Leyland, who might have been expected to produce vehicles, had turned their production facilities exclusively over to the war effort. The first Daimler chassis arrived on 26th October 1943 and was delivered to Widnes Corporation just before Christmas that year and, in fact, had a lower body number than the first Guy bodied, perhaps indicating that although the official announcement of Daimler's return to chassis manufacture was made in December 1942, staff at Northern Counties were aware of the development some time before. That Daimler was able to produce anything was a credit to wartime ingenuity as its works had been all but destroyed in air raids on Coventry in 1940 and 1941 and it resumed assembly initially in Wolverhampton, which coincidently, was the home of Guy Motors, who also produced the wartime trolleybus chassis under the Karrier and Sunbeam names, so that for a period all utility double-deck chassis were assembled in that town.

As mentioned previously, all this work was under the watchful eye of the MoS and the MoWT and, as befitted this bureaucracy, virtually everything required a licence. Thus, the first vehicle delivered in 1943, as it happens to an undertaking that was later to become synonymous with Northern Counties products, namely Lancashire United Transport (in future referred to normally as 'LUT'), was one of 36 units in MoS contract 257/VEH/1810 for lowbridge bodies on Guy chassis. Each vehicle also had a MoWT acquisition licence number, which, in the case of this bus, was No. 1056. More than one vehicle might be included in a given MoWT licence number if the operator was lucky enough to be allocated several buses at the same time. At first, the chassis delivered were of the Guy Arab I variety with Gardner 5LW engines, part of the 500 chassis initially permitted by the MoS and distributed to the various authorised bodybuilders and Northern Counties bodied 53 of these, all to lowbridge configuration (i.e. with an offside sunken gangway in the upper-deck). Subsequent chassis from Guy were designated Arab II, having an extended bonnet to accommodate, if required, the Gardner 6LW engine. The next two MoS contracts were respectively for 84 and 29 buses and these also were all fitted with lowbridge bodies, the last of these being delivered to Highland Transport in March 1944. The contract for 84 units was, in fact, the largest single one received by Northern Counties from the MoS during the period controls were in place.

By this time, as indicated above, Daimler chassis were also being bodied at Wigan Lane. Originally it appeared that plans were in hand for at least 75 Daimler chassis to be delivered to Northern Counties, but, in the event, only 56 were programmed through the factory and all were fitted with highbridge bodies. Obviously, during this period of national conflict all plans were subject to amendment and of the intended recipients of the 75 buses most more-or-less received the original allocation. However, Widnes Corporation, who received the first vehicle, was not on the original list, nor were Rochdale Corporation, who received seven Daimler CWA6s (in fact, all the Daimlers bodied by Northern Counties at this time were this model). On the other hand, Aberdeen Corporation (one), Maidstone & District Motor Services (six), and West Bromwich Corporation (four), were destined not to receive utility bodies from Northern Counties. The Daimler interlude lasted from October 1943, when the first chassis was received, until June 1944, when the last complete vehicle departed for SHMD. Within twelve days of this vehicle departing, production was being concentrated on the next MoS contract for 16 buses, which, in this instance, rather unusually were intended for a single operator, namely W Alexander & Sons and were of highbridge layout, as were all remaining Guy utility chassis that were bodied.

This wonderful line-up of wartime utility buses shows five Guys delivered to Northern General Transport. The two on the right were part of an order for ten Northern Counties bodies delivered in 1944/5. The other three buses had been bodied by the near neighbours of Northern Counties, Massey Brothers. It is interesting to compare the different approach of the two coach builders, particularly in respect of the roof lines, Massey's bodies being slightly tapered at the top of the upper-deck. *(STA)*

At this point it is, perhaps, worth pausing for a moment to take stock of the impact that the Government controlled-wartime production and allocation programme had on Northern Counties. Whilst the supply of public passenger vehicles was obviously important, in no way was it intended to divert from the overall war effort, and the vital feeding of resources to the military machine. The premises at Wigan Lane were by no means extensive, as illustrations in this book serve to demonstrate and production of all units had to take place within the limited, in terms of space, available facilities. From the slightly stuttering start in 1942, when 43 motorbus bodies were produced, production increased to 126 units in 1943, 160 in 1944 and 173 in 1945. During the period this book has been in production, Alan Condie has produced one of his excellent line drawing books devoted to Northern Counties utility production, which graphically illustrates the variety of operators who received such buses, no less than 67 different organisations taking delivery of Wigan Lane products.

The point has already been made that many of the recipients would not, in all probability, have selected Northern Counties as their preferred contractor, but equally, some 60 years on, it is perhaps puzzling to some readers to discover precisely why certain operators, with whom they might be familiar, received relatively large allocations, whilst others did not. To a degree, this has to be down to the vagaries of the civil servants carrying out the allocations, but it has to be appreciated that as far as the Government was concerned, transport for war workers was paramount. By their very nature, some of the sites chosen for war work tended to be 'off the beaten track'. Munitions factories, for example, were not ideally situated in built-up areas for obvious reasons. Furthermore, military training establishments, certainly in the earlier war years, were equally not desirable in the urban environment or the South of England. Similarly, the further away from continental Europe such establishments could be located the better. Thus, Scotland was deemed a perfect location in many respects, and accounts for the relatively large numbers of utility buses built by Northern Counties (roundly one third) being allocated to Scottish operators. After London Transport, W Alexander & Sons was the largest single recipient of Northern Counties-bodied Guy Arab utility buses.

Having made the case for building the utility buses as a means to support the war effort, it is perhaps unusual, therefore, to find Southdown Motor Services taking 46 similar vehicles. The South Coast was certainly out of bounds to most civilians, but

The Balfour Beatty subsidiaries based in Nottinghamshire received a number of utility bodies from the company. Both Mansfield District and Midland General were involved, and here two 1944 Guys for Midland General, Nos. 22 and 23, part of an order for eleven delivered that year, are seen after the war in Mount Street Bus Station, Nottingham. ***(GHFA)***

leading up to the assault on Europe military activity was at its height. After the war, Southdown found the Northern Counties bodies to be particularly sturdy for the reasons stated before, and accordingly converted many of them to open top form, to provide an interesting diversion for the significant levels of the population seeking a return to leisure travel in its area.

Whilst the war in Europe was far from over at this time, the W Alexander & Sons order having been delivered immediately after D-Day (6th June 1944), the MoS judged it possible to begin to relax the austerity specification which applied to utility buses. The first change was to permit the use of aluminium sheets for exterior panelling in place of steel and this revised specification was issued in July. Later that year it was announced that two opening windows per side per deck would be permitted and domed front and rear roof panels would be allowed. Probably of far more interest to the passengers, however, was the relaxation that once more permitted upholstered seating. Slatted seating was not the most comfortable to sit on, but it was generally accepted initially by most people, probably as an indication of the general discomfort and austere conditions forced on them by the war that had to be accepted 'for the duration'.

It was not possible for these relaxed specifications to be implemented immediately, although, as we shall see, Northern Counties was amongst the first bodybuilders to try to return to peacetime designs as soon as practicable. However for the time being the old order was sustained, a notable example of this being illustrated by the commencement of deliveries to what was to be the largest single user of the company's utility body, namely London Transport, or to give it the correct title of the time, the London Passenger Transport Board. The LPTB had been receiving utility bodies since 1942, but in April 1945 received the first of 102 utility bodies from Northern Counties. Despite the fact that the relaxed specifications had been permitted for nearly a year, the first 20 were delivered with wooden seats and ventilators above the top-deck front windows, this latter feature actually being considered unnecessary now that ten half-drop windows per side were permitted. The remaining 82 were delivered with leather-trimmed spring-filled seats, albeit on wooden frames. John Gillham, writing only a year or two after these buses entered service, described them thus: "they are of particularly handsome appearance both externally and internally and can be distinguished by the very pronounced sweep to

London Transport was the largest beneficiary of Northern Counties utility bodies, receiving 102. By the time delivery had commenced, the rather restrictive regulations concerning the construction of such bodies had been relaxed a little. London Transport G165 (GYL 304), therefore, had five half-drop opening windows per side, but still retained ventilators at the top of the upper-deck front windows. ***(ABC)***

the rear roof dome, the curved front end to the top-deck (where most bodies have one flat surface), and the radiused corners at the bottom of all windows. Their all-metal construction is the only one amongst London wartime buses." The London Transport delivery was the result of no less than four MoS contracts, all but one of which was exclusively for the LPTB. The final bus was delivered to London on 15th March 1946, by which time the national emergency was over and the MoWT licence system was coming to an end. MoWT acquisition licence No. 5087 appears to be the last issued to involve Northern Counties and was for ten Guy Arabs for Youngs' Bus Service of Paisley, the last of which was delivered in November 1946.

The speed with which the numerous bodybuilders embraced the relaxation in regulations varied considerable, but Northern Counties adopted them almost as soon as it was possible, the description of the London vehicle above indicating features that would not have been permissible a year or two earlier. In fact, by June 1945, the introduction of a bow-fronted upper-deck and a return to pre-war standards in rear-end curvature had taken place. By the middle of 1946 further improvements were possible, although not all operators took advantage of all of these relaxations. The hinged vents at the front of the upper-deck could be dispensed with and the ten opening windows per side no longer needed to be of the half-drop variety. It was even possible to merge the front roof dome with the corner pillars and to reintroduce out-swept skirt panels. Ten Guy Arabs for Potteries Motor Traction, (carrying body Nos. 3932-41) delivered between April and June 1946, and the first of many orders for this operator, illustrate these features perfectly.

Many of the wartime bodies required rebuilding after the war because of the use, in the main, of unseasoned timber. Northern Counties bodies were not exempt from this practice as has been seen elsewhere, even though some of them were of all-metal construction, as explained in the text. Midland Red's method of rebuilding was a little unusual, to say the least, but it certainly would have made maintenance of the Gardner 5LW engine fitted to this Guy Arab delivered in 1945, one of five to go to Midland Red, easier! *(GHFA)*

Readers may care to note that before the war the Scottish company described itself as Young's, but after the war adopted the more grammatically correct Youngs' to recognise that there were, in fact, several members of the family in the company.

Furthermore, before the last of the Youngs' deliveries mentioned above had been made, the two leading vehicle chassis builders in the pre-war period mentioned above had returned their factories back to a measure of peacetime production.

Both AEC and Leyland, therefore, were able to supply their vehicles once more to customers, although initially when the assembly was taking place it was, in theory, under the supervision of the MoS and MoWT. The first post-war Leyland PD1 chassis to be bodied by Northern Counties arrived at Wigan Lane on 6th February 1946, followed three weeks later by the first such post-war AEC Regent. The former was destined for Central SMT; the latter for Western SMT. Leyland was to resume its bodybuilding facilities as soon as it was able, in line with the recommencement of chassis construction. Initially, only highbridge bodies were built by Leyland, and as both orders were for lowbridge bodywork, the work came to Wigan Lane making these the first such to be constructed for two years. However, Western was to receive its first post-war bus on 25th June that year and was to continue taking deliveries on an almost annual basis until the end of the 1970s. Just three days after the AEC left Wigan, Central received its Leyland. It is interesting to note how, once again, the Hibernian influence plays a crucial part in Northern Counties history and, indeed, much of the early post-war production was destined for Scotland. England was not totally neglected, however, Leylands being delivered to Bolton, Bury and Middlesbrough before the end of the year. The Bolton and Bury buses were to highbridge design, whilst the Middlesbrough buses were of lowbridge layout. For a moment, however, perhaps time should be taken once more to look at the human element of the business.

As the body output was beginning to return to normality, standards were once more starting to resemble those that existed in 1939 and staff who had been conscripted were beginning to return to take up their employment again, although, as with all organisations, not all those who left were able to return. Reg Fone had steered the company through the difficult times as Works Manager, but one event that must have saddened all those who had been or were associated with Northern Counties was the death on Friday 9th February 1945 of Henry Gethin Lewis, the Company's founder, at the age of 72.

The Lewis family home at Porthkerry, Glamorgan, is now a private hotel. *(RGR)*

He died at his home at Porthkerry, near Barry in Glamorgan and his funeral took place one week later. His home, which had been a rectory in Victorian times, is now the Egerton Grey Country House Hotel, having been opened for this purpose in 1988. His obituaries in the local press reported that he had been one of the leading figures in the commercial, educational and cultural life of Wales and was one of the most popular of Cardiff Docksmen. He had provided money in 1927 for the purchase of the former residence of George Davidson at Wernfawr, Harlech and presented it to the founders of Coleg Harlech for the purpose of adult education of University standard. He also bought and gave to the National Library of Wales the EC Quiggan Celtic collection. He had been High Sheriff of Glamorgan in 1920/1 and in the latter year had become a Justice of the Peace for the county. In a tribute, the chairman of the Barry Court, Sir Ivor B Thomas described him as "a valued member of the bench and a most generous benefactor in the locality". He had also been a governor and treasurer of the University College of South Wales and Monmouth and was one time treasurer of the National Eisteddfod Association. In recognition of his generosity towards education, the University of Wales conferred on him, in 1928, the degree of LL. D. He had also been a governor of Cardiff Royal Infirmary and founder of the United Kingdom Commercial Travellers Benevolent Association.

At the time of his death, besides being Chairman of Northern Counties, his company directorships were recorded as being with the Glamorgan Wagon Co Ltd, the North Glamorgan Wagon Co Ltd, the Taff Wagon Co Ltd and Holmes Electrical & Engineering Co Ltd. He had married Annie Llewellyn in 1897 and they had four sons and four daughters. Unfortunately, he was only survived by three of his daughters and two of his sons, the eldest of whom, Henry Gethin Lewis, was recorded as living at Penarth at this time. Henry Junior, as he was known during the lifetime of his father, had, as we have seen, been a director and one time Company Secretary of Northern Counties and now became its Chairman.

At the same time, Gwilym Alfred Thomas, who was Company Secretary and who was also a director of Glamorgan Wagon Co, and Gwendolen Joan Lewis, both became directors. This is therefore an appropriate point at which to draw this chapter to a close.

Chapter Four

1946 - 1953

The new Chairman was faced with a number of challenges. Within months of his appointment the war was over, but it was to be some considerable time before the supply of materials needed for manufacture was to be back to anything approaching normal. Indeed, the shortage of supplies was, in some cases in the months following the return to a peace-time situation, almost worse than during the war. The national priority in the meantime was to export in order to help pay off some of the war's costs and move towards easing the balance of payments. In this respect Northern Counties was to play an extremely modest role in terms of exports, as will be seen. Whilst the government controls and allocations of the past five years had nevertheless ensured sufficient and consistent orders for Northern Counties, there was now much competition in the market place for orders for bus bodies, despite the struggles to obtain the necessary manufacturing resources.

Fortunately, or perhaps even perversely, the idiosyncrasies of government control had brought Northern Counties into contact with a number of operators with whom they had previously not dealt, but who, in the post-war period, were to become firm customers. These included LUT, Potteries Motor Traction (subsequently referred to as 'PMT'), Southdown Motor Services and Western SMT. The latter firm was still controlled by its managing family the Swords, although the sale of the bus interests of the parent group, the Scottish Motor Traction Company, within a few years, would see the company fall into the nationalised realm and for it to become part of the Scottish Bus Group. The Sword's relationship with the Lewis family had actually commenced during the 1920s when some Albions were supplied to Sword's Midland Bus Services, subsequently to become part of Western SMT when the latter company was formed in 1930. As was mentioned earlier, the first actual deliveries to Western SMT were not made until 1942. Also, two long-standing local authorities were to retain their faith in the company and orders from Wigan Corporation and SHMD were assured.

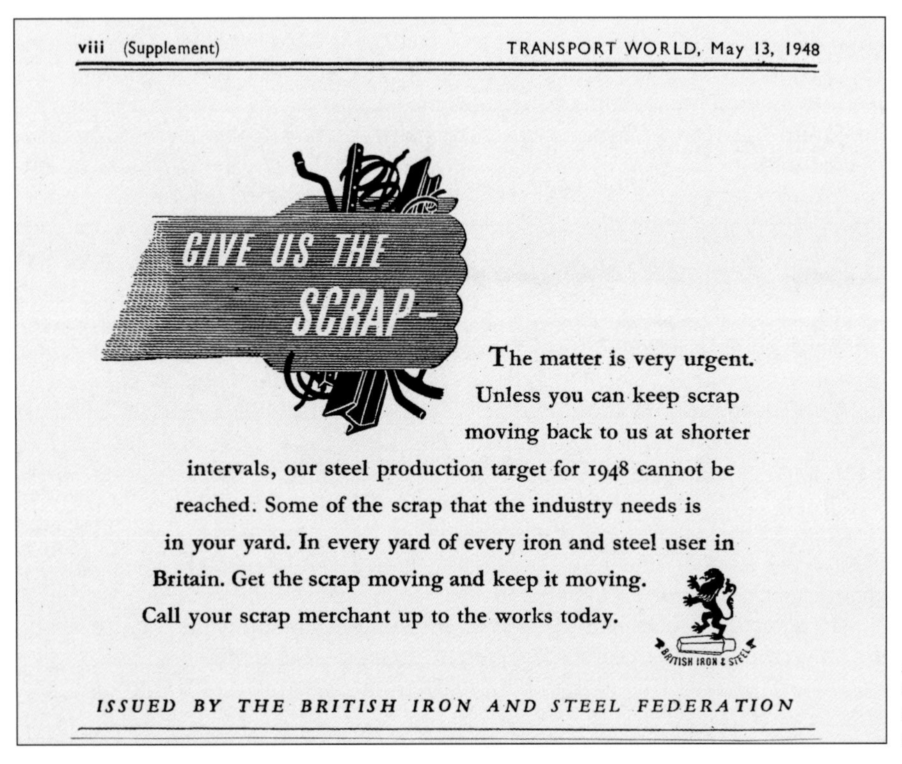
viii (Supplement) TRANSPORT WORLD, May 13, 1948

The matter is very urgent. Unless you can keep scrap moving back to us at shorter intervals, our steel production target for 1948 cannot be reached. Some of the scrap that the industry needs is in your yard. In every yard of every iron and steel user in Britain. Get the scrap moving and keep it moving. Call your scrap merchant up to the works today.

ISSUED BY THE BRITISH IRON AND STEEL FEDERATION

Almost three years after the end of the war this advert clearly spelled out the difficulties then still affecting all manufacturers requiring supplies of iron and steel. *(STA)*

In addition there were two other factors which were to help stimulate the market following the return to peace. Several major tram operating authorities which had embarked on tramway abandonment prior to the war were now able to resume their plans; for others the abandonment of trams was a post-war priority. In any event, whether following their interruption by the war or not, they would require replacement motor vehicles and in some numbers. Secondly, many operators found that several years of sub-standard maintenance had left them with buses in the fleet that required more than a reasonable amount of residual work. Since new chassis were not going to be available in more than penny numbers for quite a few years due to the restrictions mentioned above, some operators took the view that buses delivered in the late 1930's, having reasonable life left in the chassis, could benefit from the fitting of new bodies. Fortunately PMT, Southdown, Central and Western SMT were amongst those who took this view, so besides bodying new buses, there was a fair amount of work for bodies to be built and which would be placed on reconditioned chassis. Before this rehabilitation commenced, however, there were signs that things were beginning to return to normality, and what could be more normal than an order from SHMD, at that time also still (just) a tram operator. Fifteen double-deck Daimlers were supplied in 1947, but L G Stockwell's promotion from Rolling Stock Engineer to General Manager ironically coincided in orders for the next two years going elsewhere.

A further sign of the return to traditional work was an order from another of Northern Counties' pre-war customers, namely Douglas Corporation. During the war, 'holidays-at-home' were rigorously encouraged, as travel of any distance was not viewed with approval, and certainly not where it involved a sea crossing! However, the Isle of Man, whilst temporarily not a holiday destination, was home for a number of internees and displaced persons, and Douglas did, in fact, receive some utility Daimlers bodied by Duple. The Corporation's first post-war AECs were rather unusual in that the Regents it received were of the RT variety, which were by no means common away from the capital, and were in fact the only RTs bodied by Northern Counties, easily identifiable by the lower bonnet line when compared with other Regent IIIs. The balance of the order for ten, a further six units, were delivered over the next two years and were of the provincial AEC Regent variety.

Kemp & Shaw was a Leicester based independent operator who was allocated one wartime Guy utility, supplied in February 1946. It purchased a trio of Guy Arabs after the war and numbered the first, which was delivered in November 1946, as 25 (EBC 882). This bus carried a relaxed utility body. The remaining two were delivered in November 1947 and became 26 and 27 (EJF 668/9). They carried the gently curved profile body developed after the return to peacetime conditions. The company was taken over by the Birmingham & Midland Motor Omnibus Company (BMMO for short, but 'Midland Red' to all its users) on New Year's Day 1959 when the fleet was totally merged with the parent company, and Nos. 25/7 became BMMO 4839-41. The former Kemp & Shaw 26 is seen here as 4840 in company with two of its new brethren. *(GHFA)*

The Stalybridge, Hyde, Mossley & Dukinfield Joint Transport and Electricity Board (or SHMD Board for short, as shown on the side of this 1947 Daimler) was a confirmed Northern Counties customer. Number 30 in the fleet (JTU 791) was delivered in October that year and is seen here when new. This excellent nearside view shows the detail of the immediate post-war developed body. On the original print the name of the Acting General Manager, SJ Davies may be read. He would subsequently be succeeded by LG Stockwell. *(STA)*

The rebodying work commenced in 1948 for Central SMT on Leyland TS7 (single-deck) chassis which, after refurbishment, were now fitted with new double-deck lowbridge bodies. This fitting of new bodies to pre-war chassis was to stretch into the early 1950's and will be returned to later in the story. The situation of Western SMT in 1948 in respect of new chassis perhaps illustrates the industry supply situation quite well, for in that year they took delivery from Northern Counties of AEC Regent IIIs, Daimler CVG5s and Guy Arabs, the latter two models, of course, sharing in common the Gardner engine. (Guy had decided to continue with chassis production of this model after the war in view of its undoubted popularity – despite the decision to produce it in the first place not being entirely their own!)

The first year after the war when the bi-annual London Commercial Motor Show returned was also 1948 when two Northern Counties vehicles were on display. One was a little surprising, being for Liverpool Corporation, who had not previously bought products from Wigan Lane, with the exception of one unfrozen Leyland TD7 in 1942; the other was the first in a long line of buses for Southdown, examples of which were to appear at successive Motor Shows. They were respectively a Daimler and a Guy; the former was the first of a batch of 50 for Liverpool, the balance of which was delivered during the following two years. The City was one of those that had embarked on a tramway replacement programme as mentioned above. Clearly the opportunity to 'blow their trumpet' with an order from such a major customer was not going to be missed in Wigan!

The Liverpool bodies were a departure from previous styles in that they were of four-bay construction, a first for Northern Counties, but in conformity with the style on which Liverpool was attempting to standardise at the time. The body on the Guy represented a new type of design altogether, and it was actually exhibited on the Guy Motors stand. The foremost upper-deck windows were D-shaped, whilst above the lower-deck windows, of which there were still five and which were of the half-drop type, were fitted smaller sliding ventilator windows. A curved valance was fitted to the nearside front of the lower saloon, whilst both front and rear domes were generously curved. The small sliding windows later became generally termed as 'standee' windows, as they allowed standing passengers to see out of the lower saloon more easily. It was also a test bed for Northern Counties' new ventilation system. This was characterised on double-deck bodies by having a wider pillar at the front of the upper-deck. Stale air was drawn through perforations in the roof lining panels, the duct formed by the double-skin roof being connected to the engine air

(Opposite) Liverpool Corporation's order for 50 bus bodies in 1948 was the largest single order received up to then from a local authority undertaking. Delivery commenced early in 1949 and continued through to 1950. The body style was very much to the Corporation's design and was the first four-bay double-deck body built, but still recognisably a Northern Counties product. Similar four-bay bodies were ordered around the same time from Weymann, many of which were completed at Edge Lane works. *(STA)*

The correct location of the apostrophe 'S' in the Young's Bus Services fleet name would appear to be a matter that taxed those concerned over the years, see marginal note on page 55. Fleet No. 162 (XS 6414) was a 1948 Leyland PD2/1 that would pass to Western SMT on the take over of Youngs' in January 1951. ***(STA)***

The Potteries Motor Traction Company (PMT) had become a Northern Counties customer in 1946, and was to be a regular client in post-war years. The first peacetime order to NCME was for 25 lowbridge and 20 highbridge Leyland PD2/1s which were delivered to the Company's Stoke on Trent headquarters in 1947-9. Number 381 was one of the former, the bench seats in the upper-saloon being just visible through the windows. *(GHFA)*

Southdown Motor Services had become the second largest user in the country of wartime Guy Arab utility buses. Immediately after the war large numbers of Leyland buses were taken into stock, thus resuming the pre-war pattern. The Guy chassis had presumably impressed the company management, however, as had, it would seem, the Northern Counties products, with the result that in 1948 twelve buses with this combination were supplied. JCD 504 was representative of eleven of the batch, and is seen here at the well-known photographic location of Pool Valley Bus Station, Brighton. *(RNH)*

The odd-man-out of the batch was JCD 502, which was exhibited on the chassis manufacturers' stand at the first post-war Commercial Motor Show held in London in 1948. It trialled the experimental Northern Counties ventilation system, the pillar on the front of the upper-deck being slightly thicker than that on the bus above. The fact that this pillar was even thicker on subsequent buses fitted with this feature would perhaps suggest that the initial design needed some development. The vehicle was also the first to be fitted with 'standee' windows above the lower deck panes. The front upper-deck pillars were also more generous, matching the curved glass in the cab door. The pressed chrome number plate and chrome surround to the destination box were typical of fittings often added to show models. *(RNH)*

Lancashire United had also become a Northern Counties 'convert' as a result of wartime deliveries and its first post-war intake arrived in 1949, being similar to the Southdown Motor Show exhibit from the previous year. This time the body had sliding opening windows rather than the half-drop variety. Number 391 (KTE 627) was one of ten delivered that year and went on to give 15 years service with the Atherton-based independent. ***(STA)***

intake by means of piping utilising the front pillar. Although only the show model of the batch incorporated all these features, subsequently, buses with the standee type of window (more usually of four-bay construction on double-deckers) were also supplied over the next ten years to a number of other operators. These included Edinburgh, Middlesbrough and Stockton Corporations, LUT, PMT, SHMD and Youngs' of Paisley, although none standardised on this type of body completely. A small number of underfloor-engined single-deckers were also to have this feature.

As an indication of the industrial climate of the time, but also illustrating the difference in the emphasis on the celebrations at the turn of the year, an interesting entry in the company's files for the end of 1948 records that Edinburgh G3 (DWS 313) was actually delivered on Christmas Day! It was, in fact, a wartime Guy Arab chassis, one of half-a-dozen that the operator had chosen to have rebodied within six years of the original body being fitted. Whilst many utility bodies were known for their short life-span, these were probably amongst the shortest lived. Surprisingly perhaps, the new bodies were, however, of the relaxed utility style rather than the more rounded post-war style that was being built for other operators, and which Edinburgh was to take on some new Guy chassis the following year. A slightly unusual situation arose in May and June 1949 when a delivery was made to a British Transport Commission (formerly Tilling Group) company, Hants & Dorset Motor Services, who, unlike certain BET Limited subsidiaries, were not normally Northern Counties customers. They received six AEC Regent IIIs with lowbridge bodies, which, it is said, were originally intended for Western SMT. Western themselves received no less than 25 double-deck bodies that year, the majority fitted to pre-war Leyland chassis. The AEC Regent IIIs it did receive had 9.6-litre engines with epicyclic gearboxes, whilst the Hants & Dorset buses had 7.7-litre engines and 'crash' gearboxes. They remained the only new double-deck AECs purchased by the Hants & Dorset company.

Mention has already been made of the need for Britain to export at this time, and Northern Counties contribution in this respect, whilst by no means extensive, was spread over three continents. Dealing firstly with that with which it was most familiar, a right hand drive double-deck Guy Arab III, but with the stairs and the entrance on the right hand side of the vehicle also, was supplied to the Danish State Railways in 1949. The company records show that job No. 4462 was delivered to Sommer

The first post-war Leyland for Southdown to be bodied by Northern Counties (some pre-war TD5s had returned from Wigan early in 1950 with new lowbridge bodies) was this PD2/12, which received this rather impressive full-fronted high-bridge body and which appeared at the 1950 Commercial Motor Show. It is seen here in Portsmouth in its later days following demotion to Excursion duties. *(RGR)*

Single-deck bodies were not constructed in large numbers immediately following the war because Government restrictions on the use of steel were designed to restrict their build in favour of double-deck chassis and it was not until August 1950 that the first of these was delivered to SHMD. The half-canopy design is an interesting comparison with the Aberdare vehicle shown below. Number 59 (MMA 59) was inevitably a Daimler, of the CVD6 variety. *(DBC)*

Aberdare Urban District Council, by contrast, preferred the full width canopy on its single-deckers supplied by Northern Counties in 1951. There were three AEC Regal IIIs and four Guy Arab IIIs, one of the latter (LNY 856) being shown here. Urban District Councils who operated buses were not common in England and Wales, but a number were to be found in the Welsh Valleys. Whilst this chassis was being bodied at Wigan Lane, the Leylands for Wigan, seen on page 65, were alongside it, rendering the upright-engined chassis almost obsolete overnight. *(DBC)*

of Denmark (presumably an agent acting on behalf of the Railways) on 13th February 1949. The records, unfortunately, are less clear in relation to another Guy Arab bodied in the same year for Bloemfontein in South Africa. The South African Construction and Use regulations, being at the time more generous than the United Kingdom ones, allowed for a body to be built on a 17ft 6in wheelbase chassis. In the event, the bus was not exported and the chassis was dismantled. The body was, of course, too long at the time for British operation, but no evidence of its subsequent use has come to light, despite considerable research by Robin Hannay, the authority on Guy bus production. The final continent to be supplied by Northern Counties products was South America. Walker Bros of Wigan were a well known engineering firm who were capable of producing almost anything to customer's requirements. They had built up a range of cranes and light locomotives as part of their catalogue and it is understood that when approached for railcar orders for Trujillo in Peru, they sub-contracted the bodywork locally for this job to NCME. At different times similar work was also sub-contracted to Massey Bros and East Lancashire Coachbuilders of Blackburn. Eric Ogden also reported in his original history that similar railcars were supplied to the Clogher Valley Railway in Northern Ireland, and there has also been reference made to a railcar going to what is now known as Libya. Whilst such railcars formed only a small part of the factory output, Norman Green recalls part of the pattern for the cab side still resting against a wall when he started in 1957.

Before the war, annual production of buses at Wigan Lane is believed never to have reached triple figures; once the utility programme was under way it never dropped below 125 and these kind of figures continued until 1949, when 143 units were constructed. The following year saw the figure drop below 100 and this may have given some cause for alarm even if other developments were taking place. On the one hand, the first post-war single-deckers were bodied that year, being five Daimler CVD6s for SHMD and had four-bay bodies with a half-canopy. The rear-entrance was fitted with a sliding door, as was the driver's cab. This order marked

For a small Welsh Urban District Council, Aberdare's receipt of ten buses in 1951 was quite significant. The seven single-deckers mentioned opposite were accompanied by a balance which comprised three highbridge AEC Regent IIIs, with a style of body slightly different from those supplied to LUT or PMT, for example, lacking the heavily radiused upper-deck front pillars. *(DBC)*

a return to Northern Counties by SHMD, and from then on until the demise of the Board only products with bodies by the company entered the fleet. In addition, possibly the most interesting body constructed in 1950 was for Southdown on a Leyland PD2/12, being a double-deck coach which made its debut at that year's Motor Show. The body was in many ways a development of the 1948 show vehicle, but the main obvious difference was that the vehicle was full-fronted and of four-bay construction. The lower-deck windows were now of a double length appearance, being divided by a thin chromium plated strip. The sliding ventilators above these were also fitted in pairs. The upper-deck included glazed cant panels, and the platform was enclosed by double jack-knife doors. Intended for express operation on the London – Eastbourne service, unfortunately the performance of the vehicle was less than impressive, even though the passenger capacity was only 44. The bus was also constructed to the new 8ft wide dimension which had become legal for general operation that year. It was an interesting prelude to the Leyland PD3 models for the same operator which were to follow later in the decade. More Guys went to LUT about the same time with a very similar body, including the upper-deck glazed cant panels, but with a conventional half-cab and without platform doors.

Whilst orders for new bus bodies were becoming more difficult to secure, Northern Counties was able to supplement work in the factory by dealing with major repairs from operators who returned their buses to them for such purposes, usually, but not always, as a result of the vehicle concerned being involved in a major accident. During 1950, nine LUT Guys were recorded as returning for 'repairs' and the following year the number of such jobs had increased to twenty-two, the majority of which were again for LUT, who were, of course, on the doorstep. Middlesbrough, PMT, Highland Omnibuses and SHMD also took advantage of the arrangement and similar numbers of vehicles returned in 1952 and 1953.

A decision by PMT to place new bodies on some pre-war Leyland TD4s led to ten bodies as illustrated here being built in 1951 and it will be noted that they were of the then current four-bay design with standee windows developed the previous year. Subsequently, these bodies were placed on 1949 Leyland OPD2/1s, which when new, as in the case of H449 (NEH 449), had been fitted with single-deck bodies because the wheelbase of the overseas Titan chassis was, when built, too long to comply with UK regulations for double-deck bodywork. ***(GHFA)***

Salford's Greengate arches are famous in bus folklore as one of Britain's least attractive bus termini. A short walk beyond, where vehicles waited to join the gloomy stygian damp, the terrain was no better as this LUT Foden view demonstrates. The Greengate & Irwell Rubber Company's premises can be seen behind the bus while the NCME body blends in with the Foden's front end extremely well. ***(GHFA)***

The Festival of Britain took place in 1951 and whilst the transport industry input in terms of exhibits was minimal, (a Maidstone & District Leyland PD2 appeared at the South Bank site, with the prototype Lodekka) some variety in terms of chassis manufacturers and designs began to appear in the factory. Lancashire United ordered five Foden PVD6 chassis which were delivered with double-deck 57-seat highbridge bodies in the late summer. It has to be said, with hindsight, that these Fodens, the first to be bodied by Northern Counties, were somewhat more successful than the next quintet of chassis from Sandbach that were to appear a quarter of a century later, of which more in due course. Around the same time a delivery of eight lowbridge Guy Arabs to Middlesbrough Corporation, which was not in itself too unusual (Middlesbrough having been a regular customer since 1946), marked the beginning of a period of 44 years in which every new double-decker bought by the Corporation and its successors was bodied by Northern Counties. A number of further single-deck bodies were also produced in 1951, including three AEC Regals and four Guy Arab IIIs for Aberdare UDC, but with a different style of body, being five-bay with a full width canopy in comparison with the SHMD buses. The Aberdare vehicles were also unusual in that wartime-type wooden slatted seating was incorporated. It is said that this was preferred to upholstery, easing the cleaner's work in view of the number of colliery workers who normally travelled on the Council's buses.

Northern Counties had to develop a new design altogether for the under-floor chassis which entered service in 1951. Appropriately, Wigan Corporation was the first to place these new generation buses in service, and the first of the quartet, No. 18 (JP 9061), a Leyland Royal Tiger PSUC1/13, is illustrated here. Note the depth of the steps necessary to reach the high floor above the horizontally mounted Leyland O.600 engine. 'Easy access' buses were many years away. *(STA)*

The underfloor-engined single-decker had been developed significantly after the war and had been available for a year or two before the first was bodied at Wigan Lane in 1951 (if one excludes the advanced AEC Qs of the 1930s, which were technically 'side-engined' anyway). The first of this type of chassis to be ordered, for bodying by Northern Counties, was by LUT (ever the innovators!) from Atkinson of Walton-le-Dale near Preston and was for ten units, but Wigan Corporation's Leyland Royal Tigers were delivered first, the chassis arriving at the works in February 1951 with the finished buses being handed over to General Manager, Mr J McKnight, by November of that year. It is perhaps indicative of the different nature of the bodies required for this type of chassis that they were under construction for such a lengthy period; other chassis delivered around this time were completed and dispatched to their new owners in around two to three months on average.

The Royal Tigers were described in the January 1952 issue of *Bus & Coach* in some detail. The bodies seated 43 passengers and had a forward-entrance with driver-controlled doors, an offside door being provided for the driver. An emergency door was provided in the centre at the back. All seats faced forward and were in pairs with the exception that, at the front nearside, there was a single seat to allow for maximum gangway space at the stepped entrance. Framing was of the standard metal type with channel-section pillars having timber inserts for the attachment of panels by wood-screws. Exterior aluminium panelling was of 18-gauge and was not stressed. It was further reported that in the matter of torsional rigidity, a somewhat unusual construction had been adopted to ensure that the body shell was relieved of the function of acting as a girder to stiffen the chassis frame. Before the body was

mounted, the chassis as supplied was stiffened by the addition of a truss plate of 14-gauge steel of a mean depth of 18 inches. Gusseted brackets were welded to the existing outriggers and the truss plate was bolted to these. The truss extended the full length of the frame and also surrounded the back end, thus tying the ends of the outriggers and the frame together into a complete unit so that both longitudinal and torsional stresses were distributed throughout the entire structure of the vehicle.

The rigidity of the construction was said to enhance the quiet running of the vehicle on the road, particularly so in view of the fact that no anti-drumming packings or non-resonant coating preparations had been used. The unladen weight of the complete bus was 7tons 12cwt, which is hardly surprising in view of the aforementioned method of construction. This was, in fact, in excess of some contemporary double-deckers and in due course would lead Leyland to offer the lighter Tiger Cub chassis as an alternative to the Royal Tiger. Northern Counties patent ventilation system was also provided, but in the case of this single-deck body, the ducting within the double-skin roof was connected to the engine air intake by a vertical pipe within the cab frame which passed into the raised seat platform and then to a resonance box between two outriggers. The resonance box acted as a silencer and air reservoir and was coupled to a normal oil-wetted air filter, which in turn was coupled to the manifold by flexible hose. It was said that at normal engine speed, the system would extract the complete air volume of the saloon in five minutes, so providing twelve changes an hour. *Bus & Coach* concluded that 'the vehicles certainly illustrated what could be done with standardised chassis when the operators' requirements were translated into terms of practical bodywork by a specialist concern'. The same month as the article appeared, Lancaster Corporation took delivery of three single-deck Daimlers, which were to be the last half-cab single-deckers constructed by Northern Counties. (One of these was later to distinguish itself by being used as a prisoners' transport vehicle, where passengers were charged, by the police, some time after their journey!)

Lancashire United had to wait until October 1952 before the first of its new breed of single-deckers was ready, although the first chassis had been received in Wigan in May. A 44-seat body with an entrance ahead of the front axle was fitted to the first six in a layout similar to the Wigan buses. This turned out to be a lean year for Northern Counties, only 65 new bodies being constructed in 1952. What impact this had on the company's finances can only be guessed, as it has unfortunately not been possible to trace board minutes and associated detailed accounts for this period. What is known is that it was resolved in August 1952 to increase the nominal capital of the company by £50,000 beyond the registered capital of £15,000 which dated from the re-formation of the company in 1935. As in 1935, when not all of the shares

Lancaster Corporation had the distinction of taking the last half-cab single-deckers bodied by Northern Counties. Now in preservation, sister vehicle NTF 466 was later rebuilt with a front entrance. NTF 468 is seen here. *(STA)*

Lancashire United's first underfloor-engined chassis, built by Atkinson, were constructed almost a year after the Wigan Leyland Royal Tigers and were given a slightly different frontal treatment, the curve to the lower edge of the windscreen being a fashion in vogue with other body builders on early chassis of this type. *(STA)*

were actually issued, it would seem that a similar decision was taken this time, with an additional 40,000 shares being issued. The bulk of them were issued to HG Lewis, but a sizeable number were also allocated to Gwendolen Joan Lewis, his wife, who had become a director in 1945. The remainder of the new shares, accounting for less than 50 in total, were generally allocated to other members of the Lewis family, although a small number were also received by Reg Fone and Gwilym Alfred Thomas, the then Company Secretary.

The following year the balance of the LUT order, for four, was delivered, but this time a centre doorway was fitted together with seats for only 34 as seen overleaf, but with standing space for a further 27. The offside and nearside profiles varied considerably, though both had standee windows, with twin-sliding doors on the nearside, whilst the offside waistrail was raised at the centre opposite the door opening. Intended for use on workmen's services to Trafford Park, and others where low bridges restricted vehicle height but high capacity was deemed desirable, they proved unpopular in everyday service, yet LUT found a niche market for these vehicles in their private hire business; they were ideally suited for transporting weekend anglers with their long rods and copious other equipment.

This variety in bodywork for underfloor chassis was to reach its ultimate conclusion the same year when Manchester Corporation ordered no less than 24 Royal Tigers with three types of bodywork. The first 18 were fitted with rear entrances, without doors, the next four had front entrances and folding doors and the final two (one of which is preserved) had centre entrances with sliding doors. Their use on Manchester Corporation service 22 (which was operated jointly with the North Western Road Car Co) between Eccles and Levenshulme bemused drivers and passengers alike when all three types were operated at various times. Manchester's allocation on the 22 was worked from Parrs Wood depot, so all three types were allocated there at one time or the other; the front-entrance version could be used on service 110 (Dane Bank) from Hyde Road, which was the only one-man route at that time. The centre-entrance versions were tried on the famous 53 service for a short period.

Before Manchester received its first underfloor single-deck chassis, however, a further single-deck chassis of this style had been bodied, this time for SHMD, and it appeared at the 1952 Earls Court Commercial Motor Show, being a Daimler Freeline which was registered PLG 967 and attracting much attention. The Freeline

The first public appearance of a Northern Counties centre-entrance underfloor engined single-decker was at the 1952 Commercial Motor Show, where SHMD's PLG 967 is seen on their stand. The capacity of this vehicle was 60, a reduction of one when compared to the LUT vehicles, and probably as a result of meeting gross vehicle weight regulations. In the background is a Guy Arab IV for LUT. During the early 1950s the Atherton based operator maintained a tradition of having 'one-off' buses at the Motor Shows and what was to become fleet No. 489 (OTE 72) was no exception. *(STA)*

was Daimler's response to the underfloor offerings from AEC and Leyland, the Regal IV and Royal Tiger respectively. All three chassis suffered from being too heavy for the job they were designed to do and were succeeded, as mentioned, by Leyland with the Tiger Cub. AEC subsequently introduced the Reliance as its alternative. Sales of Freeline in the United Kingdom were such that no corresponding lightweight replacement chassis was built by Daimler, even though the chassis was fitted with the ever-popular Gardner engine. The body on the SHMD bus had a centre entrance much like the Atkinsons supplied to LUT, and indeed the last two Manchester Royal Tigers, with a high centre offside waistrail and two sliding doors on the nearside. It is a moot point as to which of these three operators was involved most, in what was, for the time, a ground-breaking experiment, but it is generally accepted that Mr Stockwell, the SHMD General Manager, had most to do with this new design. Sixty passengers were accommodated in three separate compartments, with 16 seats and room for seven standing passengers being provided in the front section, whilst room for twelve standees was available in the centre compartment, the rear section having seats for 18 passengers and a further seven standees. An additional intention was that the centre-entrance design would avoid the problem of persuading reluctant passengers to 'pass down the bus' from either a front- or rear-entrance and thus ensure full utilisation of the available passenger space, particularly at times of peak hour operation.

The SHMD vehicles (also probably those for LUT, MCTD and Wigan) provided the driver with his own completely enclosed cab with offside door. The twin-sliding passenger doors were intended for operation by the driver, but a lever was provided for the conductor if required. The vehicle was fitted with the patented NCME

The centre-entrance versions on the same Atkinson chassis for LUT bodied by Northern Counties utilised a straight edge to the bottom of the windscreen and No. 494 (RTC 685) was representative of five buses supplied at the end of 1953. The total passenger capacity of these buses was 61, only 34 seats being provided. *(STA)*

The variety of bodywork supplied on Manchester Corporation's 24 Leyland Royal Tigers of 1953 is perhaps indicative of the slightly uncertain view of the industry on the best way to use the still relatively-new underfloor single-deck chassis. The very first one, (top) appropriately numbered 1, is seen on the occasion of an official handing over ceremony involving representatives of the chassis and body manufacturers and the operator. Amongst the group are AF Neal, Manchester's General Manager (second from left) with his Chairman Cllr Blackwell (fourth left) next to Reg Fone of Northern Counties. Despite similar events undoubtedly being organised on such occasions, this is one of the few photographs found during the research for this book to portray Mr Fone. *(STA)*

(Centre) The first 18 bodies were of the rear entrance type and No. 4 is seen here. These vehicles had 42 seats. Mr Neal's name is displayed on the skirt panel immediately in front of the front axle. A new experience for passengers was the facility to sit alongside the driver. *(STA)*

(Lower) The last two of the delivery were provided with front entrances, which made them suitable for one-man-operation, although such a feature was by no means common in urban operation at this time. Seats were provided for 43 passengers. *(STA)*

A necessary requirement for any new bus is that it should be tilt tested to ensure stability and safety in service. Single-deck vehicles are required to reach 32º from the vertical without overturning; the figure for buses with two decks is 28º. Whilst the former could be tested within Wigan Lane, where this photograph was taken, it is clear that arrangements were needed to be made elsewhere for double-deckers. All three photographs show one of the pair of centre entrance Leylands, which in Manchester's case had seats for 33. The centre view also shows the space for the seated conductor when the vehicles were used experimentally on service 53. This was later removed and the seating capacity increased to 41. The unladen weight shown on the side of the bus of 7 tons 16cwt led largely to the replacement of the chassis in due course by the lighter Leyland Tiger Cub. *(STA all)*

Some of the most attractive bodies ever built by Northern Counties were arguably the four-bay lowbridge design of this time, ten such bodies going to Yorkshire Traction of Barnsley (their first post-war order) in 1953. Seating capacity was for 55. Yorkshire Traction was subsequently to return to Northern Counties in later years. *(GHFA)*

ventilation system by which the engine obtained the air needed for combustion by extraction from the saloon, as described previously. It was claimed for this vehicle that the interior air would be changed approximately some 20 times per hour, a distinct improvement over the frequency described in contemporary reports referred to above for the Wigan single-decker. An ingenious arrangement on the Freeline provided for the ducting for the ventilation to form a crush barrier for the twelve standees in the centre compartment in the central pillar facing the door opening.

Lancashire United was to receive a further five Atkinson single-deckers towards the end of 1953, again with centre-entrance bodies. Wigan also took four further Leyland underfloor buses during the year. However, apart from fourteen bodies on Guy Arabs that went to Western SMT (seven), LUT (six) and Grahams of Paisley (one), 1953, besides being Coronation Year, would have to be described, as far as Northern Counties was concerned, as the year of the Leyland bus. We have already noted that Manchester received 24 Royal Tigers and the balance that year of 38 double-deck bodies that were to be built were all on Leyland PD2/12 models. This model reference indicated that they were 27ft long and 8ft wide with synchromesh gearboxes and vacuum brakes. Despite the fact that they were all bodied in the same factory, the three operators concerned specified features that were by no

For their 1953 deliveries on Leyland PD2 chassis, Manchester Corporation preferred five-bay construction. Together with NCME's special air extraction system and Manchester's own square shaped windows either side of the central pillar which this needed, the upper-deck front had a unique appearance. Sixty seats were fitted to this vehicle, which was one of 30 delivered in 1953/4. They were regular performers on this limited stop route to south Manchester. *(GHFA)*

Southdown Motor Services' 1953 Leylands were also five-bay, but with half-drop windows and sliding cab door. This later feature was perhaps more reminiscent of London operation than company style at this time, although in the author's experience this feature also permitted closer parking in depots! Not visible in this view, the platform was also fitted with doors and seating capacity was 56. The upper-deck front pillars were now less pronounced giving an even neater appearance. A committed Leyland customer, Southdown's MUF 456 was one of only ten PD2 models, apart from the 1950 Show version, bodied by Northern Counties. For yet even more variety, note the position of the number plates on the Yorkshire Traction, Manchester and Southdown buses. *(RNH)*

means identical, perhaps underlining the fact that Northern Counties were more than prepared to provide vehicles to customers' exact requirements. Interestingly, two of the recipients were BET subsidiaries (not generally regular customers at this time), both Southdown and Yorkshire Traction receiving ten buses each. The latter was receiving its first post-war order from Northern Counties, as also was, in fact, Manchester Corporation as far as its double-deck bodies were concerned, the Corporation being the third recipient.

Yorkshire Traction, based in Barnsley and referred to affectionately by its regular passengers as 'Tracky' (as a matter of interest, even in the 21st Century, typing 'www.tracky.co' into a computer search engine would have found the current Yorkshire Traction website), was the first to be dealt with and received its order in March and April 1953. These were of lowbridge design of attractive four-bay construction, the opening windows being of the slider variety. The Manchester Corporation and Southdown orders were similar in that both were highbridge vehicles with five-bay bodies. Opening windows were of the half-drop type on the Southdown vehicle, with sliders on the Manchester contract. The Southdown Leylands were fitted with platform doors and a sliding cab door (a first for Southdown), whilst only the Manchester vehicles had the Northern Counties proprietary ventilation system fitted (had they given up smoking in Barnsley and on the South Coast by then?), which resulted in the customary wide pillar in the centre of the front of the upper-deck, thus necessitating the fitting of different windows from those on the Southdown order and altering the appearance somewhat.

About this time it was usual for Northern Counties to place small embossed plastic notices on the bulkhead of each saloon advising passengers of the benefits of their proprietary patented system. The Southdown vehicles seated 57; all but six of the Manchester buses seated 60, with the balance seating 61 and indeed the balance of the Manchester order, which was for 30 units, was delivered in 1954.

Close examination of pictures of the upper-deck front windows of the bodies built in this year indicated for the first time a move away from the traditional downward curves and the beginnings of the squarer style that was to be associated with Northern Counties subsequently for many years, possibly in line with the change of single-deck windscreens.

With the celebration of the Coronation and the dawn of a new Elizabethan era, this is perhaps a convenient point at which to conclude this chapter of the company's history.

Chapter Five

1954 - 1967

The dawn of the new age was also perhaps a watershed for the bus industry. The Coronation had been the impetus for many homes to obtain television for the first time, and car ownership, whilst by no means yet universal, was nevertheless on the increase. These factors were only two of several reasons why the bus operators began, almost imperceptibly at first, to look for more economical ways of going about their daily business. In turn, this was going to be reflected within the manufacturing industry. In 1954 London Transport was taking delivery of the last of its ubiquitous RTs, but as an indication of future trends, many of the final deliveries were going straight into store.

Whilst the price or supply of diesel fuel was not a particular problem at this time, (the Suez crisis was still two years away) there was, all the same, a desire to reduce fuel consumption if at all possible. We have already seen that the heavyweight underfloor single-deck chassis from AEC and Leyland had been replaced by lighter chassis, which was saving around one and a half tons per bus as a result and generally a move was beginning to be made by bodybuilders towards a reduction in vehicle weight, all in order to improve fuel consumption figures. The efforts of some of Northern Counties' competitors to achieve this weight saving were not necessarily universally praised for their appearance; the Metro-Cammell-Weymann organisation's Orion body has, over the years, come in for a fair amount of criticism in this respect. The first example of this body had, in fact appeared, at the 1952 Commercial Motor Show and had an unladen weight of 6tons 2cwt. Since 1954 was the year of the bi-annual Commercial Motor Show at Earls Court, it is not surprising to find that one of the company's exhibits at the show was a development demonstrating the weight reduction possibilities. What was perhaps slightly surprising was the recipient of the vehicle, namely Walsall Corporation. The first Northern Counties-bodied motorbus delivered to that Corporation had, in fact, left the factory in May 1954, being a Daimler CVG5 registered TDH 99 (fleet No. 400). Whilst the combination of chassis manufacturer and operator were to play a significant part in the Northern Counties story in later years, Mr R Edgley Cox, the undertaking's General Manager who had arrived in 1952, had previously tended to use bodybuilders located in the Midlands.

PMT received its first new lowbridge double-deckers for eight years in 1956. They were also the last of the standard type of half-cab sunken side gangway lowbridge vehicles to be purchased. Fleet number L6674 (XVT 674) was one of 15 Daimler CVG5s with seating for 59 passengers in the order. *(GHFA)*

The beginning of 1954 had seen the factory completing the Manchester order, delivery of which had commenced the previous year and which, with its total of 54 units, must have given Reg Fone and the other directors of the company much satisfaction. Manchester ranked amongst the big three municipal operators in the country and until then, despite the relative proximity of the city to the factory, had not taken vehicles from the Wigan organisation with any orders since 1923. For a relatively small company in the bus industry, bearing in mind that Leyland, Associated Commercial Vehicles (of which Park Royal was part) and MCW were still the big players, this must have been pleasing. Leyland's closure of its body building plant (which fortuitously resulted in some staff taking up posts with Northern Counties) undoubtedly had reduced some of the competition, but there were still plenty of others and traditional allegiances still were important. In this connection, it must also have brought a wry smile to the management's faces when ten SHMD 1948 Brush-bodied Daimlers were sent to the factory after only six years service, for the fitting of new bodies, the work being spread from February 1954 to May 1955. If Mr Stockwell had made an error of judgement in his choice of bodybuilder, he was not to repeat it. The SHMD Daimlers were not the only buses to receive new double-deck bodies after a relatively short life for the original body, for PMT carried out a similar exercise in 1954, although for somewhat different reasons. PMT had purchased a number of OPS2 and OPD2 chassis in 1949/50. Because these chassis were originally intended for overseas use, they did not meet Construction and Use regulations on the fitting of double-deck bodies at the time; accordingly single-deck bodies were fitted when new. Subsequently, the regulations were changed and PMT took the opportunity to fit 'new' bodies. In the case of this particular batch (NEH 458-67), brand new bodies were supplied by Northern Counties. Others of the overseas chassis received Northern Counties bodies that had originally been fitted to pre-war Leyland TD4 chassis, which themselves dated from 1936/7, when they were rebodied in 1951/2.

For the Motor Show, however, the Walsall Daimler CVG5 that was to be displayed, body No. 4864, (TDH 673, fleet No. 821) was built with a slightly more upright profile than previously, echoing Manchester's choice, allowing 65 seats to be incorporated in the 27ft body, improving on the 60 seats of Mr Cox's first Northern Counties body and was completed in September. Those who recall the later history of Daimlers in the Walsall Corporation fleet might just detect a pattern forming here! The finished bus weighed 6tons 19cwt. Interestingly, it was to join in the Walsall fleet its main competitor in the lightweight stakes, a Metro-Cammell Orion on a Leyland PD2 (Walsall No. 823). Wigan Lane must have been a busy place that autumn as,

The chassis of PHP 220, seen here after bodying, had been developed by Daimler as a lightweight version of its popular CVG6 model, and in 1954 was fitted with this lightweight body and used by Daimler for a while as a demonstrator. *(STA)*

in fact, three vehicles were provided for that year's Commercial Motor Show, the two others having body Nos. 4839 and 4841, either side of Walsall's earlier Daimler. The first of these bodies was fitted to LUT's last Atkinson single-decker, which in itself followed on from two similar central-entrance Atkinsons for SHMD, all of the trio being completed in July that year. The third vehicle at Earls Court was another Daimler, this time a CVG6. The chassis had been built as an experimental lightweight vehicle by the manufacturer two years previously to perform as a demonstrator for Daimler and was registered PHP 220. The body, needless to say, was also of lightweight design, seated 61 and the complete bus was subsequently sold to Burwell & District, at the time a committed Daimler user.

Mr Stockwell's apparent enthusiasm for his centre-entrance single-deckers, to say nothing of Atkinson's products, resulted in 1954 in an order that truly can be described as unique. Fortunately for us, this bus is still in existence, being one of the many fine exhibits at the Manchester Museum of Transport. SHMD No. 70 was, therefore, the only Atkinson double-decker ever built for use in the United Kingdom, and was fitted with a centre-entrance body which seated 60 and was delivered to Stalybridge in February 1955. Such must have been the impact on Mr Stockwell that before the year was out SHMD had ordered a further five centre-entrance double-deckers. This time, however, the delights of the Atkinson model did not, for one reason or another, produce a repeat order and Daimler, with its CVG6 tried and tested model, was the supplier. These buses entered service early in 1956 and were to be the last centre-entrance double-deckers to be built in the United Kingdom. Mr Stockwell had not given up on Atkinson, however, for two more centre-entrance single-deckers also entered service in 1956, although these were to be the last SHMD buses with this entrance configuration. Leslie Stockwell was to take no more deliveries from Northern Counties, however, for he shortly moved to a position with L Gardner & Sons, the well-known engine manufacturers. The new manager at SHMD was Frank Brimelow, who arrived from Middlesbrough, so he was no stranger to Northern Counties' products.

In the earliest days of the company, it has been noted how the business sometimes operated as an agent for other manufacturers, and how, conversely, it was common practice for vehicles to be supplied to dealers for onward sale to operators. This method of conducting business was still not unusual at this time in the coach trade, but was not anywhere near as common on the bus side of the industry, although it was perhaps slightly less unusual in Scotland, so the supply of three lowbridge Leyland PD2s to Milburn Motors of Glasgow in 1955, a well-known

Stalybridge, Hyde, Mossley & Dukinfield Joint Board No. 70 was delivered in 1955 and was the only Atkinson double-decker ever built. The photographer caught this unique vehicle in Piccadilly, Manchester, during a national rail strike in that year. *(JAS)*

Scottish dealer, was not quite so surprising as it at first might have seemed. In due course the three buses found their way into the fleets of Hutchinson of Overtown and Laurie of Hamilton. Interestingly, over the next three years, both operators were to come back to Northern Counties as new customers in their own right. On the subject of new customers, Northern Counties pleasure at receiving this order from Manchester Corporation has already been discussed. One can only guess, therefore, at the elation there was when a further order arrived, this time for 40 bodies, which, on this occasion, were to be mounted on Daimler CVG5 chassis. The displays of lightweight buses at the previous Commercial Motor Shows had obviously had some influence, for this batch of vehicles was to lightweight specification, and delivery commenced in April 1956 and continued through to March 1957. One of the batch, No. 4544 was displayed at the 1956 Commercial Motor Show. In appearance, the body was unlike anything else produced by Northern Counties and the style remained unique to Manchester. Possibly as part of the weight-saving process, they were not fitted with the proprietary ventilation system as on the previous order.

Photographed only a stone's throw away from the previous picture, in Parker Street Manchester, though some years later following the construction of the bus station at Piccadilly, Manchester No. 4539 represents one of 40 buses built on the lightweight principle by both chassis and body manufacturer during 1955/6. The result is a vehicle which, in appearance, is not quite typical of the latter. One of the batch achieved notoriety when it skidded and toppled over into the basement of the burned-out ruin of Messrs Pauldens store on Stretford Road. *(STA)*

Geoff Atkins stood a little further back to take the shot below of a Daimler to match John Senior's Atkinson picture, facing. Seen under the Manchester Corporation trolleybus overhead, also in Piccadilly, where today the overhead of the Metrolink may now be observed, is SHMD No. 75 in original livery soon after delivery in 1956. This bus was one of five, which were the last centre-entrance double-deckers built for operation in Great Britain. *(GHFA)*

The bus industry was changing (there are doubtless some who would say that it has never stopped evolving) and as we have already seen, there was increasing pressure to make economies, which had resulted in the production of lightweight designs. One other area that gave rise to pressure to change was that relating to vehicle size. The Ministry of Transport had always been somewhat reluctant to increase vehicle weight limits and dimensions; even the wartime concession that allowed the utility Guy Arab to be fitted with the longer Gardner 6LW engine, thus extending it over the then legal figure, was withdrawn after the war. Mr R Edgley Cox, who we have already met in connection with Walsall's Daimlers, had persuaded the Ministry to allow him to operate 30ft trolleybuses on two axles under dispensation in 1955. It was not too long, therefore, before the Ministry introduced new regulations governing the length of two-axle double-decker motor buses, so that with effect from 1st July 1956 their permitted length was also 30ft. Needless to say, a Northern Counties vehicle of this new dimension was on display at that year's Commercial Motor Show at Earls Court, although their customers generally seemed reluctant to embrace the new order immediately.

The customer base of Northern Counties was also evolving around this time. Municipal customers had tended to form the bedrock of Northern Counties' patrons, and from 1955 a number of new customers from that sector materialized. Stockton Corporation, the neighbour of the long established customer Middlesbrough, had purchased their first bodies in 1955, repeat orders being delivered in 1957 and 1958. Oldham Corporation took deliveries in 1957 and 1958, Lytham five in 1957, whilst Sunderland Corporation took eight Daimlers in 1958, the other vehicles all being Leylands. Local authorities tended by nature to be traditionalist; even after the increase in vehicle dimensions, the orders referred to here were all of the 'old size'. There was also the invaluable market in Scotland, where two of the Scottish Bus Group subsidiaries had consistently re-visited the Wigan 'shop'. Surveying the bus operating company scene in England, it has to be remembered that at this time it was divided into three distinct sections. The British Transport Commission had its own manufacturing facilities in Lowestoft and Bristol and seldom bought from outside the group. Throughout the 1950s only three BET subsidiaries ever bought from Northern Counties, although this number and quantity bought was to change during the 1960s as we shall see. The final section was the so called independent one, the largest company here being LUT, who had consistently placed orders from the factory on their doorstep. Two new customers from this section placed orders during 1957. Moore Brothers of Kelvedon took two Guy Arab IVs, although subsequent orders before the company was purchased by Eastern National went to the other Wigan bus builder. The second new customer was Barton of Chilwell, who had previously only received Northern Counties bodies during the war. Given the ensuing orders from

Stockton Corporation had become a Northern Counties customer in 1955, thus emulating its municipal partner across the River Tees, who had commenced receiving bodies in the immediate post-war period. The body on this Leyland PD2/12 shows no signs at the front of the upper-deck of the flamboyant curves so typical of Northern Counties, and whilst standee windows are fitted, the pillars between the windows below them are without the pairing of the original design. *(JMBC)*

Lytham St Annes had also become a customer, this time in 1957. This Leyland PD2 is seen in the Fylde livery which was the name the undertaking adopted as a result of Local Government reorganisation in 1974. *(GC)*

Oldham Corporation's distinctive maroon and ivory livery suited this 1957 body very well. The Leyland PD2/12 with its 'tin front' was one of six 61-seat buses in Oldham's first order from Northern Counties; a repeat order was received the following year. *(STA)*

Barton, the first two vehicles delivered were totally conventional, being lowbridge 27ft long AEC Regent Vs.

It was around this time that the next generation of the Lewis family joined the company and this has proved slightly confusing for this story, in that the party concerned was the third generation of the family to be called Henry Gethin Lewis. He was born on 21st January 1932, and educated at Shrewsbury School and Oxford, following which this HG Lewis undertook a variety of work for the company, eventually becoming Sales Director. Possibly because of his academic background, sporting activities were very much his forté and anyone who can clear a five-bar gate is worthy of respect. The story that he once cleared such an obstacle in his MG sports car is included for the sake of completeness, one vouched for by David Cherry. Despite the rather cramped facilities at Wigan Lane, space was still found for HG's vintage Bentley, which had been his father's, though it was through his golfing activities that he was later to bring David Cherry to the company. Other senior members of staff at this time included Jack Abbott, who was works manager and effectively Reg Fone's deputy. One of Fone's idiosyncrasies was said to be that the only person he spoke to in the factory, apart from his secretary, was Jack Abbott, all instructions to the work force being directed through Jack. Amongst others employed as foremen at the time were A Underwood (Panel Shop), Frank Nelson (Fitting Shop), Fred Sharrock (Body Shop), C Whitter (Paint Shop), D Chetham (Finishing), J Rawlinson (Trim Shop) and Roy Leyland (Sawmill).

The first 30ft double-decker to be built and which appeared at the 1956 Commercial Motor Show was for LUT (who else?) and was on a Guy Arab IV chassis (body No. 5107) with seating for 73 and was to become LUT 603 (320 ATC). It was actually the last body number in a batch of ten, although it was the first to be built, being completed in September for the Show. The balance of the order for

The first double-deck body to be built to the then new 30ft long dimension was for LUT and appeared at the 1956 Commercial Motor Show, the year that the regulations permitting such length were amended. The body was basically the four-bay style of the 27ft long body extended by the inclusion of an additional bay and is seen here on an LUT Guy Arab IV (No. 603 – 320 ATC). The Lancashire independent was needing replacements for the three-axle GUY BTX trolleybuses which would cease operation with its sister company SLT the following year, and thus the opportunity to take this vehicle into the fleet was timely, though in the event Leyland and MCW secured the business with Orion-bodied Titan PD3s. *(STA)*

The lowbridge version of the 30ft body is shown on this 1958 PD3/3 Western SMT, posed for photography before delivery to the Kilmarnock based operator. This body still retains some of the last vestiges of the curved upper-deck front pillars. In true Scottish style, the panel for locating the side advertisement has already been prepared, complete with cut away corners. *(STA)*

these ten Guy Arabs was completed by the end of the year and they were on 27ft long chassis with seats for 64. The absence of an invoice number against body No. 5107 in the factory records would perhaps suggest that the whole batch was ordered as 27ft long models, and that 'by arrangement' with Guy Motors, Northern Counties and LUT, a 30ft model was substituted at a late stage to be displayed at the Show. The reluctance to embrace the new dimension is perhaps born out by the fact that the next 30ft body was not ready for delivery until over a year later. Production runs of 30ft long buses commenced in earnest in October 1957, starting with more Guys for LUT and continuing throughout the winter with Leyland PD3s of lowbridge layout for Western and Central SMT. There was also one for Laurie of Hamilton, this latter vehicle being a highbridge PD3.

May 1958 saw the first of some of the best known 30ft Leylands being delivered, when on the 20th of that month two Southdown PD3s left the factory, registered TCD 825 and 827. The author must confess that on a personal note, the vista of these buses was perhaps the first time he became fully aware of Northern Counties' products, when he saw one in Fareham bus station shortly after it had entered service on Southdown's service 45 to Portsmouth and Southsea. The choice of Northern Counties for these bodies might have seemed a natural progression for the

Numerically the third Southdown PD3 to be constructed, TCD 823 is seen here in the traditional Northern Counties photographic location at Spencer Road. The short bay in the middle of the body and the curve to the top of the rear lower-deck window, defining features of these vehicles, can be clearly seen. *(STA)*

Included purely to satisfy the author's nostalgia, TCD 815 is seen here 14 years after delivery, but still in Fareham bus station, the location of his original sighting when brand new. This time the bus is on the western side of the station, waiting to depart for Warsash. *(RGR)*

south coast based company after experience with the utility Guy Arabs and the subsequent orders for both Guy Arabs and Leyland PD2s in the 1948-53 period. However, during this time Southdown had been fairly catholic in its choice of body builders, taking Leyland bodies until they were no longer available, and then, after the 'coronation' bodies, going to Park Royal, Beadle and East Lancs.

That the new vehicles had a significant impact on the industry is possibly understating the case. The first order was for 15 units, but their effect on the trade was as much because of their forward entrances, set just behind the front axle and with power-operated doors controlled by the driver, than the fact that they were also full fronted. Other operators had dabbled with such forward entrances from time to time, but it is probably fair to say that only Southdown pursued it to irrevocability. It was claimed that entrances under the control and within sight of the driver were safer and reduced accidents, again another move attempting to contain costs, although mercifully the change was not driven by today's compensation culture. The body had a number of features which made them distinctive, in particular the short window mid-way along the body and the curve to the top of the rear side window on the lower-deck, imitating that at the rear of the side of the upper-deck. Other body builders were to make use of this short window device when using designs for 27ft long bodies and stretching them for the 30ft variety, (the London Transport Routemaster obviously comes to mind), but this was not the case here. The LUT Guys and Scottish Bus Group Leyland PD3s had equal size windows and in the author's view looked all the better for it. But in due course, by far the most numerous were to be the Southdown PD3s, of which a total of 285 were eventually to be built.

For what were probably good operational reasons, or other circumstances pertaining at the time, Wigan Corporation appeared to display some prevarication during the 1960s as regards its vehicle purchasing policy. Pictured here is a Leyland PD3, with a body reminiscent of the Southdown style. The Corporation reverted to some Leyland PD2 models subsequently. *(STA)*

The first 30ft Daimler to be bodied by Northern Counties was this CVD6-30 for PMT. The 'D' in the model classification indicated that it was rather unusually fitted with a Daimler engine, the vast majority of 30ft Daimlers having Gardner engines and being designated CVG6. It was registered 900 EVT and was also fitted with what was termed a 'Manchester' front, the glass fibre assembly originally having been developed by Daimler for that undertaking. *(STA)*

The first Dennis Loline to receive a body from Northern Counties was Middlesbrough 99 (JDC 599) in November 1958. The body was a low-height version of the initial 30ft body supplied to LUT, without the fussiness of the Southdown body. It was fitted with Cave-Brown-Cave heating, as witnessed by the large air intakes either side of the destination box. The lack of a step from the platform into the lower saloon can clearly be seen in the lower picture, a feature developed by Bristol Commercial Vehicles from whom the Loline was built under licence. This was achieved by means of a dropped rear axle. Contemporaneously with this delivery, Middlesbrough Corporation was taking delivery of a batch of lowbridge Guy Arab IVs. *(STA both)*

As far as the author has been able to ascertain, the only other Leyland PD3s to have this style of body were three batches for Wigan in 1959, 1960 and 1961 which amounted to 19 in total and which also had forward entrances. Since Wigan bought the shorter PD2 model before and after the PD3s, it could be argued here that the 'standard' window could be used on both types.

Middlesbrough was also to take a similar body on eight full fronted forward-entrance Dennis Lolines in 1960; but we are racing ahead; before they ordered them they took a solitary Dennis Loline with a rear-entrance, which brings us to the 1958 Commercial Motor Show, where it was on display coincidentally with a Daimler for PMT, being the first 30ft Daimler to be bodied by Northern Counties.

Dennis Brothers of Guildford had developed the Loline under licence from Bristol Commercial Vehicles, as an open market version of the Bristol Lodekka. Its low chassis frame and dropped rear axle enabled highbridge type seating, ie, with central gangway in the upper-deck, to be contained in a body with an overall height of around 13ft 6ins. Previously, to achieve this sort of overall height, it was necessary to have a sunken (and unpopular) gangway on the upper-deck. It might have been thought that those operators who were forced to take low-height buses because of low bridges, such as Middlesbrough, would find the Loline an ideal solution, yet when one considers the number of low-height bodies built by Northern Counties, the number of Dennis Lolines it would eventually body was to be surprisingly low, no more than two dozen in total. Indeed, the total number of Dennis Lolines built was to be less than the number of Leyland PD3s delivered to Southdown. There were a number of reasons for this, though it can probably be summed up in two words: 'Daimler Fleetline'. But again we are perhaps racing ahead with the story, for the first of

Another Guy Arab IV customer, this time LUT, also took the Dennis Loline in 1959/60. Number 7 in the fleet was the first and a further five followed. It seems somewhat amazing now that, within months of the final Dennis being delivered, Northern Counties was bodying a Guy Wulfrunian for the operator, seen here in the lower pictures. Guy were attempting to produce a chassis to match the Leyland Atlantean, but retained the engine at the front. To accommodate the power unit, the extent to which the steering wheel had to be moved to the right can clearly been seen, as can the unusual nearside staircase fitted to this model. Lancashire United took only one Wulfrunian, and even that was one too many as events would prove. *(STA all)*

In what was a mixed year for Northern Counties, Middlesbrough took what was to be the largest batch of Dennis Lolines in 1960, when eight were ordered. The obvious resemblance to the Southdown full-fronted forward-entrance body may be seen. The door was, however, of the sliding type rather than the folding variety of the Southdown bus. The interior view shows the arrangement needed for the sliding door and again displays the flat floor possible with the Loline, albeit necessitating rather higher seats over the wheel arches. *(STA both)*

these did not arrive at the factory until 1961. In the meantime LUT became a Dennis customer once more. Despite taking large numbers of highbridge Guy Arabs, it too was troubled by low bridges in its operating area and took half-a-dozen Lolines in 1959/60. On the face of it, this was perhaps a strange choice for LUT, but the Lolines used Gardner engines built within their operating area and already used in the Guy Arab. What was perhaps even more surprising was the Guy chassis for LUT that emerged with body No. 5557 in December 1960. This was the only Guy Wulfrunian to be bodied by Northern Counties, and from the operator's point of view it can hardly have been considered an outstanding success, being sold within a year or two. From the manufacturers' point of view, it turned out to be a disaster, but that is another story

Nineteen-sixty had, indeed, been a year of mixed fortunes. Output was down to 73, nearly 20% of which had been Dennis Lolines, yet one of these had been the sensation of the 1960 Commercial Motor Show. It had appeared alongside a Southdown PD3, 50 of which had by now been delivered and a fellow BET Company, Yorkshire Woollen of Dewsbury, had also placed their first order that year. An interesting full-fronted Daimler had been supplied to A1 Service, the Co-operative based in Ayrshire in Scotland, the first for this combine. This bus achieved some claim to fame in miniature as the result of EFE models producing a replica of it as part of its range. Despite the original being 30ft long, having a full-front and forward-entrance, it had equal size windows on both decks without the 'demi-size' central window. To return to the show sensation, this was a Barton vehicle. Even though the chassis had the ability to achieve low-height status without the need for a sunken gangway, this Loline was fitted with one, resulting in an overall height of just 12ft 6in. It also incorporated wrap-round windscreen and upper-deck front windows, a feature also fitted to five AEC Regents Vs delivered to Barton in the Autumn of 1960. Unlike all previous Northern Counties bodied Lolines, which had been fitted with Gardner engines, Barton's bus received a Leyland O.600 engine. Like the unique SHMD Atkinson mentioned previously, this distinctive Barton vehicle is also in preservation.

After the low volume production of the previous year, 1961's total output was almost doubled. This was due largely thanks to Southdown, who added no less than 76 more PD3s to its fleet. Two 'one-off' buses were also of interest this year, one perhaps representing the old order, being yet another Dennis Loline, although this time the only one to be delivered to Belfast Corporation, and the other being the first of the new generation of rear-engined double-deckers. The Belfast Loline was of

The picture opposite is clear evidence of the amount of work that was involved when preparing a vehicle, and also the stand with all its floral appurtenances, for display at a Motor Show, in this case in 1960 at Earls Court. Woe betide the contractors if someone neglected to water the blooms. *(STA)*

Barton Transport had been a customer of Northern Counties for three years when five AEC Regent Vs were delivered in the autumn of 1960. Perhaps they have never attracted the same fame as the Barton Dennis Loline, but they were the first vehicles in the country to enter service incorporating wrap-round screens on both decks. *(GHFA)*

NORTH
PRIVATE
861
861

interest in that it followed the contemporary trend of having a forward-entrance, but unlike the Middlesbrough vehicles of this configuration had equal size windows. The rear-engined vehicle was a Daimler Fleetline and the customer was A1 Service, only its second purchase from Northern Counties. Whilst the Earls Court Motor Show in London was held every other even year in alternate years the Scottish Motor Show took place. The opportunity was therefore taken to display this bus, which was subsequently registered TAG 60, at that show. Unlike its main competitor, the Leyland Atlantean, which had been in service production since 1959, the Fleetline was designed with a flat floor in the lower-deck and could be fitted with a low-height body but with a central gangway in the upper-deck and the first chassis assembled had appeared at the 1960 show. It was also available with a Gardner engine, so its appeal to many operators was universal. Since the Atlantean first appeared, it was probably fair to say that those responsible for the body design had struggled to find a product that matched the revolutionary innovativeness of the vehicle, many designs being at best described perhaps as utilitarian. To many, however, TAG 60 represented a rather more attractive design, which, nevertheless, was an adaptation of what had become the standard NCME body on front-engined chassis.

The difficulty with rear-engined double-deckers to this time had been that the 'pod' containing the engine pack was situated below the rear of the upper-deck, with an unsightly gap in between. Northern Counties' solution was to extend a fairing from the lower of the rear deck over the engine compartment, thus improving the rear profile. This style of body was to become the norm from Northern Counties on Daimler Fleetline chassis for some years.

TAG 60 established the standard in terms of improved bodywork on rear engined chassis for some years to follow. The bus first appeared at the 1961 Scottish Show and was for the A1 Service combine of Ardrossan, entering service the following year. *(STA)*

In order to compare the relative merits of the new chassis that were becoming available, Belfast Corporation took delivery of a number of 'one-offs', which included a solitary Dennis Loline in 1961. *(RGR)*

The first actual delivery of a batch of these rear-engined vehicles was made to Middlesbrough Corporation in March 1962, followed in June by a batch for LUT. Whereas Middlesbrough and its successors were to standardise on this combination, LUT's half-a-dozen were very much a trial of the new technology, a large batch of rear-entrance Guy Arabs being put into service at the same time. Other Fleetlines were delivered that year to McGill of Barrhead (one), PMT (one), Beckett & Sons of Bucknell (one) and Blue Bus Services of Willington (two). Daimler also ordered a demonstrator which was to be registered 4559 VC. Another manufacturer to order Northern Counties bodies for its products was Dennis. Here it was a slightly different situation, for Dennis wanted to break into the Hong Kong market and was supplying a Loline to the China Motor Bus Company, and selected the Wigan builder itself, taking delivery in April. A further blend of this combination was also completed in November, seemingly for the same market, but like the South African demonstrator some years previously, it did not leave these shores, subsequently going on demonstration in the UK as EPG 179B.

In the midst of all this activity, it was almost incongruous that Harper Brothers of Heath Hayes should place in service in May 1962, a Leyland PD2/28 which had been completed the previous year. This was the first new body from Northern Counties for the Staffordshire independent, but was the beginning of a relationship that was to last for over a decade. Being an even numbered year, the Motor Show was at Earls Court and by this time there was almost an air of anticipated expectancy as to what the exhibits would be. One would imagine that the observers were not

No history of Northern Counties could be complete without including photographs of Barton 861, so no apology is made for the three views included in this chapter. It will be apparent that again Cave-Brown-Cave heating was originally fitted, although this was later removed. What was possibly the shortest staircase ever fitted to a double-deck bus can plainly be seen, whilst the previous full page picture provides further evidence of the striking appearance of 'HAL' as the vehicle, happily now preserved, almost inevitably became known. *(STA)*

Lancashire United was, like many of the major operators when the rear-engined chassis was introduced, more than a little unsure whether to commit all future orders to this type. Nevertheless, their first order, also delivered in 1962, was for a reasonably large batch (by their standards), of six Daimler Fleelines,s of which No. 102 (566 TD) is seen here. In happier days an order for less than ten vehicles could include three or four different bodymakers! *(STA)*

This Daimler Fleetline PDC 111 was one of a batch of ten for Middlesbrough built in 1962, the first such vehicles for that operator and the first multiple order for the chassis to be built by Northern Counties. Note the relatively short-lived prominent Daimler winged badge. (JMBC)

The introduction of this chassis with its attractive Northern Counties body design was to result in orders from a number of new customers, amongst which was included this example registered VHS 501 for McGills of Barrhead. *(STA)*

A certain amount of intrigue surrounds the delivery of SBF 233 to Harper Brothers of Heath Hayes in 1962, where it became their fleet No. 25. Northern Counties' factory records for 1961 contain a cryptic note that it was 'completed in December 1961 but not collected until May 1962.' It was in fact delivered on 17th May that year with another note that it was 'completed 1961 and treated as 1961 sale'. It was the first order from the Staffordshire firm and was based on a Leyland PD2/28 chassis, which indicated that it had a synchromesh gearbox and air brakes. In his comprehensive history of the Leyland Bus, Doug Jack records that this model was only in production until 1959, suggesting that Leyland either had a chassis left over or put one together from components in stock. Rennies of Dunfermline usually provided a regular outlet for such one-offs and other Leyland demonstrators. *(RGR)*

In 1962 two Mark III Dennis Lolines with forward-entrances were ordered by Dennis, and were intended for export to Hong Kong, but in the event only one was shipped abroad. The body style was fairly similar to the Belfast Dennis delivered the year before as readers can see. After resting at Guildford for a while, the remaining vehicle became a demonstrator for the chassis manufacturer and it was initially displayed in the demonstration park at the 1964 Earls Court Show. It is seen here on hire to Southampton Corporation. No orders resulted from this trial, but a comparable demonstration to the Halifax Corporation *aficionado* was more successful. *(RGR)*

disappointed when Northern Counties' stand displayed two Daimler Fleetlines and an Albion Lowlander, the chassis introduced by Leyland the previous year rather belatedly to meet the market sector that amongst other competitors the Dennis Loline had been fulfilling. It was interesting that at 13ft 4in the LUT Fleetline's overall height was two inches less than the Lowlander.

The two Fleetlines were something of a contrast, to say the least. One was LUT's 137, a further one-off to follow the previous experimental batch earlier that year and carried what even by then had become the company's standard Fleetline body. The other was for Walsall Corporation and as the industry was coming to expect from that operator's General Manager, Edgley Cox, was slightly different. The chassis was reduced to 25ft 7in instead of the nominal 30ft and a 64-seat body was fitted, with an entrance just behind the front-axle, which was placed virtually under the driving position as there was no front overhang. The frontal appearance was completed by the fitting of wrap-round screens on both decks, as introduced on the Barton vehicles two years previously. By comparison with the LUT bus, the overall height of the Walsall Fleetline was 13ft 9in. The third vehicle was perhaps, under the circumstance, somewhat more conventional, but again Northern Counties managed to produce a more attractive design where the initial bodies on the new chassis had perhaps left something to be desired. The Albion Lowlander had been developed at the behest of the Scottish Bus Group and this first such vehicle

After purchasing an initial batch of Daimler Fleetlines, LUT reverted to Guy Arabs for its next delivery. However, at the 1962 Commercial Motor Show a 'one-off' Fleetline for the company was exhibited on the NCME stand. Northern Counties' proud boast was that this was the 260th body built by the company for LUT. Also on the stand was what was possibly the shortest Daimler Fleetline ever built at 25ft 7in to the requirements of Walsall Corporation's General Manager, Mr R Edgley Cox. Production vehicles for this operator were, however, slightly longer at 27ft as shown here by the second Fleetline delivered to them and appropriately numbered as their No. 2. ***(STA both)***

registered (EGM 1), was one of ten for Central SMT, Western SMT also taking a similar number that year. More Lowlanders went to both companies the following year. The only Albion Lowlanders that were supplied from Wigan for an English operator were to go to South Notts of Gotham, who had become a Northern Counties customer in 1961, initially taking lowbridge PD3s.

In a decade that was already providing a number of interesting developments, 1963 saw the ever more popular Fleetline supplied with Northern Counties bodies to two new BET companies, Maidstone & District and Trent. Other subsidiaries of the conglomerate also took bodies from the company for the first time, but were perhaps less ambitious (or maybe more conventional!), Rhondda Transport and Western Welsh both taking ten AEC Regent Vs each. This order, despite the greater centralisation of the industry by this time, still owed something to the South Wales

South Notts was an independent operator based in Gotham and had become a Northern Counties customer in 1961 with the delivery of an exposed radiator PD3, as seen here, with an interesting set back doorway. A further PD3 was to follow the next year and double-deck requirements of one or two buses most years up to 1980 followed, including rather unusually Albion Lowlanders (the type is shown below), being the only Northern Counties Lowlanders delivered to an English operator and the only independent operator to receive the chassis. Despite a 50% interest in the company being held by Barton Transport, South Notts eventually sold out to the City of Nottingham undertaking in 1991. *(STA)*

A Central SMT Albion Lowlander had appeared on Northern Counties stand at the 1962 Commercial Motor Show and one out of the batch which totalled ten buses, EGM 6, is seen here. Because of its high driving position, the Albion Lowlander was a difficult chassis on which to mount an attractive looking body, but Northern Counties probably succeeded better than most other builders. *(STA)*

Yorkshire Traction had been a Northern Counties customer since 1953, although it was to be another seven years before further deliveries were made, which were double-deck front-entrance bodies on reconditioned single-deck Leylands. Then in 1961 new Leyland PD3s with front entrances were supplied as depicted by No.1195 seen here. The offside illuminated advertisement panel is of interest, a contemporary fitting that never really became popular. The Central SMT vehicle, above, shows the feature in use but many vehicles spent their lives with it painted over as per the Yorkshire Traction vehicle, though this manufacturer's view is pre-delivery of course. *(STA)*

The first ever order from Trent Motor Traction of Derby resulted in ten Fleetlines being supplied in 1963. Not all the British Electric Traction companies were, however, convinced of the benefits of the rear-engined design, and fellow subsidiary Western Welsh of Cardiff preferred the AEC Regent V in the same year, even to the extent that it was constructed to the then superseded 27ft length. *(STA both)*

connections of the Lewis family. A further BET company, Yorkshire Traction, who had resumed purchasing from Northern Counties in 1960 and who by now were placing an almost annual order, this year rebuilt some single-deck Leyland PS2s (as did fellow BET company Stratford Blue) and had them fitted with forward-entrance 63-seat bodies. Stratford Blue also took four Leyland PD3s, which also happened to be Yorkshire Traction's standard at this time.

The largest single order for 1963 came from Nottingham City Transport, which was taking Northern Counties bodies again after an interval of nearly 30 years, wartime deliveries excepted. A total of 31 Fleetlines were supplied initially, followed in 1964 by ten Leyland Atlanteans, which were, incidentally, the first of this model to be bodied at Wigan Lane. Nottingham was to continue taking both chassis until the manufacturer ceased providing them and was to develop a distinctive styling, of which more later. Despite appearing to embrace the rear-engined concept, even Nottingham took front-engined chassis in 1965, this time the AEC Renown being selected, yet another new chassis developed, perhaps rather belatedly, to meet to the low-height demand without recourse to sunken gangways. AEC Renowns also went to Western Welsh that year. In the meantime, LUT, who were not fully convinced about the merits of the Fleetline, were still purchasing Guy Arabs, but by 1964 even they had moved the entrance forward. That same year had seen one of these LUT Guys (of course!) and a Nottingham Atlantean as well as a Western Welsh AEC displayed at Earls Court. After the previous two Motor Shows, it was conceivably not possible to maintain the off-beat display every time!

Around this time the retirement of Reg Fone should be recorded. For over 30 years he had been the public face of Northern Counties, and whilst his management style perhaps owed more to that earlier era than the 1960's, he commanded respect from all who worked for him. He was succeeded by Jack Abbott, who had commenced with Northern Counties before the war. The latter's position as Works Manager was taken by Freddie Sharrock, who in turn was replaced as body shop foreman by L Brown. R Gregson had taken over as trim shop foreman.

Throughout this period, Southdown had continued receiving its PD3s and during 1964 had taken a batch with convertible open tops for use on its seasonal services. Ironically, they were to replace the previous open top fleet which comprised wartime Guy Arabs, many of which originally had Northern Counties bodies. Walsall

No less than 31 Daimler Fleetlines were supplied to Nottingham City Transport in 1963. At this time the body outline was a standard Northern Counties product, with only the half-drop windows indicating any special requirements from the operator, a far cry from subsequent deliveries. *(STA)*

The Construction and Use regulations had been further modified with effect from 1st August 1961 to permit buses to be built to a maximum size of 36ft long by 8ft 2½in wide. It was not until 1963, however, that the first vehicle to this length was built by Northern Counties, being mounted on a Leyland Leopard chassis for Youngs' of Ayr, one of the two partners in the AA Motor Services co-operative. Because of the unusual nature of the body, its styling owed little to other designs produced by the company though echoes of the original Manchester Royal Tigers are apparent. *(STA)*

The first Leyland Atlanteans to be bodied by NCME were supplied to Nottingham in 1964 and already the distinctive style for that undertaking was beginning to appear, the angled down glass of the front destination being a Nottingham hallmark, together with the just visible two-part fully-glazed doors. Another dozen vehicles of this style followed early in 1965. Followers of Geoff Atkins photography will recognise his classic night view. *(GFHA)*

(Opposite lower) Northern Counties, like all bodybuilders, would wish to avoid building small numbers of 'one-offs', and were not beyond offering features developed for one operator to another when appropriate. This 1965 Leyland Atlantean for Youngs' of Ayr, the same operator who took the Leopard shown above and part of the AA co-operative, quite clearly shows Nottingham influences in its frontal appearance. *(STA)*

At a time when Scottish operators were taking rear-engined buses, Garelochhead Coach Services remained faithful to the front-engined variety and took delivery of this AEC Regent V, which seated 70, in 1964. The full-fronted body is reminiscent of the Southdown PD3, but the shorter length of the body has eliminated that version's small central window. *(STA)*

Corporation too had taken further 'short' Fleetlines, but from 1965 abandoned the wrap-round front and single-entrance in favour of two doors and flat screens, on an extended, but still only 28ft 6in long chassis, the seating capacity being 70. By comparison, Southdown took delivery of an experimental PD3 in October that year with a wrap-round windscreen! It was experimental insofar as a novel Clayton heating and ventilation system was fitted which moved the radiator, thus permitting the different windscreen. SHMD had become a Fleetline convert in the same year and was in due course to take the 'Walsall' two-door body on its final deliveries. The final Dennis Lolines to be bodied by Northern Counties went to yet another new customer in 1966, five with semi-automatic transmissions being delivered to Halifax, who also took a small batch of Fleetlines. The Lolines were fitted with semi-coach seats and were to the specification of the authority's charismatic General Manager, Geoffrey Hilditch, whose philosophy was not dissimilar from Mr R E Cox. We shall meet Mr Hilditch again later. Yet another Earls Court display came round in 1966 and this time, besides the Walsall and Southdown exhibits (no prizes for guessing which models they were!). Northern Counties displayed a single-deck vehicle, the first time since 1954. In keeping with tradition, however, it was for LUT but was a Leyland PSUC1/1, with seats for 40 and standing room for 16 within its 32ft length body. The Southdown bus (GUF 250D) continued

In the same way that Dennis had produced the Loline and the Leyland Group the Lowlander, AEC had introduced the Renown, a dropped-frame chassis designed to meet lowbridge requirements without the need for sunken gangways on the upper-deck. Northern Counties' bodies for this chassis were somewhat more upright than previous styles, although still unmistakably a typical product, this example being for Western Welsh in 1966 and an interesting comparison with the AEC on page 94. *(STA)*

Lancashire United 241 (YTC 249D) was a Leyland Leopard fitted with 40 seats and two doors and which appeared at the 1966 Earls Court Show. Whilst employing larger windows than the Leopard supplied to AA three years earlier (see page 96) it nevertheless has a shorter window in the centre of the body. *(STA)*

Leyland introduced its Panther, a rear-engined single-deck chassis, in 1964 and it was designed to provide a lower entry step than the underfloor Leopard. Middlesbrough took two in 1966 and the single-door body seated 44. Number 2 (DXG 402D) is seen here. *(STA)*

The last Dennis Lolines to be bodied, in 1967, were for Halifax and were finished in that operator's distinctive green, orange and cream livery. Halifax's Manager, Geoffrey Hilditch, would later renew his association with Dennis when the Dominator rear-engined double-decker was produced at his behest whilst he was GM at Leicester. *(RGR)*

Swindon Corporation took its first deliveries from Northern Counties in the summer of 1967 when a trio of Daimler CVG6-30s entered the fleet. Further orders were placed in the following two years. As a result of Local Government Reorganisation in 1974 the municipal fleet commenced trading as Thamesdown Transport. The attractive dark blue and cream livery remained unchanged, as seen here on this preserved example. *(DC)*

Southdown 315, seen here ready for its trip to the 1966 Earl's Court Motor Show, was fitted with an experimental heating system by Clayton (its Compass system) which allowed the elimination of a front radiator and permitted a lower windscreen line, this in turn allowing a wrap-round windscreen to be fitted. Clayton were well-known as manufacturers of door mechanisms and indicator equipment. The vehicle was also fitted with a new style of body for Southdown, after eight years of the previous design, which incorporated these distinctive, and no doubt very heavy, panoramic windows. *(STA)*

Number 365 represents the final design on the Ley PD3 chassis and was fitted to the last 24 vehi supplied by Northern Counties in 1967. The panora windows experimentally fitted to the previous ye show model have been retained, but the retention radiator in the conventional position has meant tha previous windscreen layout has been kept, albeit modifications to the application of the livery. *(ST*

For its final single-deck deliveries SHMD chose the Bristol RESL6G, taking three in 1967. Number 118 was photographed before delivery whilst 117 is seen in service. Some might think the slab-sided body style, by now fashionable, is a far cry from the elegance of earlier years but it reflects the need for body designers to take on board the stresses and flexing brought about by the introduction of rear-engined chassis. *(STA)*

By 1967 Nottingham's distinctive body style had evolved into this classic design with curved screens on both lower- and upper-decks. MTO 156F was one of 35 Daimler Fleetlines, delivery of which extended into 1968. ***(STA)***

the use of the wrap-round windscreen from the previous year's experiment, but combined it with panoramic windows, which allowed the upper-deck front windows also to be of the wrap-round type, features which were to become more common on rear-engined chassis in due course. This bus remained unique in its appearance amongst the large fleet of Leylands delivered to Southdown.

Nineteen-sixty-seven could in many ways be classed as a year of 'lasts'. The last of the ubiquitous Southdown PD3s left the factory in July and LUT took their last Guy Arab too. The Southdown vehicles reverted to the traditional lower-deck frontal appearance, but this final batch of 24 all incorporated the panoramic windows. It was to be the last year that two independent body builders were resident in the town of Wigan. But in fairness, there were also some firsts. Three more BET companies took delivery of Northern Counties' products; City of Oxford Motor Services, Mexborough & Swinton Traction and Ribble Motor Services, the latter after a gap of over 45 years, if wartime deliveries are excluded. The latter two companies both took rear-engined chassis, fifteen Atlanteans in the case of Ribble and six Fleetlines for Mexborough. Whilst City of Oxford took Fleetlines in 1968, the first order was, rather unusuallly, for four AEC Renowns. These were the last such to be bodied by Northern Counties.

A new local authority undertaking also joined the 'club', Swindon Transport having three Daimler CVG6-30s bodied that year. One wonders if their 'JAM' registrations were to be prophetic, for the entire share capital of Massey Brothers of Pemberton was purchased that year. Northern Counties had, after all, been producing lots of 'bread and butter' work for many years; perhaps now they could add something more. Undoubtedly, the directors must have seen some scope for rationalisation of the newly acquired premises, although it is doubtful if even they realised that in due course the original Wigan Lane site was to be superseded by the Pemberton premises.

In the light of this development, we shall break off from the Northern Counties story for a chapter to deal with Massey Brothers.

Chapter Six

Massey Bros

It is hoped that the researches which form the basis of this chapter, carried out by Eric Ogden and Harry Postlethwaite over many years, will, in due course, see the light of day as a publication in its own right on the history of Massey Brothers of Wigan. In the meantime I am extremely grateful to them both for agreeing to provide a synopsis for inclusion in this book, for it would not be right to produce a Northern Counties story without any reference to Massey Brothers. This chapter is not intended, therefore, to be a comprehensive history of the company, but to give a flavour of the organisation and to help appreciate where it fits into the overall story.

The foundation of this well-respected company pre-dates Northern Counties by some years, and indeed had its roots in work far removed from bus building. In 1904 the three brothers Massey (Isaac, Thomas and William) formed a partnership to carry on a business as builders and contractors. The original products were greenhouses, soon followed by dwelling houses, some of which could be seen adjoining the firm's premises at Pemberton in Wigan. These buildings were actually situated in Enfield Street, Pemberton and consisted of a former bleach and dye works, together with the erstwhile Wigan company tram sheds which housed, in turn, horse, steam and electric trams.

Bus bodybuilding had commenced in 1916, this again pre-dating Northern Counties. It was done in an effort to provide work for the firm's joiners during the winter months when bad weather restricted their employment in the building trade. The end of the First World War opened up many opportunities for firms engaged in the coachbuilding industry, and the progress of Massey Brothers was, in many respects, to run in parallel with Northern Counties. Wigan, in fact, boasted a third coachbuilder, in that the Santus family also entered the industry. Wigan Corporation was, as we have seen from the main story, keen to support local industry, and at various times examples of the products of all three bodybuilders entered the municipal fleet. The first bodies supplied by Massey were obtained by the Corporation in 1920, only one year after the introduction of buses by Wigan. They were then to continue supplying the Corporation until the demise of the Transport Department in 1967.

The artillery wheels on this AEC Y-type chassis confirm that it was almost certainly an ex-War Department vehicle. The body was typical of products produced by Massey and most other bodybuilders at that time, immediately after the First World War. *(STA)*

An interesting order from Wigan in 1920 was for twelve double-deck tramcar bodies which were built on four-wheel English Electric trucks and were, as far as is known, the only tramcar bodies ever built by Massey. A notable exception to the early municipal and independent customers was Cumberland Motor Services, the first bodies being supplied in 1921 to this major operator. The introduction of the heavyweight Leyland Lion PLSC in the mid-1920s saw Massey beginning to concentrate on this type of vehicle and they had little further involvement with normal-control chassis. Massey bodies on this chassis for Cumberland Motor services were, in fact, built to Leyland's design, although they also produced a version of their own. Massey were also early in the field of constructing double-deck motor bus bodies, and although not the first such body, an interesting double-decker was provided , once more for Cumberland, on a Guy FCX six-wheel chassis in 1927. The lowbridge body incorporated two sunken gangways, one each side of the upper-saloon, this arrangement being necessary at that time to avoid infringement of the Leyland patented design with sunken offside gangway as fitted to the Leyland Titan.

An interesting Massey advertisement in 1934 claimed that Salford Corporation used Massey tramcar bodies. Again, as we have seen in the main story, such trade press copy sometimes was, in modern parlance, 'economical with the truth'. The fact was that Massey had provided materials, and indeed based staff at Salford's Frederick Road premises, to fit top covers to a total of 55 small four-wheeled trams in 1926 and 1927.

Further six-wheeled chassis were bodied for Warrington Corporation in 1929, this time based on the then recently introduced AEC Renown. The rather unusual design featured a front door in addition to the usual open rear platform and a nearside staircase which ascended forward of the front door over the bonnet. Whilst this utilised space over the engine it clearly interfered with the driver's vision in exactly the same way as 'reversed' staircases did on tramcar bodies and was to prove unpopular with operators. In fact, Warrington took further bodies from Massey in 1930 and 1931, but these were on Leyland TD1 chassis.

In 1935 an interesting project was developed jointly with Leyland Motors and the General Electric Company which resulted in the production of a unique vehicle, namely a double-deck lowbridge trolleybus, which achieved an overall height of 13ft 6in. The body was mounted on a low-loading three-axle chassis and was exhibited on the GEC stand at the Commercial Motor Show held at London's Olympia that year. It was of attractive, gently curving proportions and had an overall length of 30ft. For its time, it was of very modern appearance, featuring a set-back front-axle allowing a folding door at the front, ahead of the nearside wheel. There was also a conventional rear platform with a door to the lower-saloon. The low, flat floor was ingeniously achieved by employing two traction motors, positioned one on the outside of each chassis side member. The drive shafts from the motors ran outside the chassis members to the differential casings mounted adjacent to the wheel hubs on the rear axle. A dropped front axle with under-slung springs, and inverted springs at the rear contributed to the low floor height. The

An extremely innovative Leyland trolleybus was produced in 1935 and understandably the contribution of GEC and Leyland has been widely proclaimed. Perhaps the contribution made by Massey in producing the body for this vehicle has received less recognition over the years. The entrance, placed forward of the front axle, was not repeated on an electrically powered bus for another 18 years. *(STA)*

Cumberland Motor Services was a regular customer of Massey Bros and this 1934 Leyland TD3 shows an early attempt at a more curvaceous body styling than had previously been produced. The company across the town was not to follow this trend for another year or so. *(STA)*

composite body seated 63, with 29 in the lower-saloon and 34 in the upper one. There were two staircases, designed to permit quicker loading and unloading. Despite being tested on the South Lancashire Transport system at Atherton, this extremely advanced vehicle was later dismantled by Leyland Motors.

The design of the trolleybus was an example of the trend during the 1930s towards smoother, more curvaceous body contours incorporating a sloping front profile. Massey Brothers first attempts in this direction actually came in 1934, with bodies on Leyland TD3 chassis for Birkenhead and Chester Corporations and Cumberland Motor Services. From 1936 the sloping profile totally superseded the near-vertical profile, first on the lowbridge body and then on the highbridge version. At the same time the pronounced curvature of the rear, which was to be a characteristic feature of Massey bodies for many years to come, began to take shape. The slope of the front was carried through to the bottom of the windscreen to present a neat and modern appearance. Another feature which began to appear at this time concerned the front side windows of the lower saloon which incorporated a greater radius, the forerunner of the D-shaped window which was to become a familiar feature of future Massey bodies.

A stylish half-canopy design for single-deckers appeared in 1938 and both this and the 'municipal' style full width canopy with destination indicator featured even more rounded body contours with outswept lower side and rear panels and wide-radiused rear dome, incorporating a window of well-rounded outline. Small numbers were supplied to Cumberland Motor Services and to Leigh and Salford Corporations. This development of the single-deck design had its counterpart with the double-deck design which retained its six-bay construction, now with characteristic D-shaped front and rear side windows. Early in 1939 this design was changed to five-bay construction, thus improving the overall appearance still further. The final pre-war design incorporated front roof panelling which was continued downwards to form the front corner panelling and so provided one of the most distinctive features of Massey bodies for many years when peacetime standards were re-introduced after the war.

We have already seen how Wigan Corporation continued taking double-deck bodies to the original Leyland design well into the late 1930s. Massey also provided such bodies in a similar manner, to the extent that over the years there has been some confusion as to which of the Wigan factories actually built which bodies. In any event, the truth might be purely academic, as it is likely that the same group of workers were probably involved anyway. Over the years and right until the takeover of the Massey Company, the skilled work force tended to migrate between the various Wigan employers, and also between them and Leyland Motors. In 1937 the designer and works manager, Alfred Alcock, who we have already met in an earlier chapter, and Arthur Danson, the works foreman, left to join East Lancashire Coachbuilders of Blackburn. Harry Postlethwaite has dealt with these changes in his history of East Lancs published by *Venture* in 1999. Of the Massey brothers, William, who had been the sleeping partner, had three sons who were by this time all engaged in the business. Thomas was the eldest and became the foreman painter, Norman became works manager and Arnold, the youngest, worked on the development and construction of Massey's metal sections and framing. Isaac Massey, who had originally trained as an accountant, had a daughter, Clare, who married Arthur Tyldesley. Thomas (senior) and Isaac died within a year of each other and their respective shares passed to Clare.

After the war, in 1947, the business was formed into a limited company and subsequently, in 1950, Arthur Tyldesley gave up his position as an electrical engineer to become Managing Director, a position he retained until the company was sold, having been assisted throughout this time by Norman Massey, and George Chapman, who had joined the business in 1922 as a shorthand typist and had worked his way up to become Company Secretary.

Reverting to the period immediately prior to the outbreak of war, Massey Brothers had already established itself with a small but significant group of customers. Cumberland Motor Services and Birkenhead Corporation still regarded Massey as their main supplier. They had been joined by the local authorities in Colchester, Kingston-upon-Hull, Leigh and Salford, not forgetting ,of course, the local council in Wigan. Again as was seen with Northern Counties, the outbreak of war in September 1939 did not immediately bring production to a halt and in the case of Massey bus bodybuilding continued into 1941. By this date it has been calculated that 1,330 bus bodies had been built by Massey. Amongst the very last bodies to pre-war standards to be built was a trolleybus for Ipswich Corporation. It was mounted on a Ransomes, Sims & Jefferies chassis which had originally been intended for export to South Africa as a demonstrator. The hostilities prevented this from taking place and it, in fact, became the last R S & J trolleybus to enter service in this country. In order to maintain employment for those who had not been called for military service, the firm reverted to the original business of building and contracting work and undertook repairs and reconstruction of bomb

Ipswich Corporation was a relatively early user of the trolleybus, commencing operations with the type in 1923. The first examples were all single-deckers, but double-deck vehicles were introduced in 1933. The last trolleybus constructed by the local firm of Ransomes, Sims & Jefferies entered service with the Corporation in 1940. *(STA)*

158
ST. HELENS CORPORATION
TRANSPORT
DJ 9006

PENDLEBURY
17
"STONE-DRI"
MONTON
312
NTF 431
FTE 333

(Facing page, top) Both Northern Counties and Massey were permitted to build buses during the Second World War, to the Ministry of Supply's utility specification. One delivery that was slightly different was that made to St Helens Corporation in 1942. The Sunbeam chassis had originally been intended for export to South Africa and were built 6in wider than that permitted for home operation. In addition the bodies were constructed to the lowbridge design, requiring a sunken gangway on the offside of the upper-deck, which when combined with the extra width gave these trolleybuses a very squat appearance. *(STA)*

(Facing page, lower) In theory all utility buses should have looked identical, but all builders of such buses managed to incorporate features which made them recognisable as a product from their particular factory. Massey's bodies had a slight taper at the top of the upper-deck. The picture on page 51 illustrates this feature equally well. *(JAS)*

damaged buildings. Work on mobile auxiliary fire pumps, and bodies for Austin and Ford fire service vans occurred, before the government relaxation saw 'unfrozen' vehicles completed and allocated to their new owners.

Massey Brothers, like its fellow Wigan bodybuilder at Wigan Lane, was permitted to build to utility specification, and this work commenced in 1942. Their bodies were regarded by many as being particularly distinctive, perhaps the most outstanding features being the deep roof, inward upper-deck taper and curved lower edge to the driver's windscreen. The well-shaped rear of the upper-deck contrasted strongly with the vertical rear ends of other manufacturers, but the angled rear dome left no doubt that this was a utility product. Amongst the more interesting of contracts completed during the utility period was a batch of trolleybuses for St Helens Corporation which were constructed to lowbridge design. Again, the chassis had been intended for export, in this case to Johannesburg, and were actually 8ft wide, when the permitted British maximum width was still 7ft 6in. Special dispensation was obtained in order for them to operate. Similarly, Massey bodied a batch of Daimler COG6s which had also been intended for export to South Africa.

Like Northern Counties, Massey was quick to return to peacetime appearance in its bodies once the regulations were relaxed; indeed, it has been suggested that Massey was actually the first to achieve this. Early post-war bodies of this style were supplied to Newcastle and Rochdale Corporations before the end of 1945. Subsequent developments saw a change to the shape of the lower-deck windows which was semi-circular at first as in the 1939 design. By 1948 the rounded shape had changed to become wider at the bottom as in the 1938 outline. The early post-war highbridge body possessed a more upright front profile and the front corner pillars were more slender than in the final pre-war design. In complete contrast to the highbridge design, the new lowbridge design, which was introduced in 1947 with examples being supplied to Cumberland and Southend Corporation amongst others, notable for the extreme degree of curvature and rake to the front which made these bodies even more distinctive than their highbridge counterparts.

Perhaps the most prosperous period of Massey Brothers history was the time from 1946 to 1952, when the company standardised on composite, or timber-framed, construction. The first metal-framed body was introduced in 1950, being of highbridge pattern destined for Birkenhead Corporation where it became their No. 201 (ABG 301), part of an order for fifteen Guy Arabs, the remainder still being of composite construction. The metal-framed body omitted the then current D-shaped end windows in the lower-saloon and the outswept lower panels traditionally associated with Massey bodies. Good interior finish and appointment was always a characteristic of the make and even the wartime bodies retained the attractively grained interior window fillets and bulkhead framework. The metal-framed designs maintained the tradition, together with that of attractive external appearance. Metal-framed bodies rapidly became the standard and Massey built few composite bodies after 1952 and none after 1954.

With the advent of the metal-framed body, the lowbridge design was changed to provide a less sharply raked front profile with a shallower roof line. This design continued until the takeover, the last lowbridge body to be built going to Bedwas & Machen UDC on a Leyland PD3 in 1968, its registration mark PAX 466F identifying it as the last traditional lowbridge body to be built in Great Britain. This particular body was 30ft long, but both 27ft and 30ft versions were built with five-bay construction. However, a front-entrance version was developed for Baxter's Bus Services of Aidrie and became available in 1960 and was based on four bays with a single sliding door. The combination of front-entrance and lowbridge body required a special staircase with two sections in its upper portion.

The highbridge body had also been restyled in 1954, the most obvious change being to the upper-deck front windows which now appeared with only a small radius to each corner. Again, what might have been seen as a more modern four-bay design was offered, but most customers preferred the original five-bay construction. A front-entrance version was available from 1958 on the 30ft highbridge body, followed by the same option on the 27ft chassis in 1960.

Production of bodies on single-deck underfloor-engined chassis was available from about the same time as Northern Counties offered it and again it represented only a small proportion of total output. The first of this type was supplied to Caerphilly UDC in 1954 when a pair was delivered. The Corporations of Barrow, Birkenhead, Chester, Exeter and Ipswich and Jersey Motor Transport also took small batches during the

BIRKENHEAD CORPORATION TRANSPORT

ENGAGED
201
BIRKENHEAD CORPORATION TRANSPORT
201

(Opposite) Birkenhead was a valued customer of Massey right up to the sale of the company. The body on this 1949 Daimler shows a style which carried on from the immediate pre-war fashion, while the Guy, built a year later, has a tidier window layout around the lower-deck windows. Both the buses seated 56.

(Above) Stockton Corporation chose this 1949 Leyland, with a similar body to the Birkenhead Daimler, to promote its Festival Week in 1951. *(STA all)*

1960s. Massey Brothers' first double-deck body for a rear-engined chassis was supplied in 1964, being a Daimler Fleetline for A1 Service co-operative. It was similar to the single-deck design in that it was of square, angular appearance, possessing little in common with any previous Massey design, although it was distinctive enough for it to be instantly recognised as a Massey product. Regular Massey customers Colchester and Maidstone Corporations took delivery of a few, but interestingly other regulars like Birkenhead, Chester, Southend and the South Wales municipalities did not.

Perhaps because of its size, Massey was always ready to supply what the customer wanted. One example of this was an order in 1961 for Jersey Motor Transport for five 40-seat single-deckers. The bodies were constructed on special Leyland Tiger Cub chassis which were built to reduced dimensions of 27ft 6in long by 7ft 6in wide to comply with the maximum permitted size for buses in Jersey at the time. It is interesting to note that, notwithstanding this, in reporting their arrival the local press referred to them as 'these large capacity vehicles'.

No official reason for the sale of Massey Brothers to Northern Counties was given, but it has been suggested by people who had dealings with the firm that, having built their solid reputation on the manufacture of half-cab bodies, they did not have the same enthusiasm for underfloor and rear-engined types. It has also been suggested that as their business had been supplying small and medium sized operators they were not particularly interested in supplying the large Passenger Transport Executives which were soon to appear. Furthermore, discussions were beginning to take place on Local Government Reorganisation, and even those municipal operators that did not immediately go into one of the new Executives were to be subject to change which was to involve amalgamation in some cases and renaming, as a result of re-drawn boundaries, in others. The directors of Massey Brothers, faced with this upheaval, obviously felt that the time to sell to their cross-town rival was right.

How the Massey factory was to fare under Northern Counties after the take-over will be found in subsequent chapters.

After the standard double-deck body had been re-styled in 1954, a small number of customers, Colchester Corporation among them, favoured the four-bay layout as shown on this AEC Regent III.
Post-war single-deck orders were relatively few, but Barrow took a small number, including this 1955 Leyland Royal Tiger. *(STA both)*

Unlike Colchester, Exeter Corporation preferred the five-bay design on deliveries from Massey, as shown here on this 1963 Leyland PD2A/30. Exeter standardised on this model from 1962 until final delivery in 1965, although earlier bodies of this type had been fitted to Guy Arab IV chassis.
Colchester's final deliveries from Massey Bros arrived in 1968. This Leyland Atlantean PDR1/1, delivered in the previous year, was one of the few rear-engined buses bodied by them.
(STA both)

Chapter Seven

1968 – 1979

The year 1968 was a significant one for the transport industry and no less for the company. The major event of the year was, of course, the passing of the 1968 Transport Act, the provisions of which were to come into force over the next few years and which were to radically change the structure of the bus operating industry, with consequential effects on Northern Counties, as will be seen as the company's story further unfolds.

It has already been noted that the implications of this Act were a contributory factor in influencing the decision of the directors of Massey Brothers to sell their company to Northern Counties. At the beginning of 1968, the Pemberton premises were still completing orders previously placed with Massey. In keeping with their by then well-established customer pattern, all the deliveries made that year, with the solitary exception of that to A1 Services, were to local authorities, a total of seven councils (Burton, Bedwas & Machen, Caerphilly, Chester, Colchester, Maidstone and Wigan) being involved. Interestingly, all but one of these local authority undertakings were subsequently to place orders with Northern Counties and even the exception, that of Colchester, did initially place an order after 1967, although this was subsequently cancelled. The final Massey body was delivered to Chester in December 1968 and was based upon a Leyland Tiger Cub chassis. To assist in the management of the contracts for these orders, Northern Counties retained the services of Arthur Tyldesley, who was the only director of the acquired company to become employed by Northern Counties and who assisted Jack Abbott, although he was only to stay for a few years until he reached retirement age.

Harper Brothers of Heath Hayes in Staffordshire took the last rear-entrance bodies built by Northern Counties. Seen here in Union Street, Birmingham, the then terminal of Harper's service from Cannock, No. 24 (LRF 992F) was the first of the trio delivered in 1968. *(RGR)*

By the date this photograph was taken at the former Walsall Corporation depot at Birchills, the West Midlands PTE fleet name adorned the unique Daimler Fleetline CRC6-36, which clearly displays its dual doorways. *(STA)*

Back at Wigan Lane, 1968 also saw the last rear-entrance body being constructed. This was delivered to Harper Brothers of Heath Hayes in Staffordshire in May and completed a trio of deliveries to them that year. The final bus was based on a Leyland PD3A/5 chassis, with semi-automatic transmission; perversely the two vehicles delivered earlier in the year were PD3A/1s with manual gearboxes – perhaps another indication of the way in which requirements were changing. This was also the year of the bi-annual Commercial Motor Show at Earls Court where the Northern Counties stand displayed three vehicles. Needless to say, all the chassis involved were rear-engined – the first time this had happened as far as the company was concerned. One was a Daimler and two were Leylands and were for two municipalities and one BET subsidiary. The only other rear-engined chassis suitable for double-deck bodywork being produced, the Bristol VR, was not yet available to Northern Counties' customers. The recipients concerned were Wigan Corporation, who had been a long-standing customer, of course, although FJP 566G represented their first rear-engined bus, the first with two doors and the first double-decker intended for one-man-operation. The other municipality involved was Nottingham, whose now established styling was to be found on the bus on display and had already become synonymous with both organisations. The final double-decker was for City of Oxford Motor Services, in whose attractive livery the Daimler Fleetline looked particularly smart and perhaps represented the 'new order'. It has been seen that deliveries to BET companies had tended to be rather limited until the early 1960's, with two notable exceptions, but seemingly the advent of the rear-engined chassis was increasing the number of associated companies supplied, although Oxford's first orders from Northern Counties the previous year were, as was mentioned in an earlier chapter, on the AEC Renown chassis.

The 'star' of the show, however, was to be found on the Daimler stand, although fitted with a Northern Counties body. This Walsall Daimler Fleetline should, perhaps, be examined in a little more detail before moving on; the previous Motor Show had displayed, what was by then, one of the operator's standard Daimler Fleetlines, if such a description could be applied to that fleet. As if to remind the public at large that he was still innovating and maybe with an eye to reminding his future employers too, Walsall's General Manger, the redoubtable R Edgley Cox, possibly sensing too that this show could be his swan song, produced yet another sensational exhibit. Six years earlier, as we have seen, the first Fleetline for Walsall had been at a Motor Show. Not only was it the first Fleetline for Walsall, but it had also been the shortest. On this occasion, but not for the first time, Edgley Cox went for the longest. The chassis on which it was based, the Daimler CRC6-36, had originally been introduced by Daimler to meet a request from Johannesburg for a 36ft double-decker. Since this length was now legal in Britain, it obviously made sense to Mr Cox for him to have one in the bus fleet for which he was responsible. Even today 36ft double-deckers are not common, mainly because of the need to meet the maximum weight requirements. Since this 86-seater was fitted with two staircases (and whilst at the Motor Show it also had the luxury of a remote closed circuit television camera with monitor in the cab – not bad for 1968), there was clearly a challenge to meet the weight requirement – just the sort of challenge Mr Cox enjoyed. His (so-called) standard Fleetlines already utilised a significant amount of glass-reinforced plastic exterior panelling which was self coloured to reduce painting costs, but its use on this giant was essential. The rather plain but instantly recognisable 13ft 10in high Northern Counties profile body did not repeat the use of a wrap-round windscreen and upper-deck front windows of his earliest Fleetlines, but glass is heavy and could well have made the finished bus too heavy to meet legal requirements. It was finished in a non-standard light blue and off-white livery and was powered by a Cummins V6 engine, which proved to be part of its undoing. From the traffic department's point of view, an 86-seat double-decker represented a real opportunity to eliminate duplicate vehicle working and thus reduce costs, the same reason that was put forward by Barton when purchasing their mega-low Dennis Loline. However, a unique vehicle has to be reliable. Alas, Edgley Cox's was not and it remained the only one of its kind in the fleet, which led to one exasperated operating manager later muttering that it was a pity it wasn't painted white all over, obviously having experienced elephants of a similar hue before!

Twenty years after the unsuccessful attempt by Guy Motors to export a complete bus with a Northern Counties body to South Africa, Daimler, who found themselves by this time initially fellow subsidiaries in the Jaguar Group (from 1960) and then part of British Motor Holdings from 1966, had slightly more success. Daimler had received a request from City Tramways of Cape Town for a demonstration vehicle and in order to expedite this request diverted one of a batch of Fleetlines for Halifax to fulfil this demand. Whilst subsequent orders for Daimler Fleetlines arose as a result, their bodies were constructed locally in South Africa. In tracing the history of Daimler and in order to complete the story, it should be recorded that in this same year (1968), British Motor Holdings joined Leyland Motors to form the British Leyland monolith.

The establishment of the National Bus Company, which was to be formed as a result of the new Transport Act, had been further strengthened by the reluctant agreement by the BET to sell its bus company subsidiaries to the Transport Holding Company in November 1967. The NBC came into existence on 1st January 1969, but one other major element of the Act, namely the establishment of Passenger Transport Authorities and the formation of their operating arms, the Passenger Transport Executives, was to commence the following autumn, around the time that the final front-engined buses fitted with Northern Counties bodywork (which also happened to be the last Guy motorbuses delivered to a UK operator), were entering service in Chester.

The directors of Northern Counties must have viewed the impending changes with some concern. It was recognised that the 'in-house' manufacturing associated outlets of the new NBC such as Bristol Commercial Vehicles and Eastern Coach Works at Lowestoft were barely able to meet the requirements of the THC companies, let alone the former BET companies. It was here that during the 1960's Northern Counties had steadily built up the number of subsidiaries it supplied, but the possible future developments were not clear. Similarly, whilst the number of municipalities that had 'disappeared' into the new PTEs and which had previously been regular patrons of Wigan-built bodies was not large, (Birkenhead, Halifax, SHMD and Walsall coming to mind), it was difficult to imagine that the largest constituents of the new Executives, none of whom had been regular customers of Northern Counties and who it would seem likely would have the greatest influence

After taking such a large fleet of distinctive Leyland PD3s, the next bodies from Northern Counties for Southdown were going to be a hard act to follow. They turned out to be single-deckers on Leyland Leopards and the dual-purpose nature of the bodies is well illustrated in this view of No. 466 photographed some way out of the company's operating area at Aldershot Bus Station when working a Company Express Service. *(STA)*

on purchasing policies of the new organisations, would look towards Wigan for deliveries. The Birmingham, Leeds, Liverpool and Manchester local authorities all had longstanding relations with others in the bodybuilding field and, in any event, had tended to place orders of a volume that Northern Counties might, at that time, have had difficulty meeting. How things were to change!

For a year or two, however, there was still the backlog of outstanding orders to deal with and there were still deliveries to be made to customers who had been unaffected by all these shenanigans. Factory output for 1968 was 149, down a little on the previous year, but well below that in the peak post-war year to date of 1964. Notable absentees amongst customers for 1968 were Lancashire United and Southdown, both of whom had been annual recipients since 1949 and 1958 respectively. However, their staple diet of Guy Arabs and Leyland PD3s had dried up in the light of the new bus grant allowances, which did not countenance such chassis, but both operators were back in the figures for 1969 receiving Bristol LHs and Leyland Leopards as part of a total of 186 deliveries, which now contained the erstwhile Massey orders and was thus the highest post-war total so far.

The first order to be delivered to a Passenger Transport Executive consisted of four Leyland Atlantean PDR1A/1s for SELNEC PTE (the initials stood for South East Lancashire & North East Cheshire) in early 1970, an order that had been originally placed by Ashton under Lyne Corporation. Never has the saying 'big oaks from little acorns grow' been so true, although it is doubtful whether in the spring of 1970 the prophecy of such an idiom was recognised. Merseyside and West Midlands PTEs were also to receive deliveries from Wigan later in the year, being orders placed by Birkenhead, Walsall and West Bromwich Corporations prior to the establishment of the Executives. In the case of the West Midlands, the vehicles that entered service in Walsall did so as part of a scheme to replace the last of its trolleybuses, West Midlands having had the dubious distinction of being the only PTE to operate such efficient vehicles. Already, however, the work of the new hands at the helm of the PTE were apparent; whilst clearly recognisable as Northern Counties products, West Midlands 4013-27 were not, in appearance, how Edgley Cox surely would have had them designed! After the excitement of the 1968 Motor Show, the 1970 Exhibition was perhaps a little more mundane, Northern Counties contribution being a two-door 33ft Fleetline for LUT and an Atlantean for SELNEC, one of those mentioned above and of which more later. There was also one for

What was to be the precursor of over 1400 'standard' bodies for SELNEC (and its successor Greater Manchester) PTE was fitted to Leyland PDR1A/1 PNF 941J, which entered service early in 1971 and was numbered EX1. *(STA)*

The same year Reading Corporation took the first of what were to total 50 bodies from Northern Counties mounted on Bristol VR chassis. The lower height of the Reading bus tends to accentuate its length, but there is no mistaking the basis of the design. *(RGR)*

Nottingham, to its then standard and very characteristic style in the display park.

Out of the original Transport Executives established by the 1968 Act, SELNEC PTE was generally regarded as perhaps the most innovative of the four – if not by the industry at large, then certainly by its senior managers! The day-glow orange and white livery, adopted as the fleet colours, was certainly different from any of the municipal fleets to be found in England at this time and was indicative of its novel approach to business. So it is perhaps not surprising to discover that soon after the first four Northern Counties bodies were delivered, discussions continued take place between the two organisations, led by Harry Taylor of the PTE, which resulted, in 1971, of the entry into service with the PTE of six experimental buses numbered imaginatively EX 1-6 and carrying the prototype 'standard' body. They were also based on the Leyland PDR1A/1 model, the chassis again having been ordered by Ashton Corporation. The body design owed more than a little to the pioneering work by Manchester Corporation's previous General Manager, Ralph Bennett, which had culminated in the introduction of the 'Mancunian', a Leyland PDR1/1 with Park Royal bodywork. Subsequent buses of the type were built by Daimler as well, together with some bodies by East Lancs. In the case of the other PTEs, residual orders for Birkenhead and West Bromwich were also supplied to Merseyside and West Midlands that year.

The sales department at the Wigan company was obviously now spreading its wings, as an order from yet another new independent operator, South Yorkshire Road Transport of Pontefract, arrived for two Leyland PDR1/3s, a version of the Atlantean which was fitted with a dropped-rear-axle and permitted low-height bodywork. There were orders too from new municipal customers at Chesterfield and Reading, the style of the bodies for both reflecting the developments taking place at the time for what was to become known as the 'Manchester' standard. Reading had pioneered the use of single-deck one-man-operated vehicles for use in urban areas, although these ten were the first double-deckers to be taken into stock for such operation. They were based on the Bristol VR which was now generally available and complemented the Bristol single-deckers which Reading had been buying since 1967. The Bristol VR was thus beginning to find a place in municipal fleets, Gelligaer also taking a small batch. Reading's VRs were built to an overall height of 13ft 6in, as Reading, like Middlesbrough, had a low railway bridge close to the railway station which demanded the use of such bodies.

The Albert Bridge in Middlesbrough was 13ft 6in high (or low, as the case may be!), as was Vastern Road Bridge in Reading. Their order was the first to enter the fleet from Northern Counties but the Manager concerned, Royston Jenkins, had been Deputy Manager to George Stringer at Middlesbrough, an undertaking that had been merged with Stockton Corporation and the Tees-side Railless Traction Board to form the new Teesside Municipal Transport in 1968. It continued the well-established policy of Middlesbrough by buying exclusively from Northern Counties, and Teesside took no less than 19 vehicles from Northern Counties into its fleet that year. In addition, Southend, a former Massey customer, took 26 Daimler Fleetlines, which was a sizeable order at the time and unheard of in Massey's reign. Again, a low bridge in the town centre necessitated the use of such buses; this time the offending bridge was not under a railway line but under the pier.

The SELNEC experimental vehicles had obviously proved acceptable to the PTE, for the following year a further 15 'experimental' buses, EX 7-21, were taken into stock, this time on Daimler Fleetline chassis which had originally been ordered by Rochdale and Bury Corporations. Later in 1972, 35 more 'standards' were delivered, five on Leyland chassis and the rest on Daimlers, the former with front entrances and the latter with two doors. The Leylands were amongst the first Atlanteans with the redesigned chassis, designated AN68, to enter service, Maidstone Corporation, a former Massey customer, having also placed chassis of this type into service a month or two earlier. The AN68 had been introduced as a result of the general dissatisfaction in the operational side of the bus industry with the PDR1, the PTEs being instrumental in persuading Leyland to redesign and improve the reliability of the chassis. One of the Daimlers appeared on Northern Counties' stand at that year's Commercial Motor Show, along with an additional Bristol VR for Reading, ordered as a result of the loss by fire of a Bristol RE. Two new NBC companies joined the list of customers this year; both London Country and West Riding ordered Daimler Fleetlines.

Four low-height bodies on a Leyland PDR1A/1 and three Daimler Fleetlines shown on this and the page opposite clearly illustrate the development and variations that were available to meet customer requirements in the early 1970s. Tees-side's A41 of 1970 was the only Leyland, and the only bus with two doors. Harper Brothers went for smaller windows in their single-door body. *(STA both)*

Calderdale's Fleetline delivered in July 1972 had a wrap-round screen on the lower-deck, whereas South Yorkshire's version delivered the following year had them fitted to both decks. ***(STA both)***

By now, such was the interest coming from the local Passenger Transport Executive that arrangements were consolidated and this led to a two year contract to supply double-deck vehicles. How much any of this was to do with changes foreshadowed by the Local Government Reorganisation Bill, which was then under discussion, is not clear. At the time Wigan was outside the Greater Manchester conurbation, but under the proposed local government changes, which were to take place from 1st April 1974, a new Metropolitan County of Greater Manchester would be formed, embracing all the local authorities who had contributed to the original SELNEC authority, but also including Wigan, whose own bus fleet would become part of the new Greater Manchester Passenger Transport Executive. Wigan Corporation's Transport Department had been famed for its support for local industry, generally only buying Leyland motorbuses, which were built just down the road and ordering the bodies from local Wigan firms, which, of course, included Northern Counties, Massey Brothers and Santus. Possibly the politicians in Manchester had noted and agreed with this concept; indeed in previous years there had been considerable support for Crossley Motors, but before examining this further, it is necessary to look at other company developments taking place.

Following the acquisition of Massey Brothers, the directors of Northern Counties found themselves with two factories on opposite sides of Wigan carrying out more or less the same functions. Clearly there was scope for some rationalisation. The additional factory space had already allowed Northern Counties to increase its market share and by reorganising the premises, body construction was concentrated at Wigan Lane and trimming, glazing, finishing and painting was completed at the former Massey factory at Enfield Street, Pemberton, approximately three miles away. Thus it was not unusual at this time to see half-completed vehicles being driven through Wigan town centre. The directors realised that production would be more efficiently handled at a single location, but it was not to be until 1976 that an opportunity arose which allowed this to happen and of this, more later.

Being a family firm, it was unusual for individuals other than close family members to be directors or even shareholders of the company, but we have seen how Reg Fone became a director in the mid-1920s and when he retired in 1964, his job had been taken on by Jack Abbott, previously his deputy. It was, therefore, with deep regret that the board learned of Jack Abbott's untimely death on 8th January 1973. It was said at the time that he had played a highly significant part in the success of the Company over a great number of years and his contribution and good 'Wigan' humour would be greatly missed. As a departure from previous appointments to the board, Jack Abbott's replacement was David Cherry, who had only recently (November 1972) joined the company with the expectation of taking charge to relieve Jack Abbott of pressure, but not in the realisation of how ill Abbott actually was, though David Cherry was certainly not a stranger to the company. Fred Sharrock, who had been Jack Abbott's deputy, was no doubt a little disappointed not to step up, but continued loyally as Works Manager under Cherry, masterminding the *minutiae* of the move to Pemberton, ably assisted by Norman Green, Ken Ashall and Ted Dawber, before retiring and being replaced by Peter Deveney.

David Cherry had first come into contact with Northern Counties when, as Chief Engineer of Rhondda Transport, a BET subsidiary, his company had purchased its first ten AEC Regent Vs fitted with Northern Counties bodywork in 1963. It might be thought that this was part of the company's policy to increase the number of customers from this group, but the order owes more to the South Wales connections of the Lewis family than anything else. David Cherry recalled later, in one of the interviews for this book, that his earliest impressions of the company were that it was 'a congested and small concern', but that he marvelled at how such immaculate paint finishes could be produced under the circumstances. By the time he was approached by Henry Lewis (grandson of the founder) with a view to joining the company, David Cherry was by now Chief Engineer of Western Welsh, though still responsible for Rhondda, and thus still in the South Wales ambience. In fact, he believed, initially, that the approach from his colleague Henry Lewis was in connection with a golfing matter, rather than an offer of employment! One factor influencing his decision to return north was the fact that within the still young National Bus Company there was a feeling that Company General Managers were being recruited from the ranks of the traffic department rather than the engineering persuasion. He was also very unhappy at the centralisation of policy-and-decision making which eroded the responsibility and influence of company officers such as himself. He was not alone, and Ray Braithwaite's move from Chief Engineer of Midland Red to take charge of Walter Alexander's coachbuilding factory at Falkirk reflected very similar circumstances and concerns. David Cherry recalled that his first visit with Henry Lewis to Wigan was preceded by a flight from Cardiff Roose Airport to Liverpool in a less than smooth Dakota, sharing cabin space with the cargo and accompanied by thunder storms and generally unwelcome weather. They were met at the airport by Frank Nelson, then the fitting shop foreman, but frequently used as company chauffeur. His worst fears about the return trip were alleviated when the weather caused the cancellation of the return flight and he was able to return to Cardiff on the overnight milk train!

As the new General Manager (and director from 7th March 1973), David Cherry set about reorganising the company on lines more akin to those he had experienced in his part of the bus industry rather than the situation that had existed previously. The outline of the Greater Manchester arrangement had already been made, so the major changes that this was to bring about were not new to him. However, he was able to negotiate quite early on in his new post a two year extension to the SELNEC agreement, which guaranteed a continuous stream of orders for four years to the largest of the PTEs.

Key members of staff at this time were Fred Sharrock as Works Manager, Ron Parsons as Chief Draughtsman and Bill Turner as Office Manager, two of them long serving Northern Counties employees whereas Ron Parsons had previously been at Chas H Roe in Leeds, moving to Wigan in 1960, and was himself the son of a former Ramsbottom UDC General Manager. What the new General Manager could not have anticipated was the effect that the national unrest on the industrial front was going to have on his new employer. The restrictions on production during the winter of 1973/4 – the infamous three-day week – caused the Company to comment in its annual report that:– 'turnover was falling considerably short of what could have been achieved had chassis become available as promised. The only supplier at present of chassis on which the Company constructs bodies (ie Leyland) has been unable to produce what was promised and very much less than what was and is required'. Because of these concerns, the Company had, no doubt, been pleased to receive yet another order from SELNEC for two more experimental buses. These were a pair of integrally-constructed single-deckers using Mercedes Benz running units and were the only integral single-deck buses built at Wigan. They utilised extremely deep side windows and a shallow roof, the bodies also incorporating a heavy front bumper. They were destined to be the only Mercedes built by the Company, although, at the time, the board felt the prospects for further orders were good, a view not necessarily shared by the shop floor and drawing office, where recollections suggest a considerable degree of relief that these two remained orphans.

What was of concern to David Cherry, and he certainly was not alone in this, (Alexanders in Falkirk shared similarly unease), was the position that Leyland, as the

At a time when conventional chassis for double-deck body construction was more normal, the building of two integral Mercedes single-deckers was something of an event and perhaps reflected the more adventurous nature of the operator, SELNEC PTE, rather than the company's aspirations at the time. Ron Parsons, NCME's Chief Draughtsman, went out to Germany to the Mercedes plant with Harry Taylor from the PTE to be appraised of the mechanical features. *(STA)*

Although the standard Northern Counties body was generally associated with large fleets, it also went to smaller ones too. OK Motor Services of Bishop Auckland took three on Atlantean chassis in early 1973, of which this is one. *(STA)*

Also on an Atlantean chassis but with a unique pedigree (see text opposite), the six 1975 models supplied to Fylde carried Willowbrook badges on their obviously Northern Counties design bodies. *(STA)*

major chassis supplier, was developing which has been touched on above. Whilst in name it appeared that there was market choice, the factories seeing a throughput at the time of chassis badged by Bristol, Daimler and Leyland, in practice they were all part of the same empire and a very senior Leyland Board-level manager, Ron Ellis, went further by telling him 'off the record' at an evening function that once their plans were realised, involving their new B15 model, later to become the integral Titan, it would remove the need for the independent bodybuilders like NCME.

As chance would have it, David Cherry learnt around this time that Fodens of Sandbach, not a million miles from Wigan, were involved in staff redundancies. Following discussions with Bill Foden, then Chairman of the company, it was agreed that Northern Counties would enter into a joint venture and would fund the production of a number of prototype vehicles. Possibly uniquely within the bus industry, the independent bodybuilder was helping in the development of the chassis, Ron Parsons spending some time on this project. It was not intended that the chassis would be bodied exclusively by Northern Counties; indeed, one of the prototypes did receive an East Lancs body. With hindsight, possibly the desire to produce a chassis capable of taking both highbridge and lowbridge bodies, with the complicated drive train arrangements that this necessitated, was to be its undoing. Such developments took time and it was to be a year or so before the first Foden-NC, as its badge proudly proclaimed, appeared. This potential monopoly by Leyland had also concerned, amongst others, Geoffrey Hilditch, formerly General Manager at Halifax but by this time with West Yorkshire PTE. His success at persuading Dennis to re-enter the PSV market has been well documented, but it should be recorded that before this occurred, he was involved in some discussion with Northern Counties at the time of the Foden phase.

Following the implementation of the 1972 Local Government Act, April 1st 1974 duly saw the birth of Greater Manchester PTE and the demise of SELNEC. Thirty years on, it is remarkable to consider the impact of this organisation which was in existence for less than five years. The work that had been done previously, however, allowed the new organisation to take more than one hundred bodies from Northern Counties in its first year of existence. This devotion of resources to a single customer had other implications, perhaps predictably, for in 1973/4 only three other operators received orders in double figures; LUT (of course), Reading and Tees-side, which had become Cleveland Transit the same day as GMPTE was born. Whilst the board was encouraged by the trade reaction to the Foden chassis, it was unhappy about a dearth of Daimler Fleetline chassis, to the detriment of the business, this short-fall coinciding with Leyland's disastrous decision to move Fleetline production from Coventry to Leyland

The 1974 Commercial Motor Show, perhaps understandably, only displayed two vehicles from this limited base; one was LUT 424, an 11m (36ft) Leyland Leopard with dual-purpose 44-seat front-entrance body, whilst the other was a Leyland AN68 for GMPTE (7511 - GNC 292N). Orders for 1975 followed a similar pattern as the previous year although six Atlanteans for Fylde have generated a fair amount of debate over the years, being completed by Willowbrook and allocated body numbers by them too. The debate has centred on which body builder was the preferred contractor and which, if either, was involved in sub-contracting the work. There was one other interesting development in 1975 that was going to have significant implications in the future. Cleveland Transit, besides taking ten Daimler Fleetlines, also purchased two 25-seat Ford 'A' series chassis, which, because of their improved seating, were described as coaches. It had been a long time since Northern Counties had built buses with such a small seating capacity, but these were the first modern mini-buses to be built by the Company and they were by no means to be the last, as we shall see in due course.

The Annual Report for the period up to 31st December 1975 was of interest in that it recorded that so far £40,000 had been spent in connection with the development of the new Foden chassis and that the average weekly number of employees was 247. The Board had been strengthened during the year by the appointment of Mrs J G Cory from 21st March and Godfrey Lewis from 23rd December.

In February 1976 David Cherry was able to negotiate an arrangement that was to have far reaching implications for the business, when he verbally agreed the acquisition of Enfield Mill, a building which had become vacant, having previously been used for weaving. It was adjacent to the former Massey premises and the mill owner was prepared to sell. Eventually the land, amounting to some five acres, changed hands for £87,500 and by May it was possible to store chassis on the site. By the end of the year alterations to the building had commenced. The considerable amount of work that this project was to entail was to occupy the company for some years to come, but confidence was high. Four body numbers (Nos. 8131 to 8134) had been allocated to the first four Foden chassis and construction of the first body commenced early in 1976. One of the quartet was never destined to enter passenger service, being extensively tested at the Motor Industry Research Association's premises, but the first to be delivered to an operator arrived with GMPTE in July that year, the same month as Reading commenced delivery of its final batch of Bristol VRs, 19 in total. It had originally been decided to purchase 20 units, but the transport committee were persuaded to change their intentions so that one of the order was placed with Metro-Cammell for one of their new Metropolitan

Were this photograph to be published in a modern tabloid newspaper, it would be difficult to resist the temptation of encouraging the readers to provide their own witty caption. On a more serious, but interesting, note, the photograph depicts the rather less than 'high-tech' arrangements – even in 1976 – for undertaking the legal requirement to tilt test new buses. The block, tackle and chains to the left of the photograph show how the table was raised; the part completed double-deck body on the right (at this stage built only to upper-deck floor level) was considered a necessary safeguard in case the unthinkable should actually happen! *(STA)*

The local politicians were rightly proud of on-going developments at Northern Counties, a company they saw as very important so far as maintaining local employment was concerned. Here the first Foden is posed with officers of the company. Ron Parsons is at the extreme left, with representatives of the operator, Greater Manchester PTE, with John Brownhill (who followed Harry Taylor as Development Engineer at the PTE) then Jack Thompson is prominent third from the left, Angus Munro, Director of Planning is at number six, whilst David Cherry stands directly below the driver's mirror. To David's left in this photograph Henry Lewis looks over Fred Sharrock's head. To the right of the sole lady in the picture amongst the various elected members is Patrick Twemlow of Fodens in dark suit with prominent name badge. *(STA)*

Destined to be the only Foden operated by West Midlands' PTE, ROC 300R was the last of the type to enter service in 1977. At that time many operators were specifing that vehicles should not carry badging, either for reasons of cost or local sensitivity when buses were built outside the area and local unemployment was a concern. West Midlands regular supplier was the local builder Metropolitan Cammell Carriage & Wagon Company, of Washwood Heath, of course.
Happily, NCME were persuaded to include a Foden badge on the front panel, as seen, on the basis that the vehicles would otherwise be completely anonymous in large fleets. *(STA)*

It was not unusual for enlightened employers to arrange for visits of Trade Union representatives to manufacturers' premises. On 25th June 1976 a group of such officials from Reading (including Cyril Sharpe and 'Dick' Sandhu – who is still employed by Reading Buses as this is written nearly 30 years later) are seen here with Fred Sharrock inspecting their soon-to-be-delivered No. 45 . This batch of Bristol VRs was built to an intermediate height as can be seen when compared with that illustrated on page 116. *(RGR)*

The sensation of the 1978 Commercial Motor Show, the first to be held at the National Exhibition Centre, was Nottingham 666 which incorporated a number of new features such as bonded screens. On a purely egotistical note, the author is pleased to record the fact that he was employed by each of the undertakings at the time when the two buses pictured on this page were delivered. *(GHFA)*

integral double-deckers which were fitted with Scania running units. Metro-Cammell, too, was well aware of Ron Ellis' designs on the market as expressed to David Cherry and this resulted in their link-up with Scania. In the longer term this link proved to be unsustainable, but for the meantime it ought to have been an indication to Leyland that the rest of the industry was not going to sit idly by and see its markets disappear.

These Reading vehicles were built to an intermediate height of 13ft 10in, the offending Vastern Road Bridge having been rebuilt, partly in preparation for the introduction of the first HSTs on the Western Region of British Rail. Echoing the remarks made in the annual report of a few years previously, the construction of the Bristol chassis was not as speedy as originally promised and the final Northern Counties body for Reading was delivered after the Metro-Cammell bus, surprise surprise! Subsequent orders from the operator went to Birmingham and Northern Counties lost a potentially valuable customer through no fault of its own. With events like this upsetting his schedules and turnover it was little wonder that David Cherry sought to do business with Fodens! In the event, Ron Ellis disappeared first, being seconded from Leyland to the Ministry of Defence in 1975.

Meanwhile, the second Foden, also for GMPTE, appeared at the Commercial Motor Show, held that year (1976) from 24th September to 2nd October and the last to be held at Earls Court in London. Even at this stage, however, the board recognised that it would be some time before such chassis could be produced at a competitive market price. Also on show was a Fleetline for West Yorkshire PTE, the first of the type to be badged as a Leyland as far as Northern Counties was concerned. The final delivery from this batch of ten, of low-height specification, was not made until the following April, by which time the PTE had been the recipient of the final vehicle from the initial Foden production run. Three further Foden-NC chassis were now under construction for Northern Counties, one going to West Midlands PTE in August 1977, one to Derby early in 1978, (who also took a dozen Leyland Fleetlines that year) and the final one to Potteries, who interestingly numbered it 900, the same fleet number given to the solitary Daimler CVG6-30 in 1958! Whilst this was not the final Foden to be bodied by Northern Counties (a single-deck 33-seater was supplied for the use of the Foden Works' Band in 1979), it was the final double-decker. Financial difficulties saw Fodens being taken over by Paccar, the large American constructor, who were not interested in the joint product, which was obviously disappointing for all those who had been concerned in the project and not least for Cleveland Transit, who had provisionally ordered a batch of ten. The project had not been without its benefits, however.

By July 1977 it had been found possible to commence using the partially adapted premises in the old mill and the fitting shop and erection facility were relocated there. Total costs for the completion of all the alterations were anticipated at this stage to be around £650,000. Nevertheless, consideration was now being given by the Board to the desirability of creating additional manufacturing capacity on the new site and in August the following year plans for the new building were passed, work continuing throughout 1978 and 1979 on this project, which included the need to pressure-grout part of the site due to the existence of a former drift mine.

The year 1978 saw the first use of the then new National Exhibition Centre (located just outside Birmingham), for the new combined Motor Show. As befitted such an enterprising move, Northern Counties surprised the bus industry a little more by one of the exhibits on their stand, Nottingham 666. Having established a very distinctive style, influenced to no little extent by Nottingham's Chief Engineer, John Lowrie (and encouraged by the undertaking's charismatic General Manager Philip Groves), the 1978 exhibit was, to say the least, different. The most striking feature was probably the one-piece flat raking windscreen, although it also utilised a number of other novel features, including a very early use of bonded windows on a double-deck body. The bus styling was, however, to remain unique. During 1978/79 another noteworthy order, this time for 40 Leyland Fleetlines, was completed for Western SMT, this being their final order after five decades of association with Northern Counties, and remarkable in view of the fact that by this time the Scottish Bus Group as a whole was not favouring the Wigan builder.

But by now, events which had taken place on the national political scene were going to influence the future of the company, as will be seen in the next chapter.

Chapter Eight

1980 – 1992

Following an unprecedented vote of no confidence, Prime Minister James Callaghan set the date of Thursday 3rd May 1979 for a General Election. The leader of the opposition, Margaret Thatcher, had been calling for a reversal of socialism, less state intervention, more individual power, more competition and more private ownership. Elected Britain's first woman Prime Minister the day after the General Election, with a workable majority of 43 seats in the House of Commons, she was now in a position to pursue her policies.

It was against this background that the next chapter in the history of Northern Counties may be traced. After the initial deregulation of long distance coach services, followed by the complete deregulation of bus services outside of London, the sale of the National Bus Company subsidiaries, the privatisation of London Transport and also that of the country's municipal operators, the next decade was to be a turbulent one for Northern Counties as the Thatcherite policies impacted on the country and in no small way on the Transport Industry as well.

On a more positive note, during the first full year of the Conservative Government, there were a number of important developments for Northern Counties. Three new chassis types, detailed below, were to pass through the factory, all destined for Greater Manchester Transport, but only one of which was from the Leyland stable, thus highlighting the concerns of the board which had led to the involvement with Foden. At the same time, this illustrated the fact that others too shared this concern, but also saw the market possibilities being created by Leyland's attitude to the industry.

A valuable export order was completed before the end of the year but by May of 1980 it had been found possible for the manufacture of all new bodies to be carried out at the modernised Pemberton premises, the task of conversion and adaptation having been completed over the previous year end, the transfer of work having been overseen on a day-to-day basis by Fred Sharrock. Wigan Lane henceforth was left for chassis storage.

The phasing-out of Leyland's Atlantean chassis allowed Northern Counties to re-design the rear of its standard body, eliminating the previous engine bustle which had tended to become untidy after years in service. The new body, designed principally for the Leyland Olympian, is seen here and also suited the rear-engined Dennis Dominator. *(STA)*

The 1980 Motor Show at the NEC was the location for this rare public display of a Wigan-built bus destined for the Middle East – in this instance Kuwait. The centre doorway was set back slightly further than most NCME bodies built for the UK and the deeper sliding windows on both decks reflected the requirements of a much warmer climate. *(STA)*

The first example of the new chassis to be bodied was a Dennis Dominator, Dennis (by then Hestair Dennis) having re-entered the bus building market. The Dominator was effectively a replacement for the popular (but no longer available), Daimler Fleetline, being relatively straightforward, without the complicated sophistication Leyland was putting into its Titan and Olympian models in its efforts to woo London Transport. Dennis had been very much encouraged by Geoffrey Hilditch, who had expressed some interest in the Foden episode it will be recalled. He was now General Manager at Leicester City Transport and had bought the last Dennis Lolines when Manager at Halifax. The Dominator was completed in March and the other two new types appeared around the time of the autumn Motor Show. One was the revamped Ailsa B55 whilst the final new chassis was originally designated B45 by Leyland, although it was to become better known as the Olympian. The rather convoluted history of the Olympian, conceived at Bristol, built at a factory designed for the Leyland National and finally ending up being built by Volvo, is well covered by Doug Jack in *Beyond Reality*, published by *Venture* in 1994.

The overseas delivery had arisen as a result of Leyland Vehicles, in the face of tough competition, winning an order for ten left-hand-drive double-deck buses for Kuwait. Perhaps Leyland had not completely lost the skill for which it had once been world famous, the order following on as a result of the successful operation of a single trial bus which Northern Counties had bodied the previous year. One of the batch was exhibited at the NEC in October alongside the Olympian. The trade press was able to report that, as a result of all this activity, Northern Counties' output had risen by 75% since 1975, which had led to an increase in market share which reflected the modernisation programme being implemented at the factory. The number of employees had increased to around 330. One can share the sense of pride David Cherry would have felt when he read this item. The next year, 1981, was again to see on the one hand, significant new developments, whilst also registering changes which were to be a break with the past. In connection with the latter, Southend Transport took delivery of twelve Leyland Fleetlines which were completed in June, the last new chassis of the type to be bodied by Northern Counties. Besides being registered by Northern Counties at the Manchester local vehicle licensing office (to ensure fleet number and registration number 'matched' – a feature the local Essex office was unable or unwilling to accommodate), this group of vehicles

The last new Fleetlines to be bodied by Northern Counties in 1981 coincided with the commencement of a new body numbering scheme. Despite its destination being Southend, Chief Designer Ron Parsons, standing in the centre, conceals the fact that the bus was registered in Manchester. Also in the picture are David Cherry, Ken Mellor – Southend's GM, Fred Sharrock, and Peter Rigby from Leyland's sales team. ***(STA)***

also commenced a new body numbering series for Northern Counties at No. 2001. The previous series was eventually to reach 8998, although not until 1983 on a Leyland Atlantean for Fylde Borough.

The new development which warranted a new set of body numbers related to an alloy-framed body for Greater Manchester Transport on an Atlantean AN68 chassis. Although at first glance it resembled previous products, new production changes involved the greater use of alloy framing, including body bearers, with jig-built side frames which continued right up to the upper-deck waistrail. A change to rubber gasket glazing and a one-piece fibreglass staircase were other major visible changes. On the administrative front, it should be recorded that the address of the company's registered office was moved, which, while still in Cardiff, was now at Harrowby House in Harrowby Street. The date of this change was 16th February 1982 and it was to remain there until April 1985 when it was moved to Enfield Street, Pemberton, the site of the new factory, but under somewhat changed circumstances, as will be seen. Still reflecting the early links with the South Wales area, the directors judged it prudent this year to make provision in full, in the annual accounts, for the unsecured loans and investments in two subsidiary companies. These were the Holmes Electrical & Engineering Co and the Taff Wagon Engineering Co, it being felt that the recession being experienced nationally justified this decision. The annual board report also confirmed that Godfrey Lewis was no longer a director.

Another of the new chassis to appear was the Volvo B55. This example in February 1982 was for Derby, and apart from the give-away front grille to cool the front-mounted engine, the standard ubiquitous body seated 73. *(STA)*

This Leyland AN68D was one of three delivered to Barrow Corporation in February 1983. Barrow was not a big customer of Northern Counties, nor indeed was its fleet particularly large (around 40 units) and it was to disappear ignominiously six years later. Previous deliveries from Wigan Lane to this operator had included 18 Crossleys in 1932 and two Leyland TD3c models in 1934. *(STA)*

Another landmark was reached at the 1982 Motor Show when the 1250th standard body delivered to Greater Manchester was exhibited, fleet No. 3001 and the first of a new fleet of Leyland Olympian chassis. This vehicle (ANA 1Y) is one of many splendidly preserved Northern Counties standards to be seen in the collections of the Manchester Museum of Transport and the Selnec Preservation Society. The premises of the former, at Boyle Street, Manchester, also includes many examples from the pre-standard era, as well as fine examples of all the pre-Greater Manchester constituent authorities, including a number of Northern Counties' bodied examples. The production Olympian chassis was 3in (7.6cm) longer than the Atlantean and Northern Counties cleverly adapted its standard body by increasing the width of the first upper-deck pillar to accommodate the difference. In the light of the fact that such a high proportion of the output (around 75%) was going to one operator, conveniently situated on the company's doorstep, the next developments in this story hardly come as a surprise. Before dealing with this, however, it is perhaps worth recording that the balance of the orders were still going to municipal customers like Chester, Cleveland, Derby, Fylde, Nottingham, Thamesdown and Southend, but also included Cardiff Corporation which took 27 Volvo B55s that year (the name now given to the Ailsa B55), the first order from the City since 1942. The (rumoured) problems concerning the rise-and-fall clause for the trolleybuses must eventually have been resolved! At the time this batch of buses figured prominently in the Company's advertisement material, including a photograph of two thirds of the order lined up outside Cardiff City Hall. Finally, a handful of independent operators took small quantities, but no National Bus Company subsidiaries were on the list or indeed any other PTE; nor any longer, as a separate customer, was the Lancashire United Transport company, which had been assimilated into Greater Manchester PTE, a move not unconnected with the influence of a man we are about to meet.

David Graham, Greater Manchester PTE's charismatic Director General, was well-known for his robust approach to business and it was undoubtedly his drive, perhaps behind the scenes as much as at centre stage, which resulted in the June 1983 announcement that GMPTE had bought into Northern Counties. His previous experience as the PTE's Director of Finance, to say nothing of his time with Threlfall's Brewery in Liverpool, undoubtedly equipped him well for this task. No one could level the accusation at David Graham that he was unable to organise the proverbial celebration in a brewery. Indeed it was perhaps a mark of the man when it was reported that the deal had been made 'without reference to the Passenger

The imposing façade of Cardiff City Hall was a more than suitable backdrop for part of the large delivery of Volvo B55s made to the Principality's Capital City in 1982. The Lewis family with its extensive South Wales connections still controlled Northern Counties and the company's registered office was still in the City after over 60 years. *(STA)*

Transport Authority', which apparently resulted in some 'raised eyebrows' at a meeting when the PTA had learned of the deal.

The official announcements stated that the bulk of the shares in Northern Counties were held by a family trust (for some years the annual reports had been indicating that Mrs J G Lewis and H G Lewis Junior were acting as trustees) and that it had been decided, on the advice of an independent trustee, to sell some of the shares to obtain a better spread of investment. David Graham was quoted as explaining that the opportunity was being taken to secure bus body supplies by having much closer links with Northern Counties and he went on to praise the excellent service which the company had given the PTE over a period of ten years, during which the company had been the main supplier of bus bodywork to the Executive. He added that "support would be mutually beneficial and will sustain the company which employs some 300 staff in Wigan". The press and the public were advised that links between the two organisations were being strengthened by the creation of a joint holding company in which both GMPTE and the current management of Northern Counties would have interests. Both Henry Lewis, grandson of the founder, and David Cherry would continue to be responsible for the operation of the business and they had both invested in the new controlling company to which GMPTE would appoint non-executive directors.

The annual reports for the period in question showed that H G Lewis Senior, Mrs G J Lewis and Mrs J G Cory ceased to be directors on 2nd June 1983. They were replaced by J A Elwin, B Holcroft and L Hyman– the latter only until 2nd September, when he was replaced by A W Waterworth who was a Lewis/Cherry nominee – the others being GMPTE nominees. On 31st March 1983, the company had disposed of its interests in Lilybetana Trenchard Construzioni S P A (a 25% share had been held since around 1980 in this company, which had been engaged in a holiday village development in Sicily), Holmes Electrical and Taff Wagon. An EGM on 2nd June had authorised an increase in share capital from £65,000 to £1,523,216 and the company became a wholly owned subsidiary of Kinnigar Ltd, which in turn, although not indicated in this report, was a subsidiary of Charterplan, the PTE's coaching and holiday division. The registered address of Kinnigar Ltd was 9 Portland Street, Piccadilly Gardens, Manchester, the head office of the PTE and from where DG David Graham directed affairs.

The arrival of George Orwell's premonitional year of 1984 was not perhaps as traumatic as the author's infamous book of the same name had predicted. For

From time to time vehicles were received by Northern Counties for the construction of a brand new body. Chester 57 (OFM 957K), new in 1972, was one such vehicle and is seen here with its new January 1985 body. Other fleets to indulge in such an enterprise included Cleveland Transit, Nottingham and Southend. ***(DC)***

Northern Counties was to receive only one order for the Dennis Domino, and not surprisingly, this was from Greater Manchester PTE, one of whose 22 examples is shown outside Piccadilly rail station on the city centre shoppers' service. The chassis itself did not sell particularly well, other examples being limited to the fleets of the PTEs in South and West Yorkshire. Nevertheless, an attractive brochure was produced by NCME for the model as seen below. *(STA)*

Northern Counties it meant the demands of another Motor Show at the NEC and one of the exhibits was to be indicative of the way that the bus industry was to move in the next few years. Hestair Dennis had produced a new medium length single-deck chassis called the Domino, in effect a short-wheelbase Dominator, largely at the behest of several of the Passenger Transport Executives, who ordered varying quantities. Only Greater Manchester had their order, for 22 units, bodied by Northern Counties and the first appeared at the show. The capacity of this midi-bus was 24 seated passengers and 15 standees and the overall dimensions were 7.6m long and 2.28m wide. In order to produce this bus Northern Counties had recruited John Bloor, who had previously been in charge at Eastern Coach Works in Lowestoft and before that with Park Royal, both under Leyland ownership. The construction of these single-deck bodies represented a return to this market for the first time for a number of years. Also on display was yet another Leyland Atlantean for Kuwait, 20 more similar buses having been supplied in 1983 and a further twelve in this year, one of which was to form part of the company's display.

The final move from Wigan Lane was made around this time, which involved the locating of all the offices at Pemberton from then on. A small paint shop was completed in September and the following year the Wigan Lane site was sold to the North West Regional Health Authority. The overall appearance of Pemberton had been changing, too; in July 1983 the landmark chimney acquired with the mill had been demolished.

Although numerically a small order completed in November 1984, the significance of the three Dennis Dominators supplied to London Buses Limited that year cannot be overlooked. Numbered H1-3 in the former London Transport's quaint (and sometimes obscure) system – 'H' for 'Hestair' – they were to be the first products supplied to the capital by Northern Counties for nearly 40 years. Little could it be imagined that before the end of the century, the majority of the Wigan factory output would be going to the capital, nor, sadly, could it ever have been anticipated that the last body built would do the same.

But before all this was to happen, the words of the 1985 Annual Report were indicative of the way the future was going to be for the next few years. A reduction in operating profit 'was due to the continued depressed state of the bus industry and it was impossible to predict the future due to the effects of the 1985 Transport Bill'. Initially Greater Manchester continued to take the same high percentage of output from the factory, the Leyland Atlantean

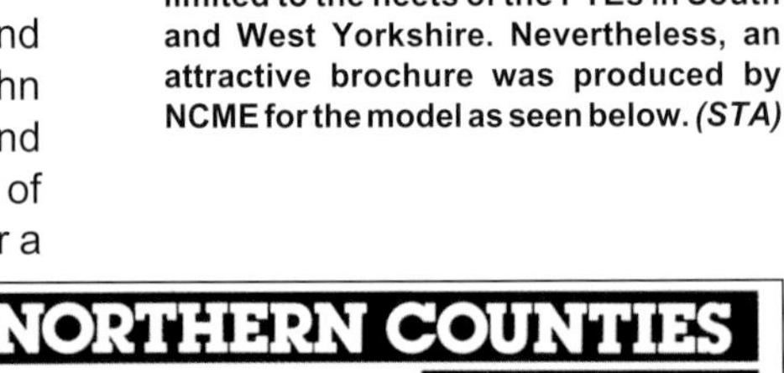

NORTHERN COUNTIES

MIDI '85

The Northern Counties midi-bus has been designed to cater for the demanding and changing operating requirements of the 'eighties - and beyond

With a normal life expectancy which will take it into the 21st Century this bus will be adaptable yet not easily dated.

Bonded glazing and panels give it a particularly neat appearance and will assist in keeping it clean and smart in service.

The wide doorway incorporates a low step height for easy access and rapid loading and unloading. Once inside passengers have a level floor clear of obstructions.

The deep side windows with high level hopper vents afford good vision for passengers, whilst the deep, two-piece single curvature screen gives excellent driver visibility.

Cab layout is particularly good, with controls neatly grouped and ergonomically located, thereby reducing driver fatigue and maintaining a safe working environment.

Great care has been taken with design to allow the vehicle – which complements Northern Counties conventional single-deckers – to be capable of adaptation for use in a variety of roles. Disabled passengers can be catered for via a wheel chair lift located amidships and conventional seating arrangements allow for 24 passengers plus 14 standees or up to 29 seated.

Designed initially for fitment to the air-suspended rear-engined Dennis Domino chassis, the body can be adapted to fit most chassis and to meet most operators requirements. Built to a width of 7' 6" [2280mm] for intensive city centre or rural work, the bus can also be produced to 8' 2½" [2502mm] as required.

All welded steel construction – with wax injected anti-corrosion protection for optimum life – gives an exceptionally strong structure and the design includes anti-roll bars fore and aft for added passenger safety.

Northern Counties will be pleased to discuss your particular requirements and to demonstrate the versatility of the design.

A series of aerial views showing the development of the Pemberton site appears in Appendix 1. This view was taken not long after the landmark chimney had been removed in 1983. *(STA)*

What was to turn out to be of significant importance was the order for body Nos. 2632-4 for London Transport which was built in November 1984. The third bus of the order H3 (B103 WUW) is seen here before dispatch to the capital. It is unlikely that at this time anyone could have envisaged the impact that this combination of chassis and body manufacturer would have on the London scene. *(STA)*

Nottingham City Transport continued to buy from both Northern Counties and East Lancs, its two main sources of bodies for the previous decade, but the styling which had been shared by both manufacturers was evolving. A699 EAU (fleet No. 699), seen above, was an Olympian with a modified window line at the rear of the lower-deck, whilst D393 TAU (fleet No. 393), below, was a Leyland Lion, a very rare breed, which entered service with Nottingham at the end of 1986. The underfloor-engined nature of the Lion enabled a seating capacity of 84 to be achieved and the body style showed a considerable departure from previous Nottingham practice. *(STA, TW)*

having been superseded by the Leyland Olympian, but dual-sourcing also saw, from March 1985, Dennis Dominators being supplied to the PTE. But as part of these changes, the PTE was destined not to remain a bus operator for much longer. Nicholas Ridley's Bill, already referred to, was to see all local authority owned operations placed into 'arms length' companies. The deregulation of the bus industry was effective from 26th October 1986, and the privatisation of those operators both locally and nationally owned was to commence soon after. It was the lead up to this situation that caused so much uncertainty and change to Northern Counties prospects. As one example of the impact on the industry, GMPTE withdrew some 600 buses overnight on 26th October, which was equal to some five year's worth of replacement production work for Northern Counties. The releasing of such a large number of modern, rear-engined, standardised double-deckers onto the open market was catastrophic. For Northern Counties and other bodybuilders looking for new business, new and old-established operators alike could fill their needs from a bus depot-cum-supermarket in a south Manchester suburb.

One initiative, developed as a result of these changes, was the greater use of minibuses. In the first instance the generic description 'bread vans' was not unfair; the manufacturers' panel van body simply being modified for passenger use. However, amongst others, Dodge produced a minibus chassis suitable for bodying by a separate builder. In the uncertainty of the time, the theory was that more frequent services operated by smaller buses would have the commercial advantage over services operated less-frequently by larger vehicles. Harry Blundred of the NBC's subsidiary Devon General, had introduced modified Ford Transit vans in Exeter in 1984 appearing to confirm the theory, which was enthusiastically taken up by certain other NBC companies. Such was the state of the industry at the time, that whilst not everyone was convinced of the argument, no-one wanted to be left behind.

Thus it was that at the 1986 Motor Show, held from 15th to 26th October at the NEC (note it closed on deregulation day!), the Northern Counties stand exhibited two Dodge minibuses and a Leyland Atlantean. The chassis now being unavailable to home customers because it could not meet new legislation on emissions, the vehicle was yet another export for Kuwait.

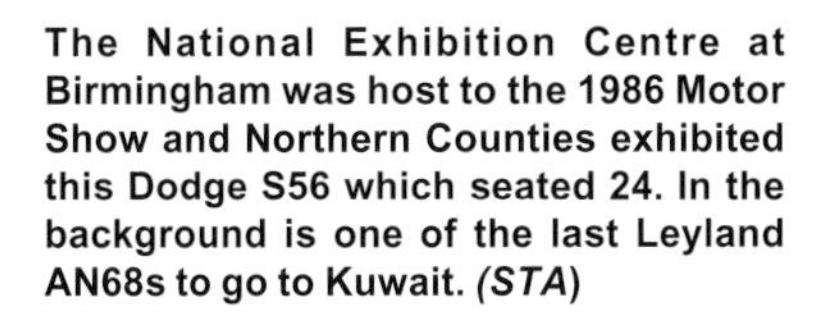

The National Exhibition Centre at Birmingham was host to the 1986 Motor Show and Northern Counties exhibited this Dodge S56 which seated 24. In the background is one of the last Leyland AN68s to go to Kuwait. *(STA)*

One of the Dodges was a company demonstrator, an S46 model, with seats for 24 and a manual gearbox. Interestingly, it carried a livery describing it as a 'Midi', even though this terminology tended to be used generally for such chassis as the Dennis Domino. The other, an S56 variety, was the first of 65 similar minibuses for Greater Manchester PTE and seated 20, unlike 40 similar S56s previously supplied that year which seated only 18. Prior to this out-pouring of Dodge vehicles, Northern Counties production had tended to concentrate on full-sized double-deckers. Only small batches of single-deck Dennis Falcons for Hartlepool and Ipswich (themselves both new customers and received within the previous twelve months), departed from a standardisation that had stretched back to 1975, when the two Fords for Cleveland were built. Now, over a third of the total vehicle output was to comprise minibuses and the proportion was to increase even more over the next few years.

After the earlier concerns regarding the availability of different chassis for double-deck bodies, the fact that 1986 also saw such bodies constructed for Nottingham, Derby and Greater Manchester on the Volvo B10M, Leyland Lions for Nottingham (both underfloor-engined double-deck models and never widespread), and on Metrobuses for Greater Manchester (the latter having been originally introduced as an integral double-deck bus by Metro-Cammell-Weymann), it must have given some heart to the company. Cleveland Transit also returned some seven early Leyland Atlanteans for completely new bodies, a move repeating one made the previous year by Southend, but in their case on Fleetline chassis. The uncertain future that deregulation was bringing to the industry was causing the company difficulties and the local press carried 'crisis' headlines in September when reporting that up to 70 jobs were at risk because of a slump in orders. The further order from Greater Manchester mentioned previously in fact averted this 'crisis', but it did lead to representatives of all ten Greater Manchester district councils agreeing to try to help, and small numbers of minibuses were delivered to some of them in due course.

The year (1986) was not without further alterations at board level either, and the remainder of the company's life was to be ruled by changes at senior level which would have been unheard of during the first seven decades of its existence and which finally severed the Lewis family links. Henry Lewis was replaced as Chairman and Managing Director by David Cherry on 4th June and his resignation as a Director was recorded on 7th November. A W Waterworth had resigned on 2nd May and John Elwin, Brian Holcroft and Ralph Roberts (who had only been appointed on 4th June), on 24th October. J W Baker (from 4th June) and G S Inskip

United Transport's attempt to re-enter the UK bus market was not a resounding success, vehicles intended to compete with the former PTE services in Manchester migrating to Preston as shown here in the town's Bus station. ***(STA)***

(7th November) had been appointed as directors. If such comings and goings appeared to destabilise the board, it has to be remembered that all these appointments were being made on behalf of the principal shareholder, which was, of course, the Passenger Transport Executive, which itself was undergoing significant changes in its role as a result of the 1985 Act. The annual report commented that the company had actually increased its market share, but that this had been achieved through reducing margins. Following deregulation, uncertainties continued, but the Wigan management team had been strengthened to meet the demands of the changing industry.

Further board appointments were made in 1987 when Mike Winter, who had been at Duple Metsec and before that with Leyland Vehicles, was appointed as the first Director of Sales and Marketing in May and Nick Parsons (no relation to Chief Designer Ron Parsons), from Hestair Duple, became Director of Production Engineering in September. Virtually all of the production that year (which in numeric terms reached heights previously unknown at Pemberton), was for minibuses. For the first time over 300 bodies were constructed, the total in fact reaching around 360, of which no less than 330 were minibuses, almost all of which were on Dodge chassis. The majority were for Greater Manchester Buses, the company set up to operate the former PTE bus services, but 50, with manual gearboxes, were for the United Transport subsidiary Manchester Minibuses, a company established to compete head on with the former PTE services. In order to stimulate the market amongst other operators, Northern Counties also offered leasing facilities, as well as offering a repainting service. Nottingham City Transport was one operator which availed itself of this arrangement.

Of the remainder of the 1987 output, which were all double-deckers, by far the largest order and clearly the most significant, was for 28 Leyland Olympians for London Buses, the one area of the country where deregulation did not apply. Cynics might suggest that Nicholas Ridley, the architect of the Act, had been a founder-member of the 'NIMBY' (not-in-my-back-yard) school of politics. Hand-in-hand with deregulation had been the privatisation of the former National Bus Company subsidiaries and the result of this was that orders began to trickle through from organisations not previously associated with products from Wigan. One of the first came from Cambus, a company that had been initially formed when Eastern Counties was divided and which itself had been one of the earliest sales to a Management buyout in December 1986. This order was reported, at the time, as being worth £1million and was ironic in that it was said that having been more than satisfied with former Greater Manchester standards (bought from the pool mentioned previously) obtained earlier, Cambus elected to purchase new vehicles of the type. Who said 'every cloud has a silver lining'?

Other former NBC companies to come to Wigan for new rolling stock in 1988 were Bee Line (the Berks & Bucks Bus Co) and Maidstone & District, whilst Eastbourne Borough Transport, still owned by the local authority, took delivery of no less than twelve double-deckers, reported to be the largest single investment ever in the 85 year life of the undertaking. All of these buses were mounted on Leyland Olympian chassis, the relative success of which was similarly ironic in that Volvo purchased what was left of Leyland in March that year. But this brighter news could not mask the underlying trends that the upheaval in the bus industry had created. The Northern Counties board was advised that due to changes in customer requirements, it had become necessary to build minibuses for stock. The minibus bubble appeared to have burst and although respectable numbers were bodied in 1988, there were many 'penny numbers' amongst them, indicative of the way the trend was going. During the following year, further vehicles were built for stock to maintain employment levels (which at the time stood at around 280), as a shortage of double-deck chassis was again experienced in the latter part of the financial year.

The annual report also indicated that the company had broadened its product base with the introduction of the manufacture of fire tenders for an affiliated company. These vehicles should, perhaps, be more accurately described as airport crash tenders and there were indeed two models produced; the Barracuda, which was the smaller of the two, and the Marlin, which was 3m wide. The chassis for these vehicles was constructed by Reynolds Boughton (Devon), based at Winkleigh Airfield. It is understood that the original chassis were to be bodied by Fire Trucks, who had gone out of business. Customers at home included Manchester and Humberside Airports, and RAF Brize Norton. Others went to the middle-east,

Confirmation that London liked the Northern Counties body came in 1987 with an order for a further 28 units, this time on Leyland Olympian chassis. This particular bus, E921 KYR, formerly London Buses No. 21, is seen here with Busways in Newcastle and was one of 21 sold to the former PTE operator in 1991.

A new customer in 1988 was The Bucks & Berks Bus Company (Bee Line) which was representative of the former National Bus Company subsidiaries free to purchase where they wished. F174 LBL was one of five Olympians purchased within a year of privatisation. *(DC both)*

including Dubai and Oman. A change in the Director of Sales and Marketing occurred in October when Mike Winter left to become Engineering Director at Cambus, to be replaced by Alan Metcalfe who had previously been with Leyland Bus. This year (1988) also saw the establishment of a further foreign connection, when a link was made with Renault Truck Industries. The intention was to import the French-built highly successful PR100 chassis for bodying by Northern Counties and to this end a chassis appeared at that year's Motor Show. Although Renault was French by ownership, it had gained a considerable toe-hold in the industry following the absorption of Dodge, who had been manufacturing the 50 series minibus at its Dunstable-based premises.

Body No. 3736 was constructed on the first Renault PR100 which was received and which duly appeared at the NEC with a 51-seat front-entrance layout. Regrettably, few orders were to be received for the model, three two-door 27-seat buses going to Luton International Airport the following year whilst a solitary example was delivered to London Buses Ltd. It was perhaps, too optimistic, to hope that a chassis produced under state ownership abroad, and therefore expensive to boot, was going to succeed in a very competitive market. The year concluded with the completion of a new paint facility, which was to lead to the spray-painting of vehicles and also the use of a tilt-table for the first time at Pemberton.

The start of 1989 still gave some reason for optimism, however. Orders were still being placed by the now privatised former constituents of the NBC, including once, again, Southdown, but now on Volvo B10M chassis, a model also favoured by London & Country, who took 25. Cambus also received the balance of a further order, whilst Kentish Bus and Eastern Counties both took Olympians. This chassis was also the choice of Merseyside Transport (the former Merseyside PTE operator which was yet to be privatised), which took 20, following on from a delivery of 15 the previous year. But within a year the press were talking of a 'Northern Counties survival plan'. The reports indicated that the company had been trading at a loss since deregulation and that GMPTE was to inject £3million. This was achieved by increasing the nominal capital of the company by that amount on 2nd April, records indicating that this was all owned by Kinnigar Limited. Such measures could not be

No prizes for guessing which show this Renault appeared at! Regrettably it was not to be anywhere near successful as the Leyland Olympian, which was placed alongside it. This was one of 25 for Yorkshire Rider (the former West Yorkshire PTE operation, which was about to pass to the employees in an EBO). Both were displayed at the NEC in 1988. *(STA)*

achieved without some heartache and trade press reports further indicated that a drastic overhaul of working practices would involve redundancies with the intention that these changes would save around £1.2 million annually. It should be remembered that maintaining local employment had been, and was, still part of the local objective.

On the personnel front, there were also a series of changes that year. In March Ian Murray had replaced Alan Metcalf as Director of Sales and Marketing. The former went to Phoenix International, the Fareham-based mini and midi-coach builder formed out of the old Robin Hood company, whilst the latter had previously been Sales and Marketing Manager with W Alexander of Falkirk. In connection with the restructuring of the company, Neil Scales moved from his post as Director of Engineering with Greater Manchester Buses to become Chief Executive and Managing Director, David Cherry relinquishing this latter post but remaining Chairman. Gordon Pennington was appointed as Financial Controller. Later in the year Frank McGhee took up the post of Sales Manager, having previously been Technical Sales Executive with Northern Counties. So, despite everything, there still seemed to be light at the end of the tunnel.

The effects in London of the splitting up of London Transport into a dozen separate companies (later to be privatised) and the introduction of competitive tendering on a large scale saw these changes bring positive results as far as Northern Counties was concerned. London General went to Wigan for eleven new buses, having won route 196 (Norwood Junction & Brixton) in the summer of 1990, while Ensign Bus (not a former part of LT) also had 24 Dominators bodied by Northern Counties for London Regional Transport services. Finally, towards the end of the year, it was announced that the company would be building a new single-deck bus featuring all-aluminium construction and that it would be launched at Bus & Coach '91 to be held at the NEC at Birmingham. Not for the first time, as seen in chapter one, a Northern Counties body would carry a name, this new design being christened 'Countybus'.

So 1991 beckoned bright. Further orders for the London scene as a result of successful tendering saw deliveries of Dennis Dominators to Frontrunner (South East), Olympians to London Buslines and BTS of Borehamwood. An extremely brief review of Frontrunner perhaps illuminates the state of the industry at the time. The operation was an offshoot of East Midland Motor Services of Chesterfield, which had been bought by its management in February 1988. Eyeing the potential for profit in London it set up a subsidiary in Dagenham and ordered new buses; it also, briefly, ran in the Glossop area. Even before they arrived, East Midlands sold out to Stagecoach in April 1989. The latter operator, perhaps more sagely, sold the Dagenham business to Ensign soon afterwards. Unlike the rest of the country, where tendering was only for services deemed not commercial, and therefore tending to be less well used, London's tendering process was covering all services, and more often than not called for new buses to have the latest national and London specifications. But it was clear that Northern Counties could not survive just on building bodies for new buses. Deregulation had brought diversification as has been seen and it was likely that this was going to be the situation for some time. Repair and accident work, which had been carried out by Northern Counties since the earliest days of the company, was now even more vital and a walk around the Pemberton premises at this time would have found Royal Mail vans being repainted as well as visits from London Routemasters for repair, to say nothing of work on buses from closer to home such as Blackpool, Greater Manchester and West Yorkshire Metro.

Even as Northern Counties was announcing further details of its new single-deck body, to appear at the NEC's Coach and Bus Show in the autumn, one event slipped by which in the light of subsequent events went almost unnoticed. Tragically, this was the death of David Graham at the age of 61 on 9th April 1991. It is not suggested that this alone made any difference to events, but almost no sooner had Ian Murray announced that three day working would have to be introduced than the company was placed in Administration on 22nd May. Grant Thornton was appointed to what one trade editorial described as the 'awesome task of finding a buyer' for Northern Counties. They immediately reduced the workforce from 304 to 127, but were quick to acknowledge that many of its competitors were also suffering a severe lack of orders. It was estimated that the orders then in hand would keep the company going until August. It was claimed that the total bus market itself was down by about 45%

Leyland Olympian J132 YRM, delivered in September 1991, reflected the new order in the capital. Capital Citybus had been successful in winning work in London and required half-a-dozen 77-seaters for the contract. *(DC)*

and that the uncertainty was clearly caused by the effects of deregulation. Grant Thornton may have been somewhat surprised, therefore, to discover that within a month they had no less than 50 enquiries from potential buyers and that companies like East Yorkshire Motor Services of Hull, in private ownership since early 1987, were more than happy to do business with Northern Counties, despite the Company being in administration.

The remaining workforce must have viewed the immediate future with some considerable uncertainty. Employees who were interviewed during the research for this book admitted that one of their greatest fears was that W Alexander of Falkirk would purchase the factory, purely with the intention of closing it. In a way their fears were confirmed over ten years later, but of this, more in due course. On the one hand orders from Greater Manchester and Ensign Citybus were still going through the factory, along with work repainting British Telecom vans into their new corporate livery, whilst the supply of two more Barracuda airport tenders, one for Hong Kong and one for the United Arab Emirates was announced as the company continued its preparation for the launch of the new single-deck body. But on the other hand a spokesman for Grant Thornton, the administrators in whose hands the company's future lay, indicated that the workforce would be further reduced to 120, that orders already in hand would be completed by August and that after that there were none. These last orders, for the time being, included a mixed bag for Greater Manchester, comprising Dennis Dominators, Volvo B10Ms and Scania N113s; there were also Leyland Olympians for Ensign Citybus, now renamed Capital Citybus, following the takeover by Hong Kong interests.

As 1991 moved inexorably closer to 1992 and the March deadline set for prospective buyers, Ian Murray was keen to appeal for loyalty from its customers in the shape of new orders and was equally anxious to point out that Northern Counties was not in receivership but administration. "There is a big difference between the two" he reminded the industry. Meanwhile, Lindsay Khan (who we will meet again quite soon) of the administrators, confirmed that the aim of Grant Thornton was to recover the company. Small orders from Leicester Citybus for some more Renault S56 minibuses, another order from East Yorkshire and one from East Kent were helping, to the extent that Grant Thornton had given their blessing to Northern Counties proceeding with its appearance at the NEC in the

The lengthy limited stop service operated by Yorkshire Coastliner, part of the Blazefield Group, linking West Yorkshire with the East Coast resorts of Bridlington, Scarborough and Whitby was supplied in 1992 with six Volvo Olympians. All six had appropriate YCL registration marks and were fitted with high-back seats. *(DC)*

Autumn of 1991. The opportunity was taken to display Ensign and Greater Manchester double-deckers, as well as the new single-deck model, with examples for Warrington and Greater Manchester available for inspection. At this stage, it is interesting to note that all four bodies were described as 'Countybus'. Before the end of the year, a significant order from London Buses for bodies for 40 Scania N113 double-deckers, which were intended for its subsidiary East London, resulted in Neil Scales announcing that 50 staff were consequently to be recruited.

Further orders early in 1992 enabled the company to clarify the situation of model names for the different types of Countybus. The double-decker was to be known as the Palatine, single-deck Countybuses as Paladins and coach built minibuses on Renault, Iveco and Mercedes chassis as Pageants. The summer of the same year saw, as the press were to describe the situation, 'a flurry of bus orders' (these included Stagecoach – for the first time – Yorkshire Coastliner and East Kent) which preceded the awarding by Grant Thornton of preferred-bidder status to the Management team at Northern Counties, an announcement that many in the industry by that time had anticipated. Then, in mid-August the formal announcement was made. The sale of Northern Counties was to be to its own senior management, led by Ian Murray and Nick Parsons and also in part to its employees, for £1.9million. And so another chapter was about to begin.

As part of its diversification Northern Counties briefly produced fire tenders, one of which is seen here for the Humberside Airport Fire Service. *(KT)*

A 'one-off' at the time for Mainline, the former South Yorkshire PTE operation, was Dennis Dart K402 EDT, delivered in September 1992. *(DC)*

The new owners of Northern Counties must have been very grateful for the large order for 30 Leyland buses received from Bristol Cityline, delivery of which commenced in January 1993. The livery of yellow, red and blue, and its style of application, was not untypical of many of the privatised former NBC subsidiaries, who wished to emphasis their break with the old, and rather drab, liveries. *(DC)*

Chapter Nine

1993 – 2005

After 15 months in administrative receivership, having been placed there by its then owners, Greater Manchester PTE (after the company exceeded its £500,000 overdraft), Northern Counties had new owners. The sale had initially been advertised by accountants Grant Thornton, but as is so often the case in such business arrangements, a number of other parties were involved before the sale was completed. The management and employees, who, in August 1992, purchased the assets, but not the company, were led by Ian Murray and Nick Parsons who became joint Managing Directors. Ian was primarily responsible for sales and Nick for production. They were joined by Lindsay Khan as Finance Director (who had previously been with Grant Thornton, the administrators), whilst a new Chief Executive, Trevor Egan, joined from Carborundum in order to satisfy the banks that additional outside expertise was at the helm. (Whilst undoubtedly not true, only the writer could imagine him as the 'hard man' of the outfit). The Bank of Boston was the sole outside institutional equity funder, providing, it was reported at the time, in excess of just over £500,000, whilst Lloyds bank provided £600,000 senior debt. Around 24% of the shareholding was made available to the workforce. Many, but not all, of the staff on the shopfloor took advantage of this opportunity to invest in the company; the brave were to be rewarded accordingly.

The Northern Counties story should really have ended at the conclusion of the previous chapter. The Northern Counties Motor & Engineering Company Limited, whose story we have been following since 1919, was no longer trading. All the investment was in the new company of Northern Counties Limited. Sadly, the Northern Counties company which actually dated from 1935 (as explained in chapter

Western National was the first operator to receive the new Volvo-built version of the Olympian. The company was at the time part of the Badgerline Group. New in July 1993, K803 ORL is seen here in Torquay. *(DC)*

Leicester Citybus L625 XFP was a Paladin-bodied Dennis Falcon delivered in August 1993. *(DC)*

By 1993 Northern Counties had begun to receive orders for single-deckers from London and one of the first substantial deliveries for single-deck buses were branded by their owners London General as Clapham Omnibus. The Volvo B10B was fitted with two doors. It commenced a new London Buses class 'VN'. *(DC)*

two), was in due time to be removed from the register of companies by Companies House. But the premises at Pemberton, whose transport connections stretched back into the 19th century, were to carry on building buses into the 21st century, so it seems only right to continue this story to, some may well say, the bitter end.

At many times it has seemed to me that events occur because the right person (or organisation) was in the right place at the right time. This is not to denigrate the efforts of those who saved, at least for the time being, over 200 jobs in the North West, where economic upheaval had hit the population as hard as anywhere else in the country. But taking stock for a moment, it has to be noted that the bus industry was now six years on from deregulation and a degree of stability was emerging. Furthermore, the one-time words of Ron Ellis of Leyland could not have turned out to be further from the truth; indeed, the opposite of what he had predicted was happening. Leyland had been sold, as we have seen, to Volvo in 1988 and the latter were now in the process of re-engineering the Olympian. Leyland bodies for this chassis were briefly switched to Workington, before that site too was closed. Nowhere could this change in fortunes be better illustrated than perhaps in the Bristol region.

Badgerline subsidiary City Line (Badgerline was yet to merge with Grampian to form FirstBus), decided to order its first double-deckers for 10 years for operation in Bristol. No less than 30 buses were required and City Line chose the Olympian. Whether this choice could be viewed as appropriate or ironic depends on one's point of view, as the chassis was originally developed and built in the city by Bristol Commercial Vehicles, until Leyland closed the plant down. The 30 Palatine bodies (to be followed later in the year by another 14), seemed to reflect the new prosperity that Northern Counties was enjoying. In addition, a variation to the double-deck body, called Palatine II was announced, the major difference on the all-aluminium body being a re-styling of the upper and lower deck screens. Initially, this body was intended for the new Volvo Olympian only.

All of a sudden, Northern Counties was looking at a total production for 1993 of around 250 units, the new Paladin single-decker accounting for almost 100 of this figure. Dennis Lances for London Buses' subsidiary Metroline and also for Eastern Counties accounted for part of the order, other Paladin bodies going to Trent on Volvo B10B chassis. And before the year was out, the first Volvo Olympian chassis were being received from Irvine in Scotland for bodying. Other customers for 1993 contributed to a truly impressive list, namely Bluebird Buses, East Midlands, East Yorkshire, Leicester Citybus, Gemsan (Huyton) subsidiaries Liverbus and London Suburban, Maidstone & District, North Devon, Southern Vectis, Stagecoach (South),

Tillingbourne Valley represented the long-established independent operator which, following deregulation, found itself running services that were once part of the NBC (and before that, BET/Tilling) empire. L103 EPA was a Dennis Dart new in February 1994 and is seen here in Reading operating on such a service. *(DC)*

United Counties, Warrington Borough Transport, Western National (now part of Badgerline too, and incidentally the first operator to place Northern Counties Volvo Olympians in service) and Whitelaw of Stonehouse. As a reversal of the labour position of only a year or so before, employee numbers were back up to 250 from the previous low point of 110.

Coach & Bus '93, held as now was the custom, at the NEC in Birmingham, saw the unveiling of Northern Counties re-styled Paladin body for the new Volvo B6 chassis, as well as the first appearance of the new Palatine II on a Volvo Olympian. Such a turn around in fortune was almost unthinkable only 12 months before. But so great was the confidence of the new organisation that before the end of 1993 plans were unveiled for a new 19,000 sq ft production unit, together with a 5,000 sq ft stores building incorporating 2,400 sq ft of mezzanine flooring. There was also to be an extension to the drawing office, a new rolling road and a new entrance with a security lodge. The pace of change was such that in February 1994 the trade press was able to report on the opening of these new facilities by the then Public Transport Minister, Roger Freeman. It was stated that the £1.9 million redevelopment programme had been part funded by a Department of Trade and Industry grant of up to 45% and the extension was expected to increase production capacity by up to 25% – up to a maximum of nine full-size buses per week. The total number of staff employed was now at 390, of which 39 were apprentices.

Sales of buses in 1994 were in line to match the previous year's total of around 250 units. Considering that none were minibuses, if one, therefore, excludes this type from comparative figures, this was probably the best production total for 15 years. Principal recipients that year were Kentish Bus, with 57 single-deckers (mainly Dennis Darts but including a dozen Volvo B6s) and eight double-deckers; Luton & District, with 32 B6s; Trent, with 18 Volvo B10Ms and Yorkshire Rider, with 25 double-deckers, all Olympians. The latter company, incidentally, had been the first of the former Passenger Transport Authority-owned companies to be privatised, in October 1988. By March 1994 all such PTA companies had been sold to their employees; by February 2000 they were all part of one or other of the big four groups that had emerged in the industry. This inevitable polarisation would not seem to have been, amazingly, what either Nicholas Ridley or Margaret Thatcher envisaged as a result of their Transport Act. Indeed, on one visit to an operator prior to deregulation, he was overheard to ask the management "how many of your drivers own their own buses?"

Yet two more new makes of chassis became available for bodying by Northern Counties during 1994. DAF, who hitherto only had their DB250 double-decker

East Yorkshire was a regular customer throughout the 1990s, its main contribution from Northern Counties being double-deck buses. The company also took a solitary single-decker in 1994. L261 AKH was a Volvo B6, delivered in March of that year. *(DC)*

Kentish Bus had originally been part of the NBC, and before that had its antecedents in the Country area services of London Transport. By the time these deliveries were being made, the company belonged to the Proudmutual Group, owners of Northumbria, which accounts for the Newcastle registration marks. In due course Proudmutual was to form part of Arriva. The two vehicles shown here were new in the spring of 1994. The double-decker carries a Palatine II body on a Volvo Olympian and is seen at Chislehurst Common. At the same location is Dennis Dart L137 YVK with a Paladin body. *(DC)*

bodied by Optare, came to an agreement with the Cleckheaton-based dealer Stanley Hughes whereby a new company, Hughes DAF, would supply both single- and double-deck buses with Northern Counties bodies. The 53-seat Countybus Paladin body would now be fitted to the DAF SB220, whereas it had previously only been available on Dennis, Volvo and Scania chassis. The DB250 would now be available as an 82-seat Palatine II, previously only available on the Olympian chassis. The first of these DAFs entered service with Eastbourne in October that year and Hughes were to supply three dozen buses to no less than a dozen operators during the next twelve months. Press reports indicated that they had anticipated selling around 50 units in that period, so by the standards of the time, it was not too bad a result. The other new chassis was from Scania, it having exhibited one of its new L113 CRL FlexiCi chassis at the previous October's Coach and Bus Show. Unlike its main competitors, the Dennis Lance and the Volvo B10B, it was not a true ultra-low floor bus. Yorkshire Traction, nevertheless, took five bodies from Northern Counties, no doubt encouraged by the fact that it was some £3,000-£4,000 cheaper than its competitors' offerings. Subsequently, Northern Counties customers did not significantly favour either DAF or Scania L113 models.

Changes to Northern Counties personnel in 1994 saw Andrew Tilstone join the company in February as Southern Sales Manager. Ian Murray, in announcing the appointment, commented that Northern Counties had, over the previous five years, become the largest supplier of double-deck buses to London Buses' subsidiaries. Whether this would continue in the future was perhaps open to speculation, as during 1994 all the bus operating subsidiaries of London Buses were sold, half going to employees (through either Management or Employee Buy Outs) and half to other groups, such as Stagecoach or Cowie. Ian Murray claimed that the company now had a 30% share of the double-deck market and 10% of the single-deck market. Andrew Tilstone joined the sales team headed by Frank McGhee, who was now Sales Manager and who could justly be proud of his staff as sales continued to increase, 1995's figures continuing the trend.

This obvious success at Northern Counties was not going unnoticed within the bus industry, for the year brought a further significant development. Whether it was this development that was to lead to the ultimate closure of the factory is perhaps for the reader alone to judge, but pessimists might point to the purchase of the company by the Henlys Group, which occurred in May 1995, as a pivotal point in the

Further orders from Bristol came in 1993 in the shape of 24 more Olympians, this time with Palatine II bodies. *(DC)*

In August 1994 Scania had a L113CRL bodied by Northern Counties, the Paladin body seating 49. It passed to Maynes of Manchester subsequently, and M113 RNK is seen here in Piccadilly in the City centre. *(DC)*

North of the border, Dodds of Troon took a trio of Dennis Darts in March 1995. M388 KVR is depicted in this view. *(DC)*

history of the Pemberton factory. The final episode in this history, which covers the next decade, is not one that can be written about with any enthusiasm by the author, unlike the events of the previous 80 years which never failed to make an impression. It is recognised, however, that in telling the story of Northern Counties the events of the final ten years should obviously be covered, albeit with this *caveat* about the lack of enthusiasm. Whereas all the events of the previous ten years had been caused, it could be argued, by changes wrought by legislative influence, it is now the situation that economic forces take over and their effect on Northern Counties and its staff needs to be considered.

It is appropriate, therefore, to look at the Henlys deal and see what it meant for the workforce. The reported price paid for Northern Counties by Henlys was quoted as £10million. Since coming out of administration three years before, Northern Counties had consistently been profitable, the figures for the year ending March 1995 showed the company making a profit of £1.4million on a turnover of £16million. Those members of staff who had invested in Northern Counties were already reaping the benefit in terms of dividend payments, so much so that many had covered their original outlay simply from the dividend payments they received. This had obviously been achieved as a result of a lot of hard work by all concerned and an acceptance of significant changes to working practices. For those who did have the courage to invest in the company in 1992, the return in 1995 was nothing short of stunning. From conversations with staff (as part of the research for this book), some who were in receipt of this good fortune were perhaps understandably reluctant to reveal the exact scale of the premium. It would be uncharitable in the extreme to suggest that this was in any way connected with the possibility that other members of the recipients' family might not fully share in the knowledge of the yield!

Turning away from Pemberton for a moment, it is necessary to review how the Henlys Group fit into this narrative. Fortunately for the author, other luminaries such as Stewart Brown and Alan Millar have covered this and subsequent machinations in some detail, which has been more than helpful. Events really need, briefly, to be traced back to 1987, when the coach and car dealership of Kirkby Central took over Plaxton, the long-established coachbuilder based in Scarborough. It is perhaps fair to say that this acquisition strengthened Plaxton's position in the market and by 1991 the Group was trading as Henlys, the original name of the car dealership. This change coincided with the stewardship of a new Chief Executive, Robert Wood. Soon afterwards, Henlys were the subject of a hostile takeover bid by Cowie (later to become Arriva), also the owner of car dealerships and also a bus operator.

The bid was unsuccessful, but the Henly Group, perhaps appreciating their vulnerability, opted to undertake a joint venture with Volvo in North America. At home they obviously saw Northern Counties' double-deck building capacity, which Plaxton did not have, as desirable. The stock market obviously agreed, as upon the announcement of the acquisition by Henlys of Northern Counties, the shares in the former company rose 44p to 380p. Undoubtedly, the deal also appealed to the owners of Northern Counties, who, to say the least, had experienced somewhat of a roller-coaster ride over the last few years. This was by no means the end of the story as regards takeovers and change, but as indicated above, 1995 was an extremely successful year as far as bus production at Pemberton was concerned and therefore befits this resume.

In case there was any doubt that Northern Counties would continue supplying to the now privatised London market, an order from Stagecoach for 100 buses soon answered any uncertainty. No less than 52 Palatine-bodied Volvo Olympians were for Selkent (one of the two London Buses companies bought by Stagecoach), the balance of eight double-deckers in the order going to Hull and Cleveland Transit, which, in the case of the latter, were their first double-deckers since deregulation. Forty B10Ms with Paladin bodies were shared between Hull, Hartlepool, Cleveland Transit and Stagecoach (South). London Central (now sold to the Go-Ahead Group) and CentreWest (at this point still owned by its managers, but later to become part of FirstGroup), also took Olympians for London work. Another market which Northern Counties began to develop at this time was in Hong Kong. Dennis had for some time enjoyed considerable success in the Crown Colony, and ten 43-seat Paladin-bodied versions with tinted glazing, on Dennis Dart chassis, now joined previous orders with the Kowloon Motor Bus company and marked the first Northern Counties exports for over 30 years. The Kowloon Canton Railway Corporation also took a number of Darts. At home customers during 1995 also included East

East London had become a Stagecoach subsidiary in September 1994 and two years later took its first batch of Olympians from Northern Counties totalling 26 buses. P803 GMU (VN3) is seen here at work on the 175 service. *(DC)*

Yorkshire, Fowler of Holbeach, Greater Manchester North, Maidstone & District, Merseyside Transport, Southern Vectis, and the Yorkshire Traction Group. The move towards low-floor single-deckers was demonstrated at the Coach & Bus '95 exhibition at the NEC, when a low-frame DAF SB220 was displayed.

Inevitably, further changes in company structure and personnel were to occur. It was unthinkable to imagine that having invested heavily in bringing Plaxton and Northern Counties together that Henlys would not wish to see a fusing of roles. The first visible sign of this was the announcement that David Quainton, Plaxton's Sales and Marketing Director, would oversee the sales effort of both subsidiaries. David Quainton had joined Plaxton in 1988 after nearly 20 years with Leyland, including a spell in charge of the Leyland National plant at Workington. For the time being at least, Ian Murray and Frank McGee would assist the team.

A press release early in 1996 perhaps underlines the significance of the take-over on Northern Counties. 'Plaxton Coach and Bus' it stated, 'along with sister company Northern Counties, has won a record £9.5million order for 263 buses from British Bus, one of the country's biggest bus operators.' The Wigan share of the order was to be for 65 Olympians with Palatine bodies (ie, that part of the deal that could not be built by Plaxton). The Scarborough and Anston factories would be constructing 127 Plaxton Pointers on Dennis Dart SLF chassis and 71 Plaxton Beavers on Mercedes-Benz 709D chassis. It was not difficult to see that the overlap in single-deck body production was not to be perpetuated and gradually the Northern Counties name was to be phased out, starting with bodies constructed for overseas operation, of which the first were soon to be leaving Pemberton.

These were 20 tri-axle 12m Olympians for Citybus Hong Kong with Palatine bodies seating 99 passengers. They were fitted with air conditioning and were to replace the remaining vehicles in the fleet without this facility. As Citybus required windscreens to be interchangeable with other vehicles in the fleet, they were fitted with Alexander glasses and screens, thus further disguising their factory origin. The Northern Counties badge was still to be found, however, on a batch of Citybus Olympians. These were for the north-east London Capital Citybus operation, which ironically had been purchased from its former Hong Kong owners in a MEBO the previous year. Yet another Citybus operation was to take Wigan-built products for the first time in 1996; this time the operator was based on the south coast and was the trading name of Southampton's former municipal fleet, which had been the subject of an employee-led purchase in 1993. These six Olympians were the first double-deckers obtained for seven years. Those staff employed at Enfield Street who were responsible for applying decals to the almost finished buses could have been excused for believing that almost every other customer was called 'Citybus'!

Inevitably, further changes in personnel were to take place; in the autumn of 1996 David Hodgetts took up the new post of Plant Director. He arrived from Johnson Controls where he had been Plant Manager; previous to that he had spent some seven years with Land Rover. His arrival was to coincide with yet another burst of investment on the site, although even the trade press seemed to get itself confused as to exactly what was happening, describing the alterations to the former mill site as having been inherited from Massey. Nevertheless, these additional alterations would further modernise the factory, along with significant changes to working practices which would see production methods move away from the traditional craftsman-built processes to a situation where vehicles were merely assembled. The Northern Counties factory was not alone in this transformation; the only bus assembly plant to be built at a brand new location in the latter part of the 20th Century (by Leyland at Workington), relied on assembly by unskilled workers, whilst resistance to such change had been a contributory factor resulting in the closure of the Park Royal and Eastern Coach Works facilities. Whilst this would ultimately allow annual production figures to increase even more (it was intended to raise output from seven buses per week to eleven), many of the staff who had remained throughout all the upheaval found it very difficult to accept all this change. Not far away East Lancashire Coachbuilders in Blackburn were progressing along the same road, to the same end – increased output.

The market forces that had seen emergency vehicles constructed for the Fire & Rescue Service were to see a further unique vehicle constructed for the service, when in April 1997 Greater Manchester Fire Brigade took delivery of a mobile incident command unit, which was based on a Volvo B6 chassis with equipment provided by Saxon Specialist Vehicles. The use of this chassis was interesting, to say the least, particularly in view of its early promise and the initial high hopes for volume production. It lost significant market share to its rival the Dennis Dart, large numbers of which were bodied by Plaxton with its Pointer body. It was not too surprising, therefore, when it was announced that Paladin production was to re-locate to Scarborough as part of Henly's Group rationalisation, which also saw the inevitable move to the badging of all Wigan built buses as Plaxton. The Northern Counties body on the DAF SB220 was rebadged as the Plaxton Prestige on its transfer to Scarborough.

The star of Coach & Bus '97 held at the NEC was, according to Stephen Morris writing in the December 1997 issue of *Buses*, the Volvo/Plaxton President. Internally, he wrote, it was based on the London Transport requirement for a low-floor double-decker and was the first British market double-deck bus to carry the Plaxton badge. In the euphoria over this exciting new design, the fact that the body had originated in Wigan seems to be totally incidental, or maybe it was conveniently played down to satisfy the new order. Described at the time as a 'concept' bus, as far as the chassis was concerned it was to turn out to be just that. Volvo had mounted the engine longitudinally on the low-floor chassis, as had Bristol with the original VR. The extra overhang this created was certainly not to everyone's liking and certainly not that of London Transport, who eschewed extra-long double-deckers in the Capital. So Volvo's engineers redesigned their chassis (funnily enough, Bristol had to do the same for the VR), the result being the B7TL and a substantial delay before the first production President body was to appear on a Volvo. Further twists to the story led to Volvo no sooner announcing that this new chassis would be built at Irvine, than the parent company announced the closure of the plant, albeit not before 2000. Cynics might claim *deja-vu*, recalling Leyland's similar perplexity at times.

Whilst all this was going on, Dennis, which had produced a variety of double-deck chassis over the previous few years, such as the Lance and the Arrow, introduced its most successful double-decker to date, the low-floor Trident. The obvious empathy between Henly's subsidiaries and Dennis had become self-apparent, so much so that in July 1998 plans for the merger of the two were announced. In this history of a Wigan company that for so long had its private shareholding tightly managed by a single family, it still seems strange to have to record the interests of the wider post-Thatcher ubiquitous public investors, but it was a fact that following this merger announcement, the value of the shares of both organisations shot up by around 10%. Publicly Volvo's view on this merger was not recorded at this time, but it will be recalled that only a few years before, Henlys and Volvo had set up a joint North American venture. At this point in the story I can do no better than repeat Stewart Brown's immortal words in *Bus Review 14*; "then in sailed Mayflower".

Yet again it is necessary to review, briefly, the history of a group that previously had no connection with the Wigan factory. It is also necessary to tread cautiously when recounting these affairs, as, even as this is being written, the Accountancy Investigation and Discipline Board is still reviewing events, in particular probing allegations surrounding Mayflower's auditors, PricewaterhouseCoopers. The Mayflower Group was a United Kingdom automotive engineering concern which had bought Walter Alexander in 1995 from the team of outside managers who in turn had bought the company from its founding family in 1990. Amongst its subsequent claims to fame was the fact the former Prime Minister John Major became a non-executive director, although he had resigned by 1993. In a war of bid and counter-bid Mayflower was eventually to trump Henlys' offer for Dennis by a significant margin, claiming the Henlys bid significantly under-valued Dennis, which claim was obviously supported by the Dennis shareholders. The result was that in October 1998, Mayflower took control of Dennis. In the light of subsequent events, one has to wonder exactly how true the estimates about value were. In the meantime Volvo had lent its support, unsuccessfully as it turned out, to Henlys' bid for Dennis. Subsequently it has strengthened its links with East Lancs and Wrights. Henlys, meanwhile, had seen the chassis builder with whom it had very close links now part of a group that had its own bodybuilding facilities.

In some ways the machinations of these groups and their direct effect on the former Northern Counties factory are beside the point. In the meantime the rebuilding programme at the Wigan site had been completed and was opened by Deputy Prime Minister John Prescott. Dennis and DAF had also got their 'low-floor' act organised so that by April 1999 the first Dennis Trident Presidents were entering service with Metroline London Northern, soon to be followed by significant orders for

One early consequence of Northern Counties being part of the Henlys Group was the opening up of the Far East market to the factory. Although badged as a Plaxton product and with Alexander screens, this is a Wigan-built bus and was one of 20 supplied in 1997. *(AWD)*

Almost the last single-deck order for PMT from Northern Counties comprised three Dennis Lance delivered in early 1997. A similar order for 13 was supplied to Essex Buses (both FirstBus companies by then) at the same time. Only Scania and DAF single-deckers were to be bodied after this, the final ones being completed by early 1998, including a solitary DAF for PMT in February 1998. Henceforward single-deck vehicles produced by the Henlys Group would come from the former Plaxton factories. *(DC)*

Southern Vectis had become a Northern Counties customer in 1993. This Olympian was one of eight delivered to the Isle of Wight in May 1998 and was fitted with high-back seating for greater passenger comfort. *(DC)*

CentreWest, Capital Citybus, First Capital and, perhaps surprisingly, Lothian. Arriva London North took a DAF in September of that year, the same month as West Midlands Travel took numerically the fourth B7TL to be built, followed by a further 100 units, a somewhat surprising order all round.

The natural consequence of this was that 1999 saw the last of the Palatine 1 bodies built. They were placed on Volvo Olympian chassis and went to CentreWest by April, still finished with Northern Counties Countybus badges affixed. Henceforward, until closure in 2005, all deliveries from Wigan would be of President double-deckers built on low-floor chassis. By far the greatest numbers of these were to be Dennis Tridents, followed by Volvo B7TLs. Only Arriva and Capital opted for low-floor double-deck DAFs. So the goal identified by Henlys had been achieved. The premises were amongst the most modern in the country to be used for the assembly of buses and the product range was limited. Quantity, however, was not. But the amazing production figures, when compared to the final years of pure Northern Counties output, could only be obtained by parts being largely constructed elsewhere and brought together at a location to be known for the time being as Plaxton Wigan. Henlys were obviously still fully aware of their vulnerability and had once again turned to North America, this time buying Blue Bird, the largest manufacturer of yellow school buses in the USA. At home matters could have been better; 60 compulsory redundancies at Enfield Street were announced in July. But the next move surprised the industry totally. In the summer of 2000 Mayflower and Henlys announced a merger, under the rather grand sounding Transbus International name. In actual fact, the merger was more of a joint venture, with the organisation being owned 70/30 in favour of Mayflower. It did not take long for the most battle-scarred of employees in Wigan to realise that their factory was now part of an organisation with production facilities in Anston, Belfast, Falkirk, Guildford, Scarborough and Wigan, all but one of which built bus bodies. Inevitably, something was going to have to give. But for the time being the former Northern Counties premises in Enfield Street, Wigan continued to churn out President bodies like no other body had ever been produced before in the town. The majority were still for the London market and the annual production totals, over four hundred each year for 2000, 2001, 2002 and 2003, were impressive. In April 2002 John Simpson, Chief Executive of Mayflower, advised the Wigan press that his group had won a £70m order for 320 buses for

Low-floor double-deckers started entering service in London in large numbers during 1999. By far the most popular choice of chassis was to be the Dennis Trident, but Capital Logistics opted for DAF chassis and its T135 AUA is seen here passing under the Tramlink overhead in Croydon. *(DC)*

London. As with all these proclamations, it is difficult to be totally clear how many of these vehicles were actually to be built in Wigan or over what period of time the work would take.

The market outside of London was still important, however, and during this period new customers included Blue Bus, Horwich; Burnley & Pendle; Go Northern and Pete's Travel of Smethwick. As was quite often the nature of things at the time, these latter Dennis Tridents of Pete's Travel passed to Reading Buses soon afterwards, thus bringing Wigan-built bodywork back into the still-owned municipal fleet after an absence of many years. Further deliveries were made to previous customers such as East Yorkshire and Southern Vectis. During the Transbus period there was also more export work on tri-axle Tridents, on one occasion on behalf of Duple Metsec, which was part of the group. And toward the end even some Alexander ALX400 bodies were assembled.

Within the monolithic group there was obviously overlap in models, but when John Fleming of Mayflower insisted throughout 2002 that there were no plans to close any of the plants, many in the industry were somewhat sceptical. The older ones felt they had seen this all before, and not once, but twice. Hadn't Leyland said the same thing when Bristol, Daimler, Eastern Coach Works, Park Royal and Roe were all part of the stable; and hadn't Volvo more recently repeated the claim, despite owning plants at Workington and Irvine? But when the inevitable announcement did come, there was again surprise. Scarborough, the only true coach building facility, was identified as being surplus. A few industry commentators viewed this announcement as a negotiating ploy and sure enough, within weeks of the announcement being made, agreement had been reached for a scaled-down Scarborough plant to stay open and fresh, more flexible working arrangements had been agreed with the staff.

During 2003 John Fleming repeated the 'no closures' policy, but the industry was moving on. London's buying spree was slowing down. In June 2003 the success of London Mayor Ken Livingstone's congestion charging scheme was blamed for a reduction in orders for Transbus Plaxton, as the Wigan site was now known. As fewer vehicles were entering the congestion charging zone in London than had been predicted, income was only half that which was expected. It was this income that was largely funding new bus orders. Predictably, 90 more Wigan redundancies

West Midlands Travel 4023 (V423 MOA) was the first Northern Counties-bodied bus to be delivered to the former PTE operator, entering service in September 1999, and was a very early production example of the Volvo B7TL. Over 100 were to enter service with the operator in due course. *(DC)*

Buses which were factory-built for open-top use have never been common, but Lothian 32 (W632 PSX) was one of four 77-seaters delivered in July 2000 for use on its Edinburgh Tour. *(DC)*

Unlike sister company Arriva London, which preferred DAF chassis, Arriva Yorkshire 681 was a Volvo B7TL which entered service in January 2001. *(DC)*

The two vehicles pictured on this page display the alternative glazing arrangements available to President customers which could either be supplied with traditional gasket fitting (upper) or bonded (lower). The operators concerned had somewhat different antecedents; X761 ABU belongs to Finglands, a long-established South Manchester coach operator primarily, but now part of the East Yorkshire Group. Y2 NBB was new to North Birmingham Buses, a post-deregulation company set up by former managers of West Midlands Travel. *(DC)*

were revealed. More importantly from the group's overall position, was the financial albatross which the high price, financed largely through loans, originally paid by Mayflower to acquire Dennis, needed servicing. In moves beloved by bean counters, but fraught with risk to everyone else, many of the sites were sold off and then leased back. Tragically for this story, the plant at Pemberton in Wigan was one of them. Early in 2004 profit warnings for Mayflower (the one announcement the city has an aversion to) started the alarm bells ringing that very rapidly heralded disaster. Fairly soon John Fleming and John Simpson resigned and just afterwards Mayflower was declared insolvent. As a subsidiary of Mayflower, Transbus was placed in administration, allowing it to continue trading pending a sale, the same situation that Northern Counties had found itself in during 1991. In Scotland *The Scotsman* declared that the brunt of the inevitable cuts were to be carried by the Falkirk plant – well, they would say that, wouldn't they? In Wigan the local MPs stepped into the battle – why do they only get involved when it's always too late?

This time there was not be the same road to recovery. Plaxton fairly quickly passed to a management buyout and quite happily resurrected its name. The bus body and chassis business of Transbus became Alexander Dennis when sold by the administrators, Deloitte Touche, in May 2004. It was purchased by a consortium of Scottish investors including the founders of Stagecoach. Former Alexander managers, Bill Cameron (who became Chairman) and Jim Hastie (who became Chief Executive), spear-headed the new organisation. There were enough pointers there for the staff at Wigan to see the Alexander ogre at last triumphing. Immediately, Alexander Dennis announced further redundancies which would leave just 120 employees on the extensive site at Pemberton in Wigan – this was down from the

An interesting vehicle ordered by the Parasol Project of Oxford during 2001 was this Dennis Trident which was to be registered YS51 LSV. It was delivered to MASS Engineering of North Anston for conversion to a Playbus (during this sojourn it was photographed for the cover of *Venture's* 2001 book on the new registration system) but is seen here at the annual Duxford Showbus Rally. *(DC)*

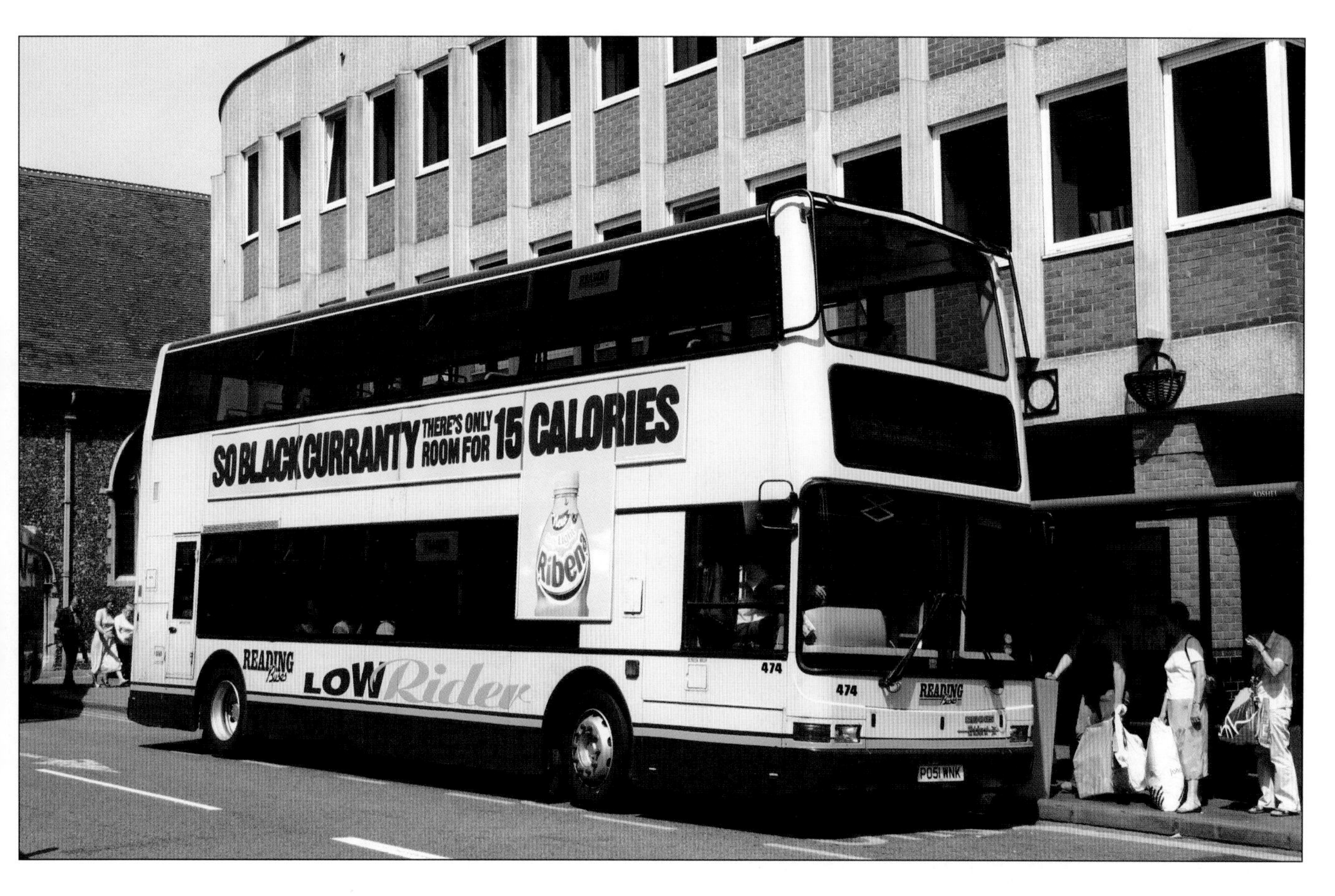

Vehicles with second owners have long-existed in the bus industry, but the operation of six Dennis Tridents new to Pete's Travel of Smethwick by Reading Buses when barely eighteen months old nevertheless caused some eyebrows to be raised. PO51 WNK is depicted. ***(DC)***

Brighton & Hove took two batches of President-bodied Dennis Tridents in 2001 and 2002. Number 875 (PK02 RFJ) named *John Rastrick,* of the second order, is seen here. ***(DC)***

Metroline VP 521 (LK04 CSV) was produced in March 2004, just before Transbus was placed in administration. A total of 637 units of the Volvo B7TL/President combination were to be delivered to the Harrow-based operator, including the final bus built at the Pemberton factory. *(DC)*

Lothian Transport, for many years a faithful Alexander customer, commenced taking bodies built in Wigan on Trident chassis in the summer of 1999. Lothian 664 (SN04 AAJ) was supplied for the Edinburgh Airport shuttle service in March 2004 and had bonded windows, other Lothian vehicles having gasket glazing. By this time the Trident was badged as a Transbus product. *(DC)*

London Central PVL394 (LX54 HBA) was built in the final month of production, January 2005, and, therefore, should be attributed to Dennis-Alexander and not even Transbus. It is seen here within two months of entering service. *(DC)*

440 who had been employed only a few years earlier. Then, in a document circulated to staff in September 2004 came the terminal news.

Jim Hastie cited a number of factors which had led to the decision to close the Wigan site. In the first six months of the year the UK market was down 13%. It had not been possible to secure significant forward-sales for the President body. There was too much build capacity. It was also claimed that significant orders for the President had been lost during the period of administration and that it not been possible to make up the ground lost, to amongst others, East Lancs and Wrights. Once current orders for the President were completed, the remaining staff at Wigan would be made redundant. It did seem a trifle strange that after producing over 2,000 President bodies in just over five years, suddenly no one wanted to buy another. Recalling Doug Jack's book on the final years of Leyland, it seemed 'beyond reality'. At the time of the announcement a batch of Volvo B7TLs was being produced for Metroline; before the close a batch of similar buses was completed for London Central, but the final bodies in January 2005 were on Volvos for Metroline, the third last being ceremonially photographed by the local media on 24th January, two days before the factory finally closed. The final bus built was, in fact, Metroline PVL 637 (LK54 FWT) carrying the highest body number in the new series (commenced in 1981) which was to be No. 8692.

This sorry scene inside the once-busy Pemberton factory after its closure should be compared with that on page 171, in its heyday.

The size of this one building gives an idea of the problem the vendors face in finding suitable clients to move into the complex. *(JAS both)*

Epilogue

After surviving the depression, a world war, economic boom and bust, administrative receivership and four sets of owners, the 21st[t] century finally saw the end of Northern Counties. As this is written, in 2005, the year bus body-building in Wigan finally terminated, it seems almost too soon to be able to take a balanced view of the full picture. Whichever of the two alternative options one believes in, either coincidence or conspiracy, there was enough incident contained in the final fifteen years of the Northern Counties story to surely satisfy both sets of supporters.

In some ways the story is still not finished. Reference has been made to the Accountancy Investigation and Discipline Board, whose work is still ongoing. The Board had decided in July 2004 to commence its investigation into Mayflower Corporation Plc and its subsidiaries. In particular three areas were highlighted for investigation:

(i) the conduct of the audits of the financial statements of Mayflower for 2000, 2001, 2002 and 2003;

(ii) the conduct of a review of the interim financial statements as at 30th June 2003 by PricewaterhouseCoopers; and

(iii) the conduct of David Thomas Donnelly, a former Director of Mayflower and Transbus International.

In September 2005 the *Manchester Evening News* reported that Pricewaterhouse Coopers was to face a disciplinary tribunal following the AIDB's year long inquiry into events. It also reported that a disciplinary complaint had been laid against Mr Donnelly. This must be heartening news indeed for all those former employees who received redundancy payments.

Reference to one of the other 'saviours' of Alexander Dennis will reveal the name of David Murray, who had been a major supplier to Alexander, having made his money in metals. A recent 'rich list' of football club owners reveals David Murray at number nine (he is Chairman of Glasgow Rangers); needless to say, top of this list is one Roman Abramovich of Chelsea. It is an indication of how money has come to influence industry. But in fairness, in some ways Henry Gethin Lewis might well have been regarded as the David Murray of his time. So maybe the wheel has turned full circle.

Perhaps no finer tribute to the staff at the Enfield Street premises can be paid than to repeat a comment made by an observer of the closure. 'The same pride was put into the last bus out of the factory as if it had been the first one; the tragedy was not going to dilute standards and personal self-respect'. These were the people who had given their all, or were working in the expectation of a secure future, and were left to make whatever arrangements they could – once again the men and women on the shop floor paid the price for the ambitions (and follies) of the money-men.

Over the years a number of bus and coach-building firms have existed in and around Wigan; Beccols, Massey, Northern Counties and Santus can be recorded. Today only one of these names is still involved in production – Santus – but Uncle Joe's Mint Balls will never catch the writer's attention in quite the same way that a Palatine II did.

And what of the remnants of the site? Ironically, the relatively-new tilt-table was removed and sold to, of all people, East Lancs! Other equipment was removed quite quickly, so that today an empty, modern shell is all that is left. Some of the staff did indeed go to Alexander Dennis at Chorley, amongst them being Dennis Smith and Frank McGee. The streets of London at least will continue to see for some years to come, products from Enfield Street in large numbers, in locations that were for so many years associated with an icon of the bus world, the Routemaster.

Appendix 1 – Premises

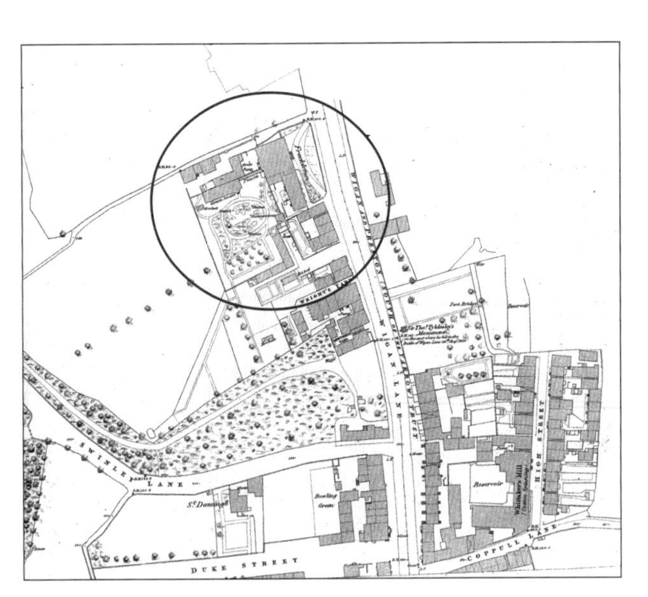

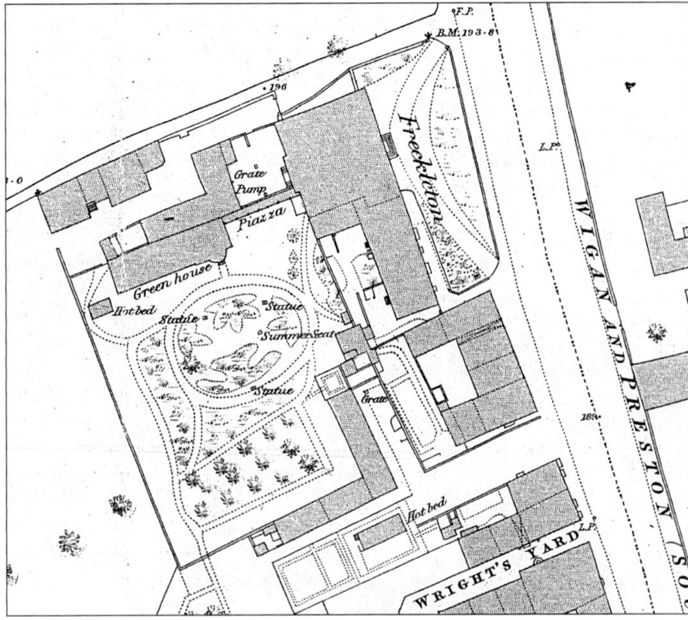

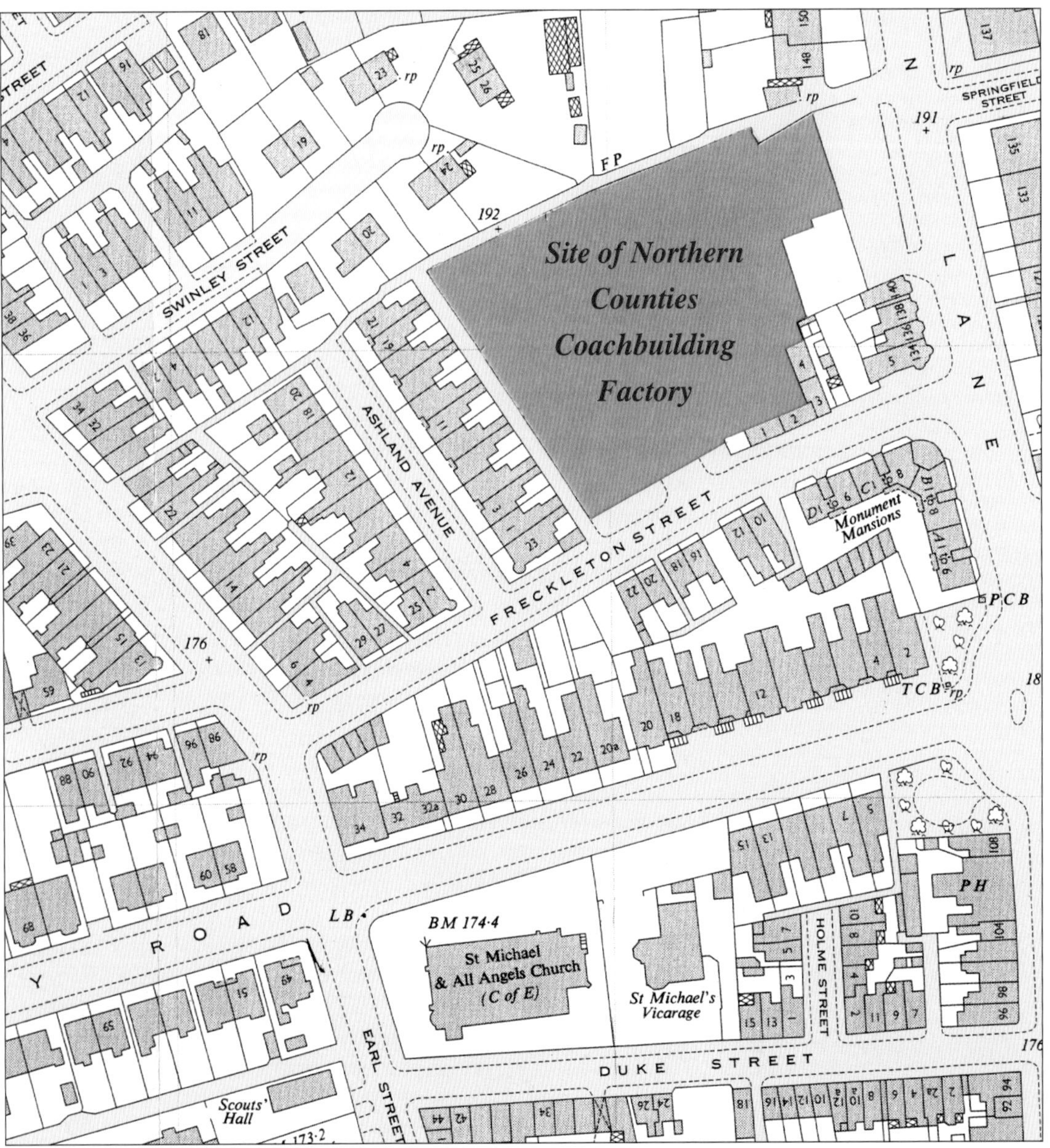

It is most regrettable that early 20th Century pictures of the exterior of both the premises at Wigan Lane and at Pemberton have proved elusive. This Appendix attempts to give some impression of the extent of the factories, and the way in which they developed.

The plans reproduced here indicate the rural nature of the Wigan Lane area in the mid-19th Century before the building of Northern Counties' premises, and the extent of the gardens behind the house upon which the factory was built can clearly be seen. The lower plan, dating from a century later, shows the fullest extent of the complex.

(Wigan History Shop)

The picture above shows the view of the Wigan Lane premises as many people would have seen it from a passing bus or car. The Company name is proudly displayed over the doorway leading into the works and thence into the factory. Esso petrol is still on sale, reflecting the site's origins as a garage. Just visible in front of the prototype Foden bus is a chassis waiting its turn to be bodied. *(RGR)*

Below we see the frontage in all its glory; the pumps and the staff have all gone and the agents boards will soon be put up. The site was eventually purchased by the North West Regional Health Authority, to be used as a car park for staff from the nearby hospital, a function it still performs. *(EO)*

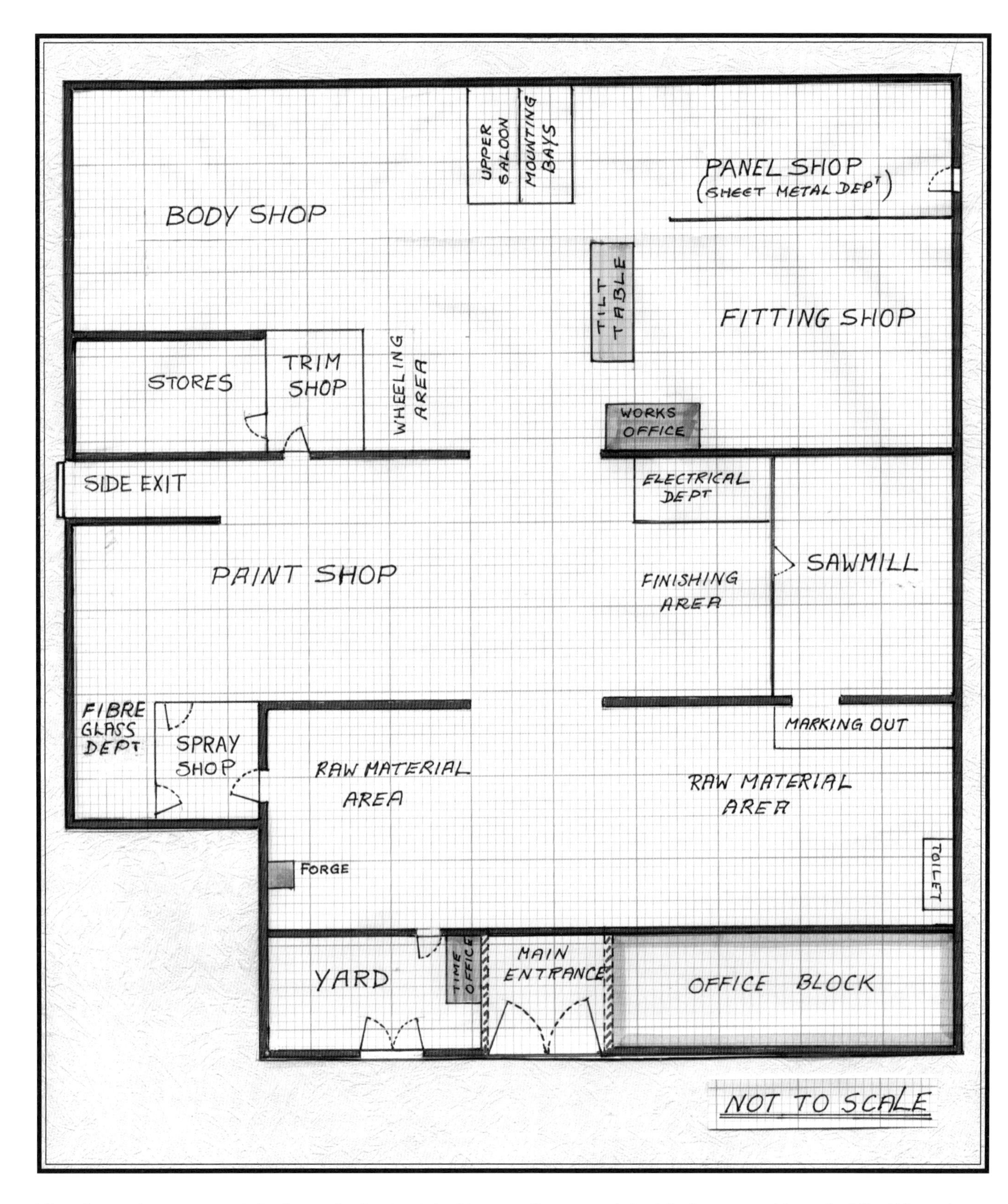

The above plan was specially drawn for the book by Norman Green, and depicts the general layout of the Wigan Lane premises during the late 1950s. It should be noted that on this plan Wigan Lane runs along the *bottom* of the plan, whilst Freckleton Street runs down the *left hand* side.

In the very early 1960s, changes were made in order to create more floor space. Firstly, two mezzanine-type floors were installed in the raw-materials area; this allowed the trim shop and the small fibreglass department to be relocated on the mezzanine floor nearest to the office block. The other, smaller, mezzanine floor was used for the storage of floor-covering materials. Later, a further similar floor was erected which covered a small part of the fitting shop. This was used for the preparation and storage of heating system components. After the purchase of Massey Bros. In 1967, the trim shop and fibreglass departments were relocated to the Pemberton site, thus creating space on the mezzanine to relocate the electrical department and create even more storage space.

The interior of the Pemberton premises seen on page 166 when double-deck production was in full swing. ***(JMB)***

Four views showing the development of the Enfield Street, Pemberton, site after Northern Counties purchased Massey Bros and, later, the mill. *(Harry Wall all)*

Opened By
The Rt. Hon.
JOHN PRESCOTT M.P.
DEPUTY PRIME MINISTER
TUESDAY 14th SEPTEMBER 1999

Appendix 2 – Staff

People are the life blood of any organisation and Northern Counties was no different from any other business in this respect. In gathering information for this book it has been the author's privilege to meet some of the personalities who coursed through the veins of the company. Many anecdotes have been shared, such as the argument between the apprentice and his journeyman, when measuring a length of timber for a particular job. "I told you to cut it 42ins long" – "No you didn't; you told me to cut it 3ft 6ins!" Many other stories, regrettably, to avoid either embarrassment or even legal action, can not be repeated!

Former employees have also loaned or provided material, and in this respect I have to thank Norman Green, who commenced his employment with the company in March 1957 in the panel shop and who retired in January 1996 as Production Manager. Not only did he provide the original of the Wigan Lane plan included in the previous appendix, but he also supplied profuse information, drawn from his 40 year career, to enable the organisational charts included in this appendix to be produced. Should any errors have crept into during their compilation, however, they are entirely my responsibility.

During the production of this book, it was my pleasure to be able to attend the Commemorative Event organised by the Manchester Museum of Transport at their excellent premises at Boyle Street in October 2005, to celebrate the work of the Northern Counties factories, and I am pleased to be able to include photographs of that wonderful occasion.

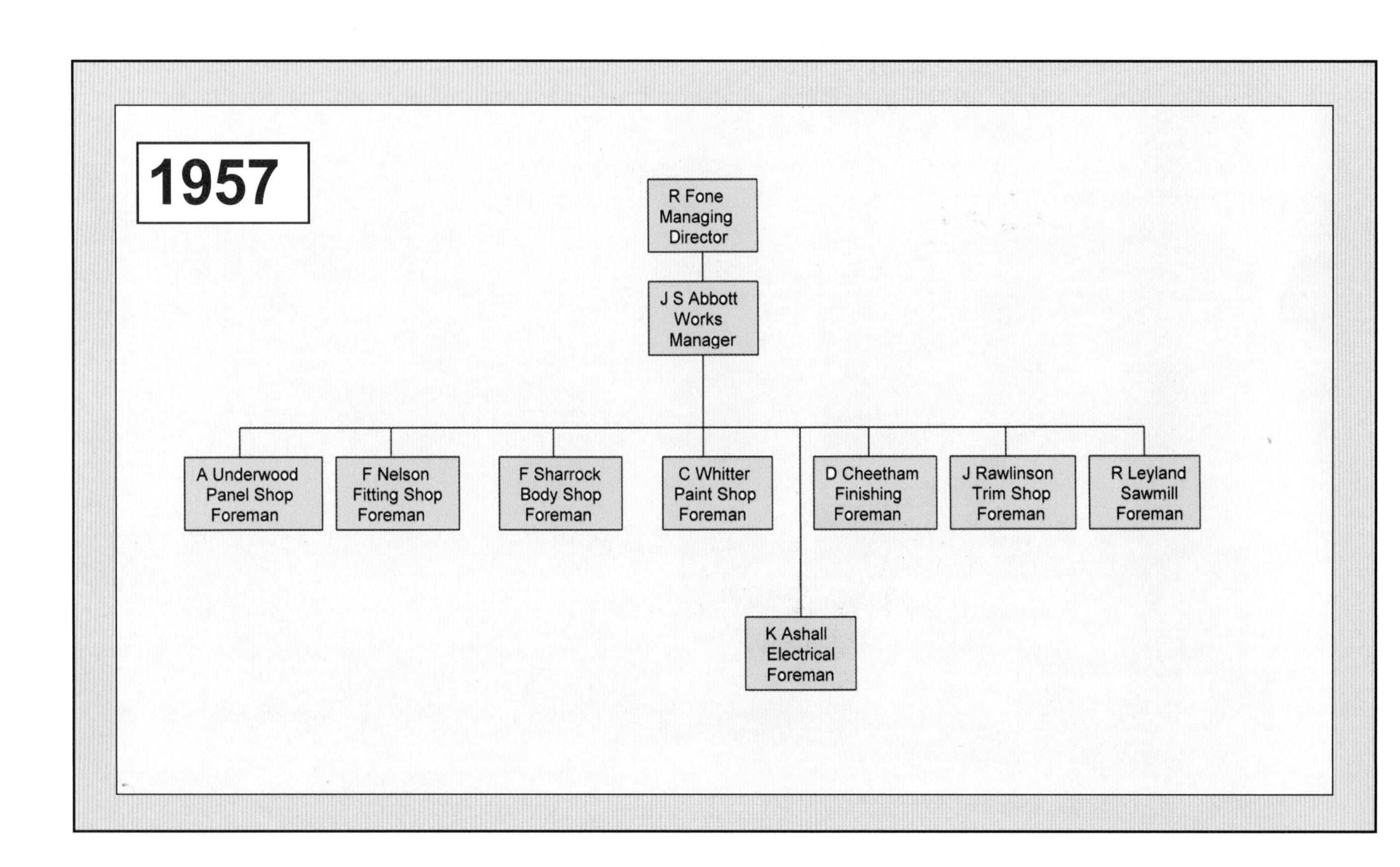

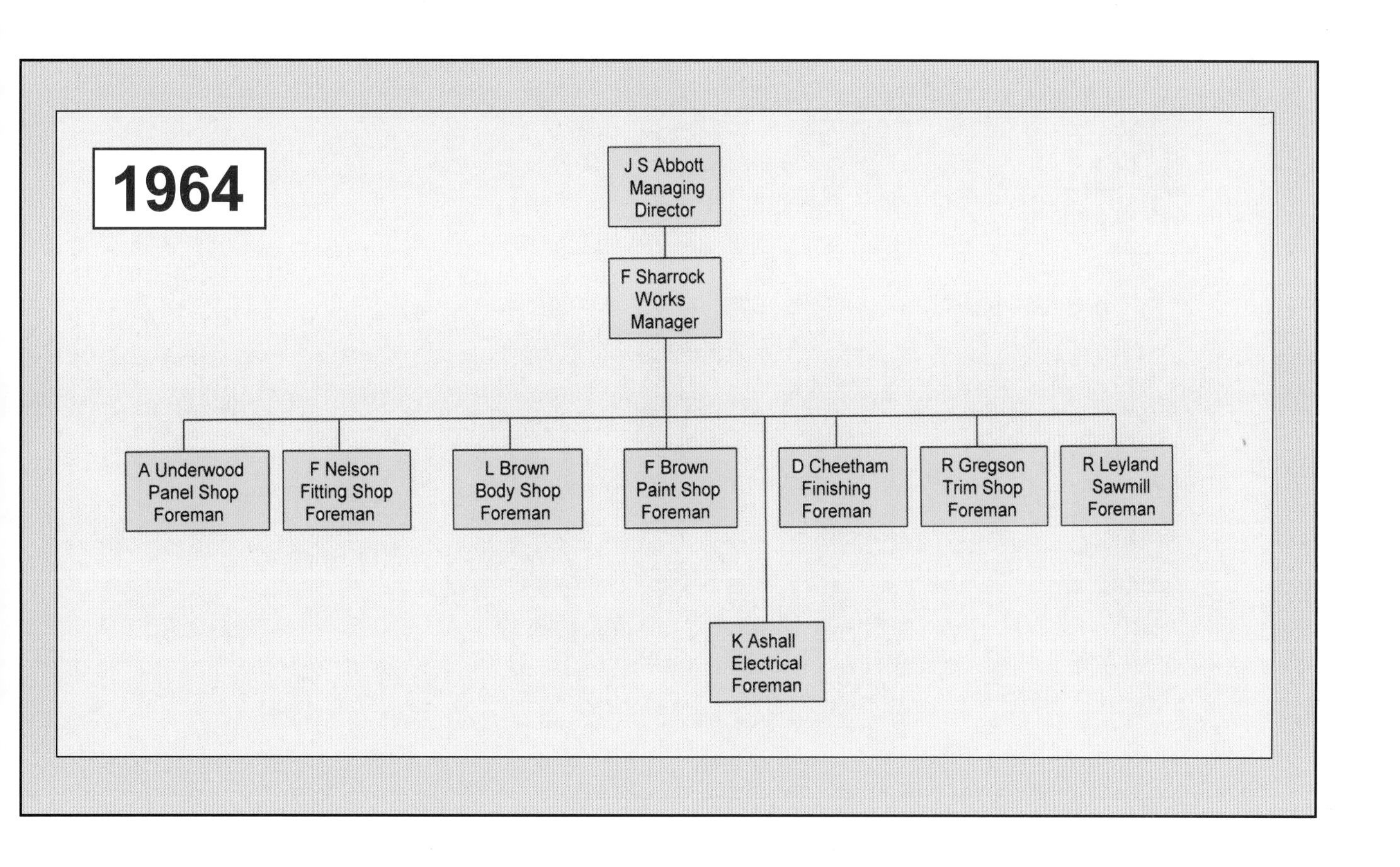
1964
J S Abbott
Managing
Director
F Sharrock
Works
Manager
A Underwood
Panel Shop
Foreman
F Nelson
Fitting Shop
Foreman
L Brown
Body Shop
Foreman
F Brown
Paint Shop
Foreman
D Cheetham
Finishing
Foreman
R Gregson
Trim Shop
Foreman
R Leyland
Sawmill
Foreman
K Ashall
Electrical
Foreman

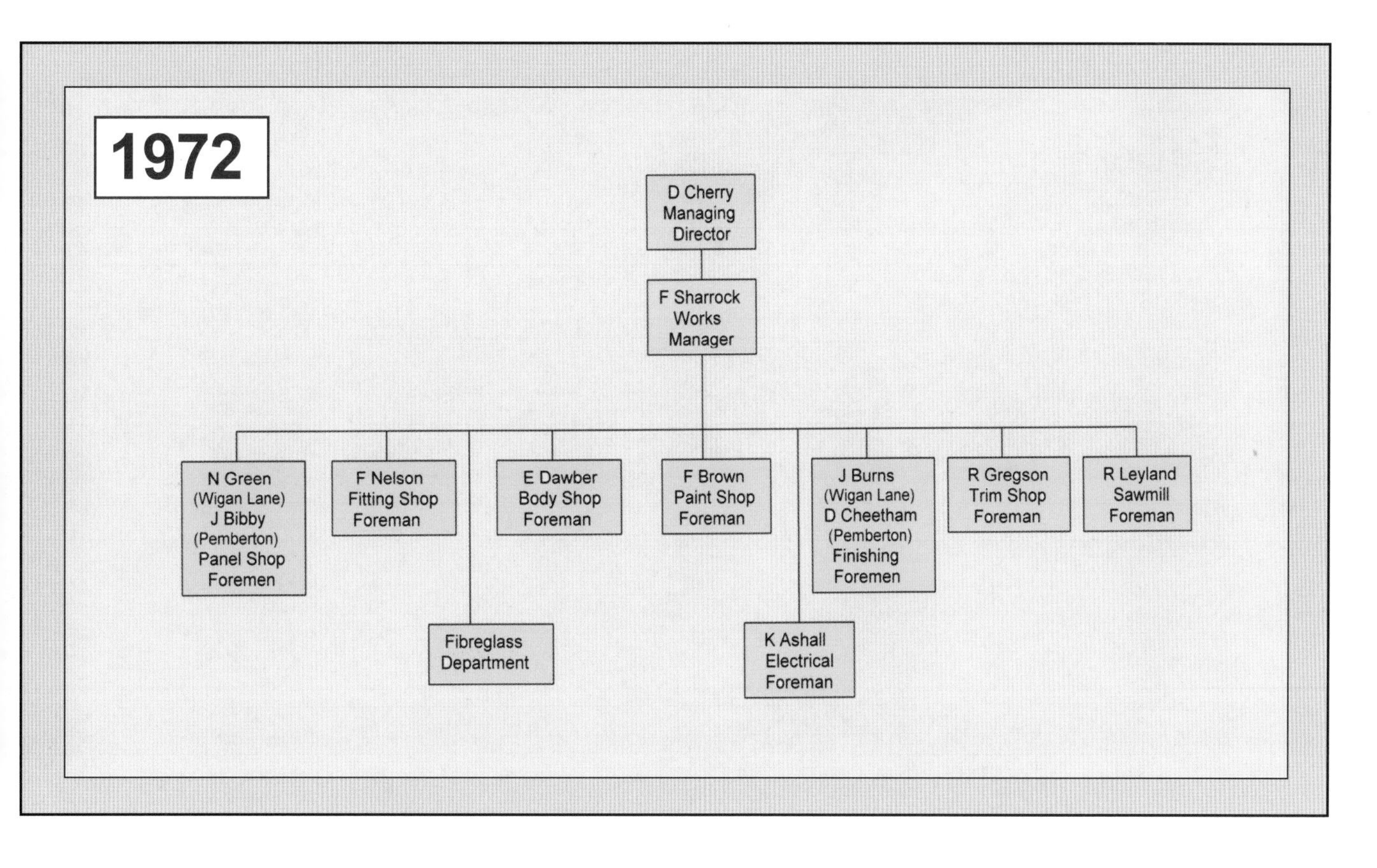
1972
D Cherry
Managing
Director
F Sharrock
Works
Manager
N Green
(Wigan Lane)
J Bibby
(Pemberton)
Panel Shop
Foremen
F Nelson
Fitting Shop
Foreman
E Dawber
Body Shop
Foreman
F Brown
Paint Shop
Foreman
J Burns
(Wigan Lane)
D Cheetham
(Pemberton)
Finishing
Foremen
R Gregson
Trim Shop
Foreman
R Leyland
Sawmill
Foreman
Fibreglass
Department
K Ashall
Electrical
Foreman

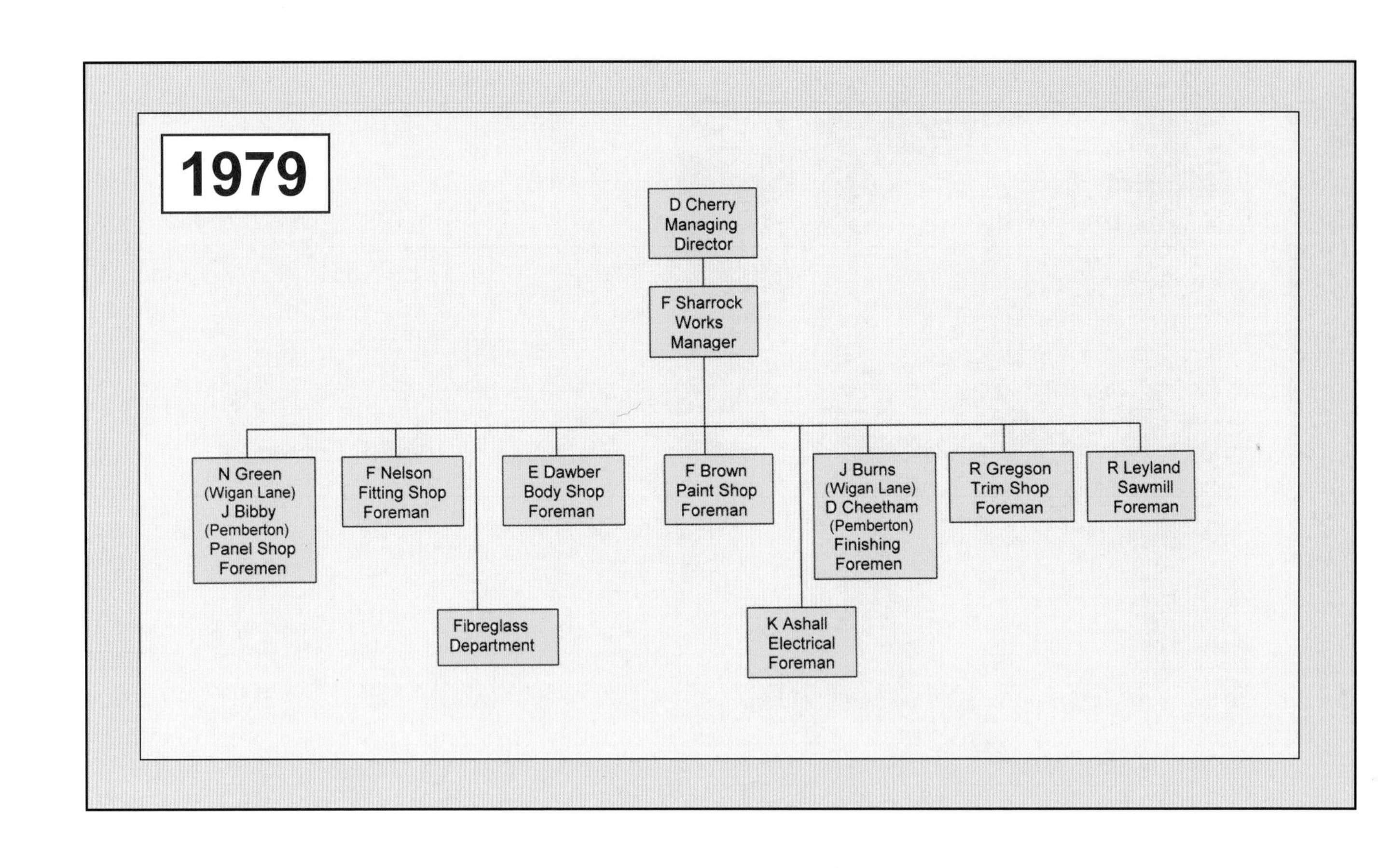
1979
D Cherry
Managing
Director
F Sharrock
Works
Manager
N Green
(Wigan Lane)
J Bibby
(Pemberton)
Panel Shop
Foremen
F Nelson
Fitting Shop
Foreman
E Dawber
Body Shop
Foreman
F Brown
Paint Shop
Foreman
J Burns
(Wigan Lane)
D Cheetham
(Pemberton)
Finishing
Foremen
R Gregson
Trim Shop
Foreman
R Leyland
Sawmill
Foreman
Fibreglass
Department
K Ashall
Electrical
Foreman

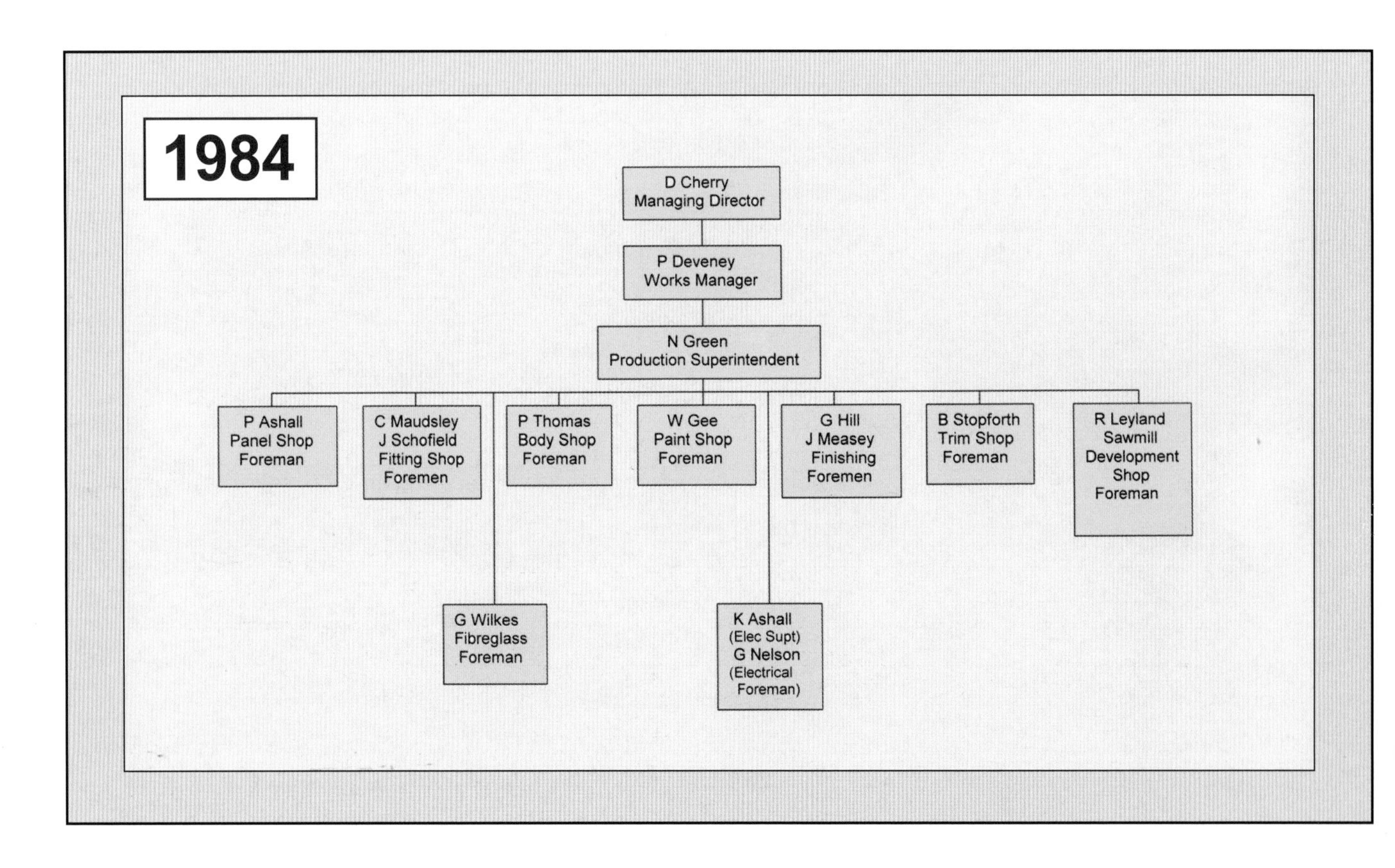
1984
D Cherry
Managing Director
P Deveney
Works Manager
N Green
Production Superintendent
P Ashall
Panel Shop
Foreman
C Maudsley
J Schofield
Fitting Shop
Foremen
P Thomas
Body Shop
Foreman
W Gee
Paint Shop
Foreman
G Hill
J Measey
Finishing
Foremen
B Stopforth
Trim Shop
Foreman
R Leyland
Sawmill
Development
Shop
Foreman
G Wilkes
Fibreglass
Foreman
K Ashall
(Elec Supt)
G Nelson
(Electrical
Foreman)

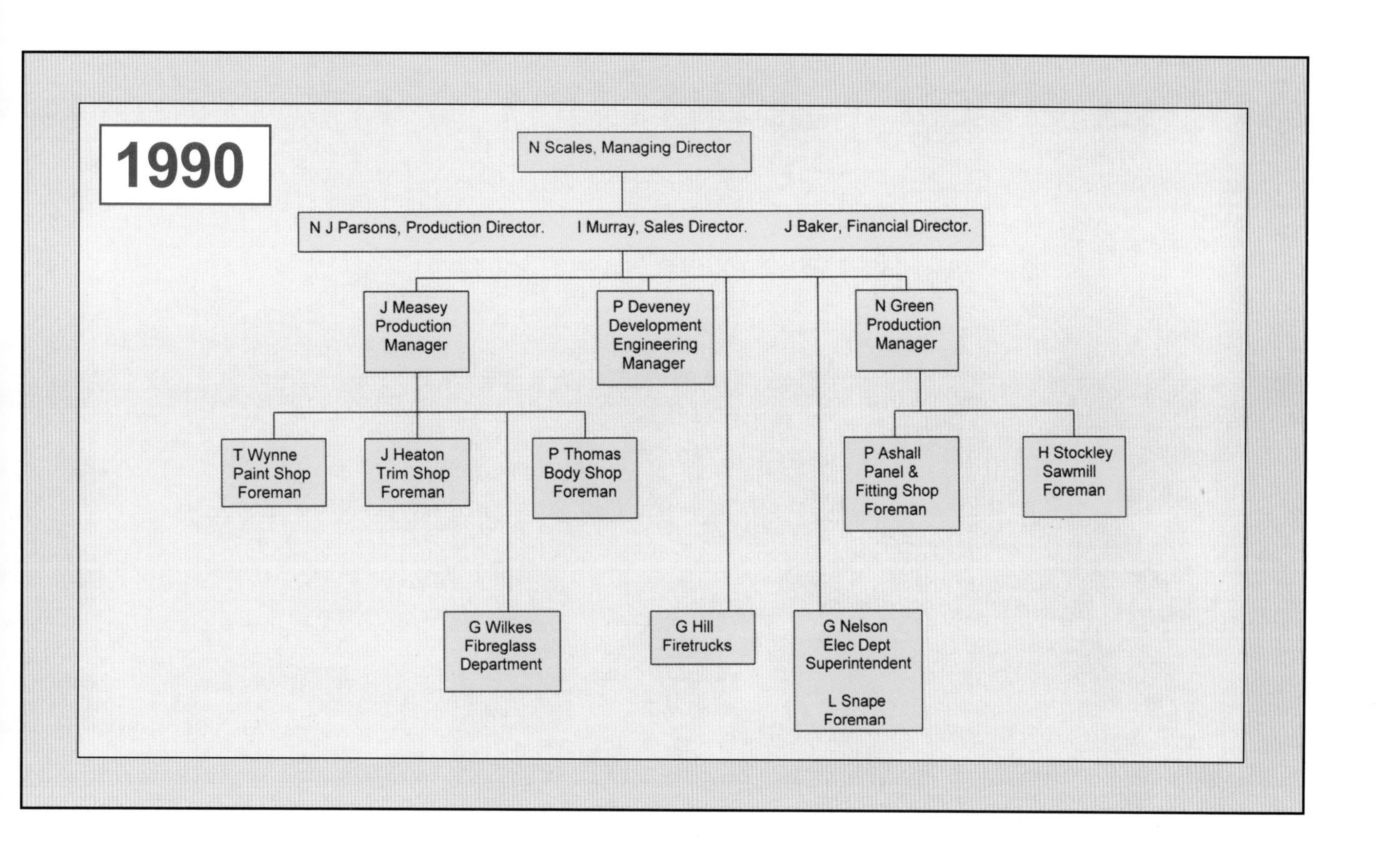
1990
N Scales, Managing Director
N J Parsons, Production Director.
I Murray, Sales Director.
J Baker, Financial Director.
J Measey Production Manager
P Deveney Development Engineering Manager
N Green Production Manager
T Wynne Paint Shop Foreman
J Heaton Trim Shop Foreman
P Thomas Body Shop Foreman
P Ashall Panel & Fitting Shop Foreman
H Stockley Sawmill Foreman
G Wilkes Fibreglass Department
G Hill Firetrucks
G Nelson Elec Dept Superintendent
L Snape Foreman

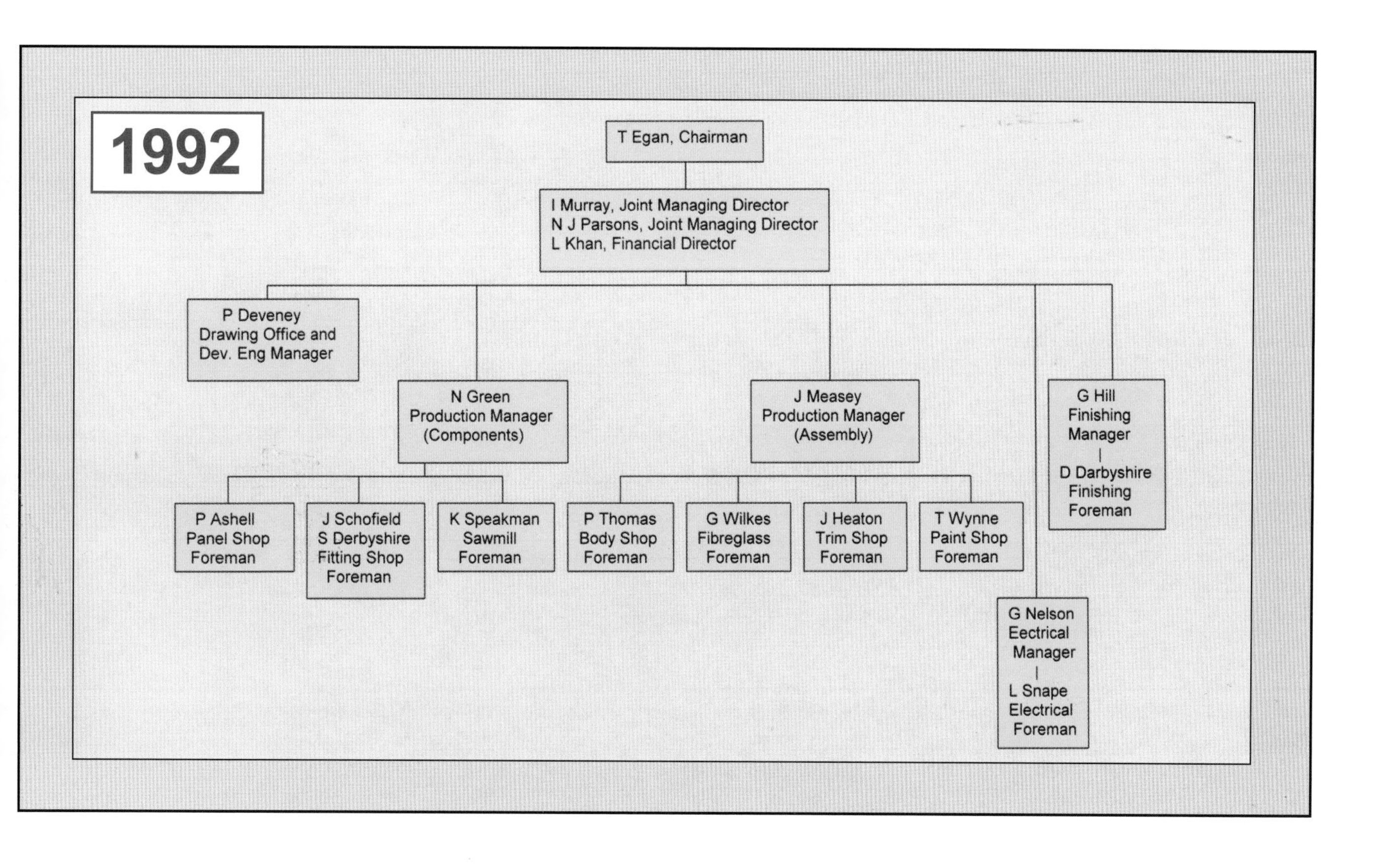
1992
T Egan, Chairman
I Murray, Joint Managing Director
N J Parsons, Joint Managing Director
L Khan, Financial Director
P Deveney Drawing Office and Dev. Eng Manager
N Green Production Manager (Components)
J Measey Production Manager (Assembly)
G Hill Finishing Manager
D Darbyshire Finishing Foreman
P Ashell Panel Shop Foreman
J Schofield
S Derbyshire Fitting Shop Foreman
K Speakman Sawmill Foreman
P Thomas Body Shop Foreman
G Wilkes Fibreglass Foreman
J Heaton Trim Shop Foreman
T Wynne Paint Shop Foreman
G Nelson Eectrical Manager
L Snape Electrical Foreman

Appendix 2 – Staff

The assistance of Norman Green in providing information for use in this appendix is acknowledged on this page. Here Norman is seen with the splendid vintage Bentley sports car which had been given to the grandson of the founder, Sales Director Henry Lewis, by his father, and kept in the works after Henry's death during the settling of his estate. Many stories are told about the exploits of both vehicle and driver, most of which are unsuitable for inclusion here! His antics in his MG have already been mentioned elsewhere. We should also apologise to those whose sensitivies are upset by including a vintage Bentley and a minibus in the same photograph. ***(NGC)***

Retirement presentations to employees took place from time to time at Northern Counties, as they do in most organisations. This picture was taken in 1987 at the retirement of Graham Santus, who had joined Northern Counties from Massey. Thus in one picture, the three principal bus building firms in Wigan are linked, for Graham's forebears had founded the family business that carried his name. ***(NGC)***

On the occasion of the Manchester Museum of Transport's Commemorative Celebration of Northern Counties in October 2005, a number of former employees were able to attend this reunion. Included in these pictures are former employees Carl Porter, Alan Spencer, Bill Halliwell, David Ashall, Ken Speakman, Brian Turton, Roy Tithes, and Brian Halliwell (Bill's son). Amongst the Museum's officials who looked after the party and are seen here with them were Chairman Dennis Talbot, together with Chris Lonnergan and Harry Wall (proud owner of the Wigan bus seen in the pictures). *(RGR)*

Appendix 3 – Production

These production figures are based on known-information as at the time of publication, May 2006. In particular it is recognised that the figures used for pre-war production are almost certainly incomplete. Nevertheless, it is hoped that these charts give an indication of the split of production undertaken by Northern Counties during its life.

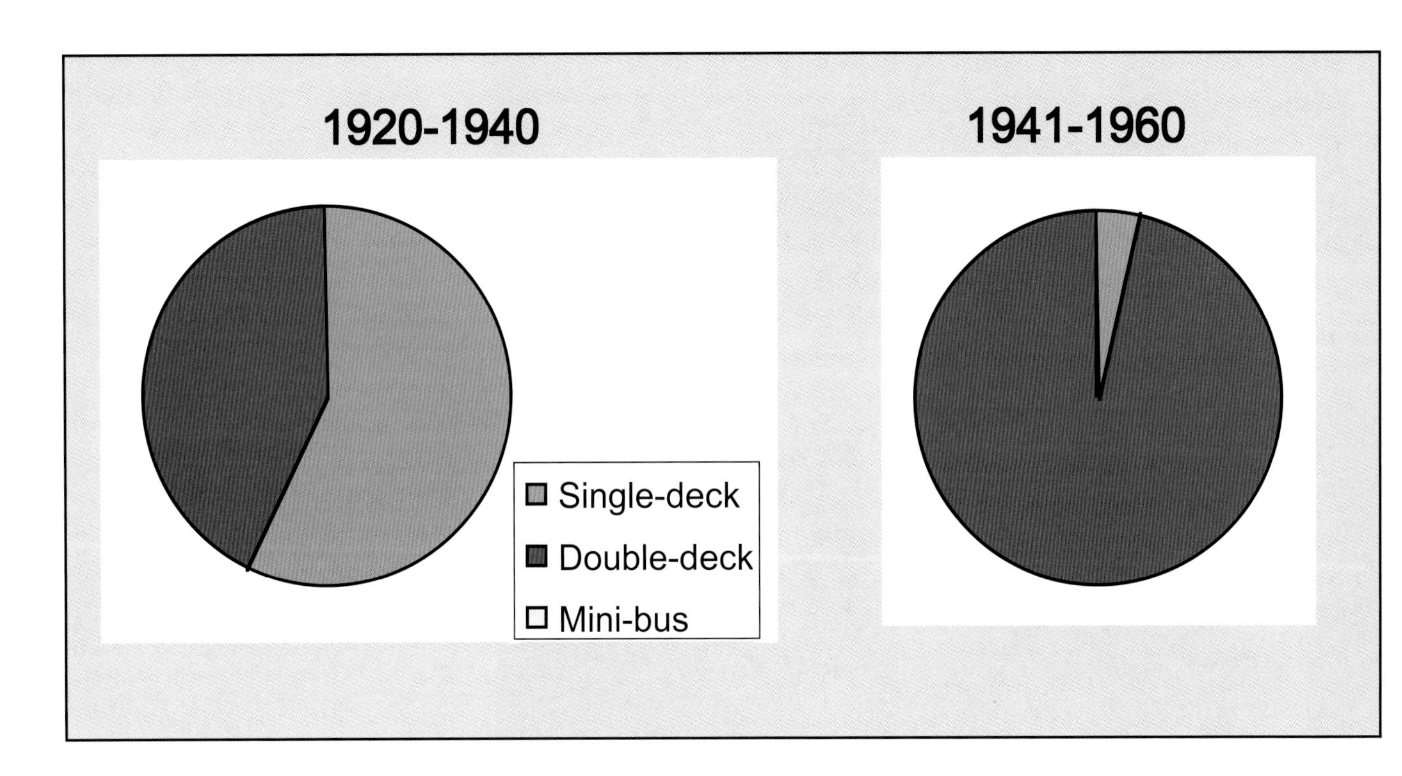

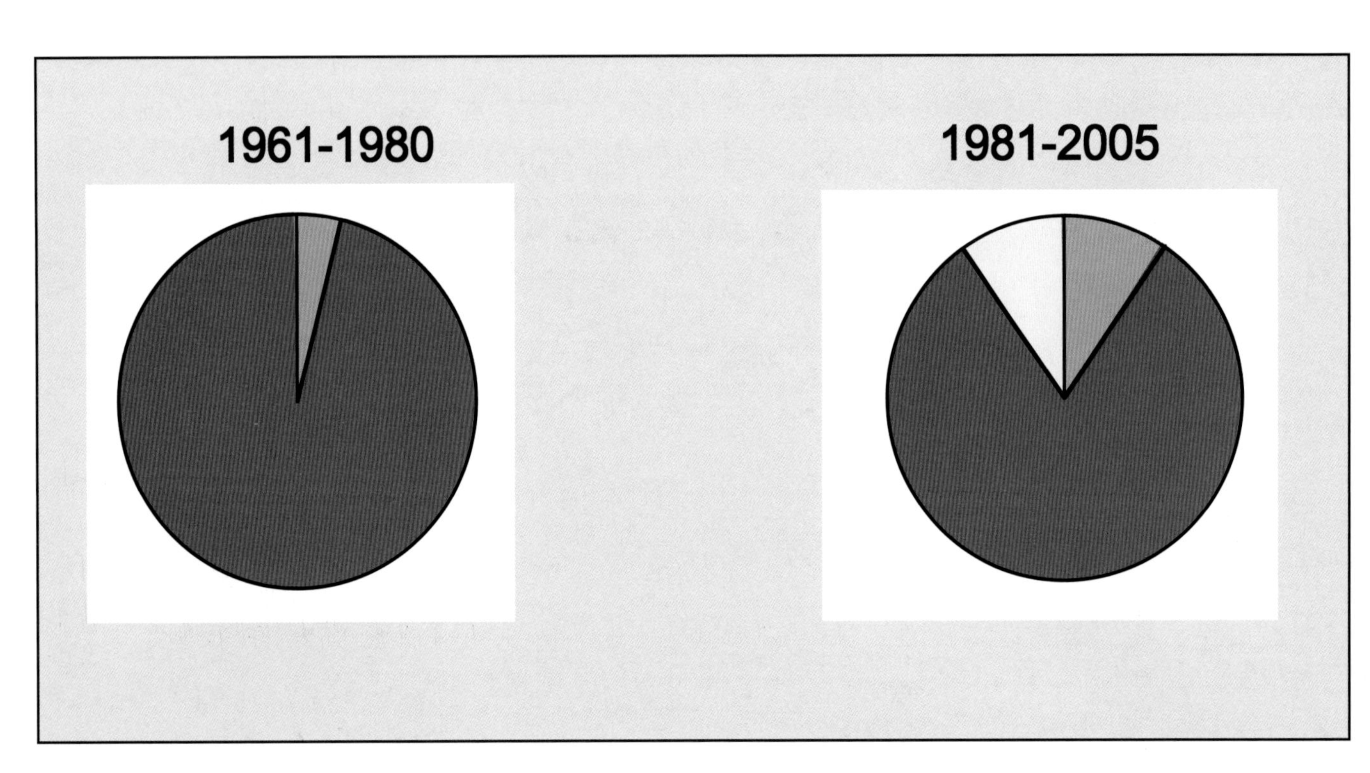

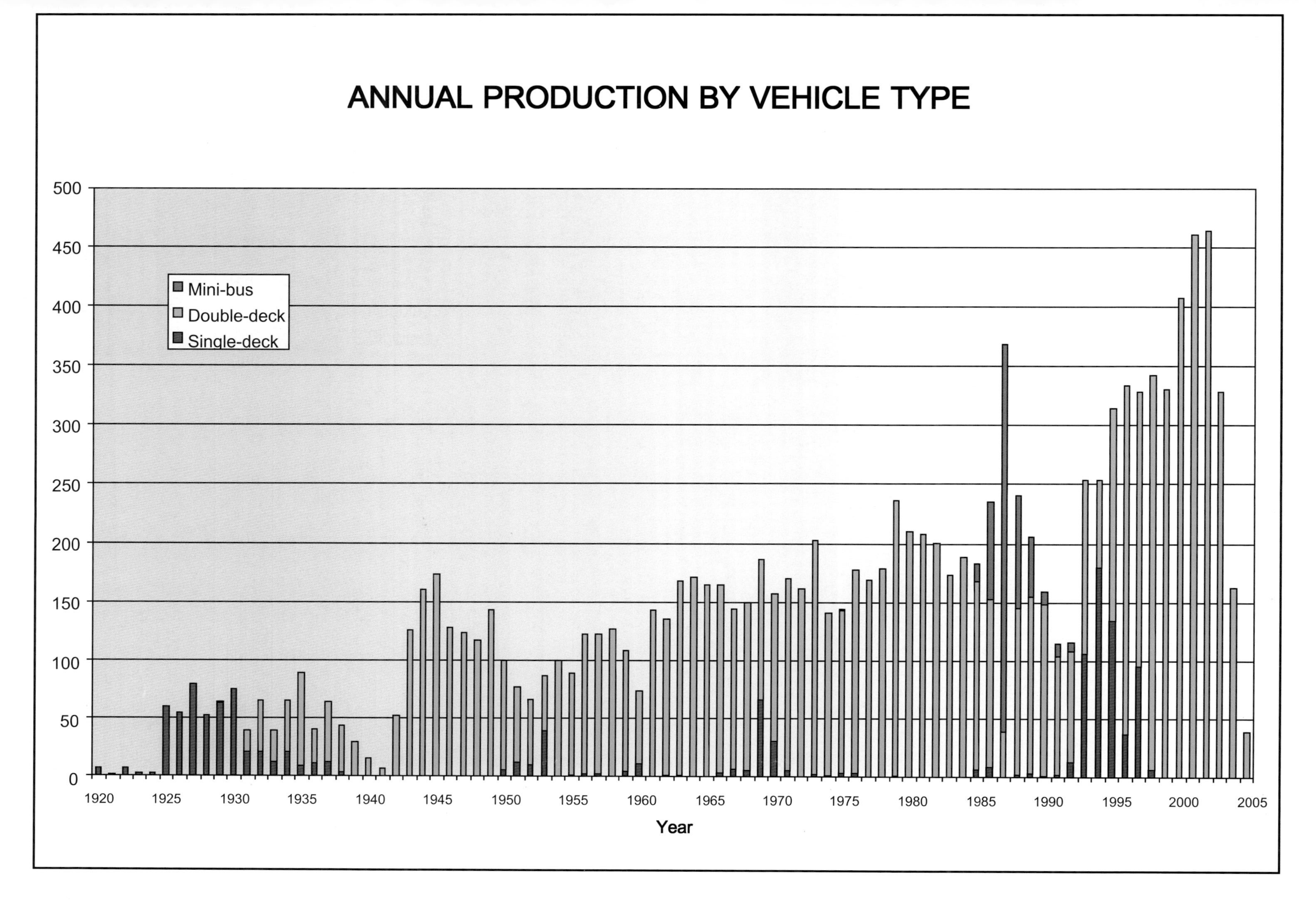

ANNUAL PRODUCTION BY VEHICLE TYPE
Mini-bus
Double-deck
Single-deck
500
450
400
350
300
250
200
150
100
50
0
1920
1925
1930
1935
1940
1945
1950
1955
1960
1965
1970
1975
1980
1985
1990
1995
2000
2005
Year

Appendix 4 – Identification

Tracing the production of the early years is always difficult when producing manufacturer's histories such as this one, and, true to form, Northern Counties has proved no exception. We were fortunate in having a detailed list of vehicles built from the first wartime productions, Cardiff's trolleybuses in 1941, but before that the picture is somewhat incomplete.

Whilst it is believed that the Northern Counties numbering series commenced at No. 1, so far no evidence has been found to confirm this. What does seem certain is that it would seem that one series was used for all work. The fact that the numbers traced with certainty for 1931 have reached 2588-90 which were used for three Huddersfield Corporation single-deckers in that year clearly implies that many other jobs were allocated numbers in the same series. These may well have included minor – or major – repairs, as well as production of cars, lorries and buses as well as, for example, cabs constructed for Walker Bros.

If 2588 vehicles had been built by 1931 that would imply an average of over 220 per year in the eleven years from 1921, which is clearly unrealistic. More especially as in the next eleven years, up to1941, the series had only reached over the 3200 mark, 3200-9 being used for Cardiff's trolleybuses above which were ordered just before the war, giving a production rate of some 40 plus per year. The next number traced is 3358, which was allocated to an unfrozen AEC Regent of Sheffield Corporation. So perhaps they didn't start at No. 1?

A considerable amount of war work was carried out as has been mentioned in the text, and so it is assumed that many of the missing numbers from then on were used for military vehicles. The only ones that have been traced, however, were for three Albion General Service lorries built in 1942 (Nos. 3284-6). Thus although the numerical sequence has been referred to as 'body Nos.' throughout this book, they were always referred to as 'job Nos.' by Northern Counties, and this presumably explains the enigma.

In his Historic Bus Profiles series, Alan Condie has so far produced two books dealing with Northern Counties. Each lists body numbers for the period concerned; the first deals with double-deckers 1942-6, and the second with 1946-55 and we have found these useful in association with our lists which came from the Northern Counties drawing office. Unfortunately they give no clues as to what happened before the war. As more information concerning the vehicles built in the pre-1939 period comes to light we shall continue to up-date our records and, hopefully, we may one day be in a position to produce a more definitive record, perhaps in the form of an illustrated body list, of what was actually built in those early years.

The landmark number of 5,000 was reached in 1956, when an SHMD Daimler double-decker was the recipient. A new series was commenced in 1981 at 2001, as explained in Chapter Eight. The original series eventually reached 8998 by 1983. The last number in the second series was 8692. In general terms the numbers were allocated on receipt of an order, with the result that when chassis were received late or were delayed, consecutive numbers could be delivered some years apart. Some gaps in the series occurred from time to time, as a result for example of cancellations and there is some evidence of numbers being reissued, which tends to prove the exception to the rule previously stated.

From early days, external Maker's transfers were fixed to Northern Counties buses, usually behind the front nearside wheel at the foot of the body panels, in the form of an oval with lettering contained within a line and giving the maker's name in gold lettering. This was common to many manufacturers in the 1920s and '30s, though some also used a logo (Burlingham used a representation of Blackpool tower, for instance, giving the link to their location), and the sharp-eyed may detect the NCME version in some of the photographs. Subsequently a plastic maker's plate was used, later replaced by a metal plate as shown above, usually being fixed in the cab, as also was the small round plate carrying the body number.

For a short period in the late 1980s the stylised transfer shown was used, but this design was quickly superseded by a black plastic badge, chrome-finished, also shown, which was fixed to either the front or rear of buses. When the County Bus name was introduced in 1991, this was displayed alongside it. Perhaps the most prominent badge displayed on buses was the President name, but this of course was under Plaxton (and subsequent) ownership.

It is fairly certain that Northern Counties also displayed their name in embossed lettering on the flywheel casing in the lower saloon, in the manner common to most bodybuilders, but photographic proof of this is was not available in time to include.

Northern Counties were certainly amongst the early metal-framed bus builders, for 1933 was the year that major manufacturers including Leyland and MCW began marketing their metal-framed vehicles. The wartime claim from the above advertisement is interesting, however; indeed they built all the metal-framed wartime buses since no one else was licensed so to do!

Appendix 5 – Customers

This list contains all vehicles of which we are aware as at the time of publication in May 2006 but details of any we have missed would be gratefully received via the Publisher in Glossop

Customer	1st order del	Final order del	Comments
A1 Ardrossan	1960	1968	
AA Motor Services	1943	1978	
Aberdare UDC	1951	1951	
Aberdeen C T	1920	1928	
Accrington C T	1945	1945	Utility only
Albion Motors, Scotstoun	1926	1934	
Alder Valley (South)	1987	1988	Minibuses only
Alexander (Fife)	1971	1971	1 order for 5
Alexander, W & Sons	1925	1945	
Armchair	1997	1998	
Arriva Derby	1998	1998	
Arriva Fox County	1998	1998	1 order for 10
Arriva London	1999	2002	
Arriva The Shires	1998	1998	1 order for 15
Arriva Yorkshire	1998	2001	
Arrowline, Knutsford	1994	1994	1 order for 3
ART East (Hong Kong)	1997	1997	1 order for 5
Ashton C T	1969	1969	Last order to Selnec
Aztecbird, Guiseley	1999	1999	1 only
Barrow	1932	1984	
Barton	1943	1963	
Beckett & Sons, Bucknell	1962	1962	1 only
Bedwas & Machen UDC	1952	1971	Massey customer
Bee Line (Manchester)	1997	1997	sd only
Belfast C T	1961	1961	1 only
Berks & Bucks (Beeline)	1988	1988	1 order for 5
Birkenhead C T	1934	1969	Massey customer
Birmingham C T	1935	1935	1 order for 15
Blackpool Transport	1994	1994	1 order for 6
Blue Bus, Horwich	2001	2001	1 order for 3
Blue Triangle, Rainham	2003	2003	1 order for 2
Bluebird Buses	1993	1993	1 order for 6
BMMO	1942	1945	Unfrozen and utility only
Bolton C T	1946	1947	
Bowen, Musselburgh	1930	1930	1 only
Bradford C T	1927	1944	
Brays School, Birmingham	1988	1988	1 minibus only
Brookside Garage, Chorlton	1923	1923	1 only
Brighton Hove & District	1969	2001	
Bristol Omnibus	1992	1998	
Bristol Tramways	1930	1930	1 order for 15
BTS Borehamwood	1991	1991	1 order for 14
Bull, Rochdale	1988	1988	1 order only (Minibuses)
Bullock & Sons (Cheadle)	1943	1999	
Bullock, Featherstone	1924	1924	1only
Burnley & Pendle	2001	2001	1 order for 15
Burnley Colne & Nelson	1948	1970	
Burton C T	1970	1970	1 order for 3
Bury C T	1933	1947	
Busways Travel Services	1991	1994	
C & M, Aintree	1995	1995	1 order for 7 sd
Caerphilly U D C	1970	1971	
Calderdale	1972	1974	
Cambridge Coach Services	1998	1998	1 order for 2
Cambus/Viscount	1988	2003	
Capital Citybus	1991	1999	
Capital, West Drayton	1999	1999	1 order for 10
Cardiff C T	1925	1984	Inc only Trolleybus order

Customer	1st order del	Final order del	Comments
Carlisle & District	1929	1930	
Catherwood, Belfast	1929	1934	
Central SMT	1942	1963	
Centrewest	1995	2003	
Chambers, Bures	1995	1995	1 only
Cheltenham District	1943	1943	Utility only
Cherry, Bootle	1996	1996	1 only
Chester	1969	1989	Massey customer
Chesterfield C T	1943	1971	
China Motor Bus	1962	1962	1 only
City of Oxford	1967	1972	
Citybus (Hong Kong)	1996	1998	Badged Plaxton
Cleveland Transit	1978	1997	
Clydeside	1995	1995	1 order for 2 sd
Connelly, Eldeslie	1928	1928	1 order for 2 sd
Cottrell, Micheldean	1972	1979	
County	1997	1997	1 order for 9
County Bus & Coach	1990	1994	
Coventry C T	1942	1944	Unfrozen & utilty only
Cowie	1995	1996	
Cox's Blue Bird, Neath	1928	1943	
Crosville M S	1942	1998	
Crosville Wales	1998	1998	1 order for 7
Cumberland	1942	1943	Unfrozen & utility only
Cunningham, Paisley	1972	1973	
Cynon Valley	1989	1989	Minibuses only
Daimler	1930	1962	
Danish State Railway	1949	1949	1 dd only
Darlington Triumph	1943	1943	Utility only
Davidson, Banff	1929	1929	1 only
Dearsley, Barking	1992	1992	1 order for 3 sd
Delaine, Bourne	1973	1973	1 only
Delta, Kirkby in Ashfield	1995	1995	1 order for 2 sd
Dennis, Guildford	1962	2000	Loline demo & Dublin 6473
Derby	1944	1998	
Dodds, Troon	1995	1995	See also AA Motor Services
Douglas C T	1926	1949	
Dublin Bus	1999	2000	
Dundee C T	1944	1944	Utility only
Dunston & Bruckshaw	1989	1989	1 minibus only
Durham Travel Services	2001	2001	1 order for 20
East Kent	1990	1993	
East London	1996	1998	
East Midlands	1992	1993	
East Yorkshire	1990	2003	
Eastbourne	1938	1994	
Eastern Counties	1989	1993	
Edinburgh/Lothian	1942	2004	Some Alex built at Wigan
Emerson, Throckley	1929	1929	1 only
Ensign, Purfleet	1989	1989	1 order for 5
Esssex Buses	1997	1997	1 order for 13 sd
Everingham Bros	1942	1944	Unfrozen and utility only
Exeter C T	1929	1931	
Fareway, Kirkby	1988	1989	
Ferguson, Renfrew	1928	1928	1 order for 2
Ferguson, Stirling	1925	1925	1 order for 3
Finglands	1996	2002	
First Capital	2001	2003	
Foden, Sandbach	1979	1979	33 seat band coach
Forest, Aintree	2001	2001	1 only
Fowler, Holbeach	1995	1995	1 order for 3 sd
Fr of Woodford School, Salford	1990	1990	1 minibus only
Frontrunner S E	1990	1991	1 sd only
Fuggles, Beneden	1994	1994	1 sd only
Fylde	1975	1993	

Customer	1st order del	Final order del	Comments
Garelochhead	1959	1972	
Garnett, Ainsdale	1996	1996	1 sd only
Gatshead & District	1997	1997	1 order for 6 sd
Gatwick Motors, Horley	1994	1994	1 order for 2 sd
Gelligaer U D C	1929	1971	
Gemsan, Huyton	1993	1993	
Glasgow C T	1943	1944	Utility only
Glossop Carriage	1929	1929	
Go Coastline	1998	1998	
Go Northern	2001	2001	1 order for 15
Gough, Mountain Ash	1935	1935	1 only
Graham, Paisley	1948	1957	
Greater Manchester Buses	1986	1989	
Greater Manchester Fire Ser	1996	1996	Incident Unit
Greater Manchester North	1994	1995	
Greater Manchester PTE	1974	1986	
Greater Manchester South	1997	2003	
Greenock Motor Services	1943	1944	Utility only
Grey, Kinrossie	1928	1928	1 only
Greyhound, Bristol	1930	1930	1 order for 15
Griegs	1945	1947	
Griffin Motor Co	1943	1943	1 utility only
Griffin, Brynmawr	1930	1930	1 only
Grimsby C T	1944	1944	Utility only
Halifax C T	1966	1972	
Hall, Lewis & Co	1923	1923	
Hants & Dorset	1949	1949	Diverted order
Harper Bros	1961	1971	1st not deliv until 5/62
Harper, Peebles	1926	1928	
Harris Bus, West Thurrock	1996	1998	
Harrogate Road Car	1924	1924	
Hartlepool	1985	1995	
Haslingden C T	1942	1942	1 utility only
Heaton, Hindley Green	1988	1989	Minibuses only
Hebble	1926	1966	
Hedingham	2003	2003	1 order only
High Wolds C B, Huggle	1988	1988	1 minibus only
Highland Transport	1944	1947	
Hong Kong Air Cargo Ter	1997	1998	
Huddersfield C T	1926	1932	
Hughes-DAF, Gomersall	1994	1998	
Hulley, Baslow	1930	1931	
Hutchinson, Overtown	1958	1993	
Ipswich	1986	1987	
Irvine	1956	1956	1 only
Isle of Man R S/ T B	1934	1990	
Iveco, Winsford	1988	1988	1 minibus only
James, Aughton	1988	1988	1 order only (Minibuses)
Joiner & Grail, Stratford	1929	1929	1 only
Jones, Pontypridd	1995	1996	
Keighley & District	1990	1990	1 order for 6
Kemp & Shaw	1946	1947	
Kendall Motor Bus Co	1928	1929	
Keneally, Waterford	1999	1999	
Kentish Bus	1989	1994	
Kilmarnock Corporation	1927	1928	
Kingston upon Hull	1942	1995	
Kowloon Canton Rly Corp	1995	1998	
Kowloon Motor Bus	1995	1995	1 order for 5 sd
Kuwait Transport	1979	1986	
Ladbrooke & Boor	2001	2001	1 only
Lake District R T	1920	1920	1 only
Lambeth L B	1988	1988	1 only
Lanarkshire Traction	1930	1930	1 only
Lanarkshire Tramways	1925	1925	

Customer	1st order del	Final order del	Comments
Lancashire United	1942	1980	
Lancaster	1929	1952	
Laurie, Hamilton	1957	1957	
Leaside Bus Co	1995	1998	
Leicester	1937	1994	
Leigh C T	1928	1943	
Leon, Finningley	1978	1978	1 only
Lewis & James, W Valleys	1927	1927	
Liddell, Riddrie	1926	1926	1 order for 2
Liverbus, Huyton	1994	1995	
Liverline	1990	1990	1 order for 10
Liverpool C T	1942	1950	
Liyell, Willenhall	1995	1995	1 order for 2 sd
LNER (Aberdeen)	1926	1927	
London & Country	1998	1998	1 order for 13
London Buses Ltd	1984	1994	
London Buslines	1990	1990	1 order for 17
London Central	1995	2005	
London Country	1972	1972	1 order for 11
London Country Buses (SW)	1989	1989	
London General	1997	2003	
London Suburban	1993	1994	
London Transport	1945	1946	Utility only
London United	2000	2000	
Londonderry Corporation	1927	1927	1only
Longstaff, Mirfield	1982	1982	1 only
Luton & District	1994	1997	
Luton International Airport	1989	1990	
Lytham St Annes C T	1957	1970	
Maidstone	1971	1995	Massey customer
Maidstone & District	1963	1997	
Manchester C T	1923	1957	
Manchester Minibuses	1987	1987	1 order only (50 minibuses)
Mann, Whitwick	1926	1926	1 only
Mansfield District	1944	1944	Utility only
Matthews, Ystrad Mynach	1924	1924	1 only
Maudslay	1929	1929	D/d demonstrator only
Mayne, Clayton	1989	2003	
McGill, Barrhead	1962	1995	
McGill, Crosshill	1927	1927	1 only
Merseybus	1988	1998	
Merseyside PTE	1970	1971	
Merseyside Touring	1929	1929	1 only
Merseyside Transport	1986	1998	
Metrobus, Orpington	1995	1998	
Metroline	2001	2005	
Metroline London Northern	1999	2004	
Mexborough & Swinton	1967	1968	
Mid-Cheshire, Northwich	1919	1920	
Middlesbrough C T	1943	1967	See Teesside
Midland Bus Services	1925	1925	
Midland Fox	1996	1998	
Midland General	1944	1945	Utility only
Midland Red (North)	1990	1991	Minibuses only
Milburn Motors (dlr)	1955	1957	
Moore Bros	1957	1957	Massey customer
Morecambe & Heysham CT	1930	1970	3 sd in 1970
Morgan, Armthorpe	1945	1945	1 utility only
Morris (Gliderways)	1942	1942	1 unfrozen only
Mott, Stoke Mandeville	1994	1994	1 oder for 2 sd
Muirhead, Glasgow	1927	1930	
Mullen & Thompson, Elgin	1929	1929	1 order for 6
Musterphantom (Solent B L)	1998	1998	1 order for 4
Naylor, South Normanton	1932	1932	1 only
New World First	1998	2000	Frames only

Customer	1st order del	Final order del	Comments
Newcastle C T	1939	1939	1 order for 2
North Birmingham Buses	2001	2001	1 only
North Devon	1993	1993	1 order for 3
North Western	1988	1997	
Northern Counties	1986	1992	
Northern Gen, Arbroath	1929	1929	1 order for 2
Northern General	1944	1945	Utility only
Northern Ireland RTB	1943	1943	Utility only
Northumbria	1992	1997	
Nottingham	1935	1994	
O'Hara, Newton Mearns	1925	1927	
OK Motor Services	1973	1992	
Oldham C T	1957	1958	
Orr, Little Lever	1929	1929	1 only
Paisley & District	1946	1947	
Pan Atlas	1989	1989	1 order for 9
Parasol Project, Oxford	2002	2002	1 only (Play Bus)
Parry, Knaresborough	1987	1987	1 order only (Minibuses)
Penmans, Bannockburn	1925	1925	1 only
Peters, Brislington	1995	1995	1 only
Pete's Travel, Smethwick	2001	2001	Later to Reading Buses
Plaxton, Scarborough	1996	1998	
PMT	1946	1998	
Pontypridd UDC	1942	1945	Utility only
Port Glasgow M C	1925	1925	1 order for 6
Preston	1987	1991	
PSA, Faslane	1989	1989	1 order only (Minibuses)
Q Drive Buses	1994	1995	
Ralph's Garage, Abertillery	1927	1927	1 order for 2
Rawtenstall C T	1933	1933	1 order for 2
Reading	1971	1977	All VR's
Red & White	1932	1936	
Reynard, Tadcaster	1988	1988	1 order only (Minibuses)
Rhonnda	1963	1969	
Ribble	1922	1996	
Ring & Ride (GMPTE)	1987	1987	Minibuses only
Ritchie, Ayr	1928	1928	1 order only
Robson Bros, Sm Syke	1932	1932	1 only
Rochdale C T	1943	1944	Utility only
Sanderson, Glasgow	1925	1925	1 only
Scania, Milton Keynes	1994	1994	
Scarborough District M S	1929	1929	1 order for 2
Scottish General Omnibus	1928	1928	1 order for 9
Scottish General Transport	1927	1927	1 order for 10
Selby & District	1996	1996	1 order for 3
Selkent	1995	1997	
SELNEC PTE	1970	1974	1970 Ashton order
Serveverse, Mile Oak	1997	1997	1 sd only
Sheffield C T	1941	1944	Unfrozen and utility only
SHMD	1925	1968	
Shropshire Services	1988	1988	1 minibus only
SMT	1927	1944	
Sommer (Denmark)	1954	1954	1 only
South Notts	1961	1989	
South Shields C T	1942	1942	1 unfrozen only
South Wales Comm Motors	1923	1923	1 only
South Yorkshire PTE	1983	1983	1 order for 10
South Yorkshire Transport	1989	1992	
South Yorkshire, Pontefract	1971	1988	
Southampton	1996	1996	1 order for 6
Southdown	1943	1989	
Southend C T	1971	1985	Massey customer
Southern Vectis	1993	2002	
Southport C T	1944	1944	Utility only
Sovereign (London)	1998	2001	

Customer	1st order del	Final order del	Comments
Speedlink	1995	1997	
St Helens & District	1921	1925	
St Helens C T	1942	1943	Utility only
Stagecoach South	1993	1995	
Stevenson, Paisley	1927	1927	1 only
Stewart & McDonald, Carluke	1927	1927	1 order for 7
Stockton C T	1942	1958	
Stratford Blue	1962	1967	
Strathclyde	1995	1997	
Strathtay Scottish	1995	1996	
Strothers & Strangeways	1995	1995	
Suddaby, Malton	1926	1926	1 only
Sunderland C T	1958	1958	
Sunderland District	1945	1945	Utility only
Sutherland & Co	1943	1944	Utility only
Swindon/Thamesdown	1967	1989	
Sword, Aidrie	1925	1925	1 only
Tailby & George	1962	1966	
Tandy, Moseley	1988	1988	1 minibus only
Tayside	1983	1983	1 order for 10
Teesside	1969	1977	See Cleveland Transit
Thames Transit	2003	2003	1 order for 6
Thamesway	1993	1993	1 only
Thornycroft, Basingstoke	1926	1927	
Tillingbourne, Cranleigh	1992	1994	
Todmorden J O C	1934	1934	1 order only
Trent	1944	1994	
Turner, Brown Edge	1967	1980	
Tynemouth	1946	1946	1 order for 5
United	1942	1943	Utility only
United Counties	1992	1993	
United Welsh	1943	1946	Utility only
Vale, Cheetham	1988	1988	1 order only (Minibuses)
Volvo, Warwick	1993	1999	
Wall, Sharston	1995	1995	1 order for 6
Walsall C T	1954	1969	
Walsh, Alkrington	1988	1989	Minibuses only
Walthamstow C B	1991	1991	1 only
Warrington B T	1987	1994	
Waveney Playbus	1997	1997	1 only (Play Bus)
West Bridgeford UDC	1926	1927	
West Midlands PTE	1970	1977	Inc Walsall & W Brom orders
West Midlands Travel	1997	2000	Inc Smiths
West Riding	1942	1972	
West Yorkshire	1934	1934	1 order for 13
West Yorkshire PTE	1974	1980	
Western Buses	1997	1997	1 order for 11 sd
Western National	1942	1993	
Western SMT	1942	1979	
Western Welsh	1930	1969	
Whetton, Coalville	1931	1931	1 only
Whippet, Fenstanton	1973	1990	
Whitelaw, Stonehouse	1993	1993	1 order for 5 sd
Whittle, Kidderminster	1992	1992	1 order for 2 sd
Widnes C T	1943	1943	1 Utility only
Wigan C T	1927	1972	
Wigan Education Department	1988	1988	1 minibus only
Wigan Social Services	1988	1988	1 minibus only
Wilson, Stainforth	1977	1977	1 only
Yorkshire Coastliner	1992	2002	
Yorkshire Rider	1988	1994	
Yorkshire Terrier	1995	1995	1 order for 6 sd
Yorkshire Traction	1944	1995	
Yorkshire Woollen	1934	1960	
Young's Bus Service	1925	1950	

Index

Figures in **bold** indicate an illustration.

To commemorate the building of
at Enfield Street, Wigan

ALEXANDER P
ANDERSON M
ASHALL M
ASHCROFT D
ASHCROFT P
ASHTON P
BARLOW K
BARTON K
BELL T
BENNETT M
BERTRAND C
BORKOWICZ B
BROWN I
BYTHEWAY A
CAMERON R
CASH N
CHEETHAM R
CLARKE D
CLEW S
CONNOLLEY T
CONNOR W
COOPER G
COX S
CUERDEN M
DARBYSHIRE D
DARBYSHIRE P
DOLDERSON M
DONALDSON D
DORAN C
DOWNING L
DYSON G
EATON D
EDWARDS K
EVANS O
EVANS P
GALLAGHER M
GILL D
GLADWIN N
GREGSON S
GRIFFITHS C
GRIMES D
HAMILTON N
HANKINSON J
HARRISON A
HAWLEY D
HEYES D
HEYES F
HILL G
HILTON C
HILTON P
HITCHEN W
HOLMES A
HOUGH A
HOUGHTON M
HURLEY M
JACKSON A
JACKSON D
JENNINGS B
JOHNSON P
JONES C
JOYCE S